Lectures on Finite Precision Computations

SOFTWARE · ENVIRONMENTS · TOOLS

The series includes handbooks and software guides as well as monographs
on practical implementation of computational methods, environments, and tools.
The focus is on making recent developments available in a practical format
to researchers and other users of these methods and tools.

Editor-in-Chief

Jack J. Dongarra
University of Tennessee and Oak Ridge National Laboratory

Editorial Board

James W. Demmel, *University of California, Berkeley*

Dennis Gannon, *Indiana University*

Eric Grosse, *AT&T Bell Laboratories*

Ken Kennedy, *Rice University*

Jorge J. Moré, *Argonne National Laboratory*

Software, Environments, and Tools

Lectures *on* Finite Precision Computations

Françoise Chaitin-Chatelin

University Paris IX Dauphine, CEREMADE and CERFACS
Toulouse, France

Valérie Fraysse

CERFACS
Toulouse, France

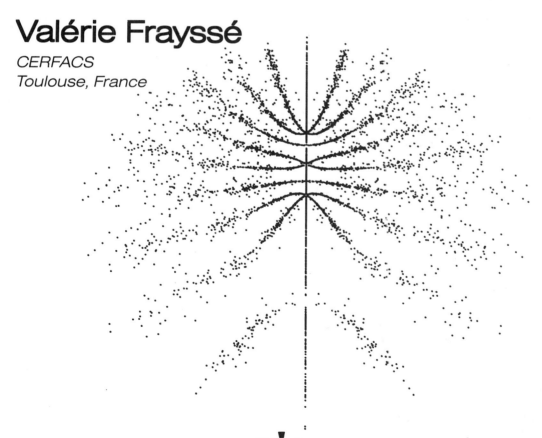

siam®

Society for Industrial and Applied Mathematics
Philadelphia

Library of Congress Cataloging–in–Publication Data

Chaitin-Chatelin, Françoise.
    Lectures on finite precision computations / Françoise Chaitin
-Chatelin, Valérie Frayssé.
        p.   cm. -- (Software, environments, and tools)
    Includes bibliographical references and index.
    ISBN 0-89871-358-7 (pbk.)
    1. Numerical calculations--Data processing. 2. Error analysis
(Mathematics) I. Frayssé, Valérie. II. Title. III. Series.
QA297.C417 1996
519.4'0285--dc20   95-45140

Figure on dedication page reprinted from the *Dictionnaire raisonné des Sciences, des Arts et des Métiers*, edited by Denis Diderot, published by Pellet, Imprimeur Libraire à Genève, rue des Belles-Filles, 1778.

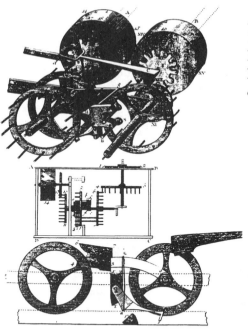

A Blaise Pascal,
1623–1662
Né à Clermont, mort à Paris.
Inventeur de la machine arithmétique
dite "la Pascaline."

Machine Arithmétique de Pascal

De l'esprit géométrique
(fragment rédigé en 1655 ou 1657)

La méthode de démonstration idéale consisterait à n'employer que des termes clairement définis et à n'employer que des propositions démontrées par des vérités déjà connues et admises. Bref, il s'agirait de tout définir ou de tout prouver. Cependant, c'est une méthode impossible puisque toute définition* s'appuie nécessairement sur des termes déjà définis. Et, en remontant cette chaine, on arrive à des mots indéfinissables: temps, espace, nombre ou homme, être, etc.... Il serait vain de vouloir les définir car ils désignent des choses qui ont un nombre infini de qualités. Or il n'est pas nécessaire de les définir car ils s'entendent de soi. Tout homme, par "lumière naturelle," sait ce qu'ils désignent, bien que les idées que chacun se forme de la nature de la chose désignée soient fort différentes. Tout raisonnement—et même le plus parfait, celui des mathématiciens ou "géomètres"—s'appuie nécessairement sur ces "mots primitifs" qui lui échappent.

*Il s'agit ici uniquement de ce que la logique scholastique appelle les définitions de mots ou définitions "nominales." Les définitions de choses, ou définitions "réelles," seraient dans ce contexte, des propositions ou jugements, donc des "vérités" sujettes à l'épreuve de la démonstration.

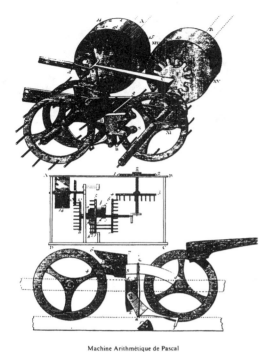

Machine Arithmétique de Pascal

To Blaise Pascal,
1623–1662
Born in Clermont, died in Paris.
Inventor of the calculating machine
called "la Pascaline."

On the geometric spirit
(fragment written between 1655 and 1657)

The ideal method of proof would be to use only clearly defined terms and use only propositions that have been proven from truths that are already known and accepted. In short, it would be necessary either to define everything or to prove everything. However, this is an impossible method since any definition* necessarily relies upon terms that are previously defined. And, by going through this chain, one arrives at undefinable words: time, space, number or man, being, etc.... It would be pointless to try to define them because they refer to things that have an infinite number of qualities. But it is not necessary to define them because these words can be understood by themselves. Any person knows, by "intuition," what they mean, though the ideas that each person builds about the nature of the designated thing are quite different. Any reasoning—even the most perfect, that of mathematicians or "geometers"—necessarily relies on these "primitive terms" that escape him.

*We refer here only to what scholastic logic calls definitions of words or "nominal" definitions. The definitions of things, or "real" definitions, would, in this context, be propositions or judgements and as such "truths" subject to the trial of proof.

Contents

Foreword

I am very pleased that Françoise and Valérie have invited me to write this foreword for their book on finite precision computations.

It has been my pleasure to have known Françoise for more years than I can respectfully admit and to have been a colleague of both Valérie and Françoise within the Parallel Algorithms Project at CERFACS since Valérie joined us from the Turbulence Modelling Project in 1989, an appropriate training given the nature of the some of the current work. For many years a major preoccupation of the Qualitative Computing Group has been the determination of the confidence that a user can place in computed results. This not only is a challenging intellectual exercise but also is of crucial importance to industry, where large sums of money or even issues of human safety may hinge upon complicated numerical calculations. The analysis and implementation of robust methods for assessing the reliability of computations are very much still in their infancy, and this book is an excellent effort in establishing a rigorous basis for this domain and moving it to adolescence.

As the authors explain in their preface, this book owes its genesis to a series of seminars and workshops that the authors have organized primarily but not exclusively under the CERFACS banner. These events have involved both academic researchers and industrial scientists and engineers, and the appeal to this mixed audience is also present in this current volume. Indeed, it is the blend of fundamental and rigorous definition with intensely practical experimentation that characterises this present work.

Continuing on this theme, this book will, I believe, have a very wide appeal to many, from the trainee numeratician who wants to understand issues of backward and forward analysis and the influence of norms and the various measures for determining and analysing error, to the engineer who wants to see practical examples of the horrors of finite computation thus motivating a very healthy interest in matters numerical. While it is difficult to see this book being used as a stand-alone teaching text, it has a wealth of information and examples, which I feel make it an invaluable companion to teaching and self-study and an excellent reference source for research. Indeed, I have already found the tables of condition numbers and backward error estimates (Chapter 5) a handy aide-mémoire.

Other aspects of the book attract me greatly. The boxed principles, while not, like the Ten Commandments, showing the way to Paradise, might at least guide one to a better computational life. The bibliographical comments section at the end of most chapters is a most useful and focused pointer to very up-to-date, detailed current work.

This book is timely in two quite different senses. In the first case, it is really the first time that computational aids and computers have been sophisticated enough to enable the detailed description and investigation of the phenomenon under study. In the second sense, the study and understanding of chaos are among the most dynamic fields for both specialists and laymen alike, in their respective ways and levels. Indeed, a title of *Order from Chaos* would not be inappropriate and may, I should add, have sold more copies! In fact, the timeliness is most urgent when we consider the influence of large computations on public life and safety, some recent examples being the accuracy (or rather lack of accuracy) of Patriot missiles, anxiety over fly-by-wire systems, and the importance of accurate control in nuclear power stations.

One aspect that is absolutely captivating is the notion of obtaining meaningful information from what might be considered wrong results. This contradiction of the "garbage in, garbage out" principle is seen very clearly in their work on computing Jordan forms from scatter plots of eigenvalues of perturbed systems. Indeed, as the authors say, one power of finite precision computations is that they mirror reality in a way that exact arithmetic cannot.

If there is a drawback to the book, it is the effect that it might have on some of its readers. There are so many examples of deceptively simple computations going haywire that one's confidence in the reliability of computation could be significantly eroded. In some sense, that awareness is no bad thing, so long as the positive aspects of the understanding of finite precision computation also are appreciated. Maybe the remedy to any loss in faith is the PRECISE prescription.

If you want to attribute the blame for natural disasters to other than the proverbial butterfly, then I can recommend this book as a good launchpad and fully believe that, at the very least, a few hours spent browsing this volume will be both entertaining and instructive.

Iain S. Duff
Project Leader, CERFACS
Group Leader, RAL
Visiting Professor, Strathclyde
Toulouse, 17 May 1995

Preface

The book is devoted to the assessment of the quality of numerical results produced by computers. It addresses the central question, *how does finite precision affect the convergence of numerical methods on the computer when convergence has been proved in exact arithmetic?*

The book describes the principles according to which the general picture of stability and convergence in theoretical numerical analysis, established with exact arithmetic, can be distorted on the computer by finite precision. It shows that such a distortion should be expected for *reliable* software only in the neighbourhood of *singularities*. It also shows that the distortion can be severely amplified by certain parameters in the problem, such as high nonnormality for matrices.

The book gives a rigorous theory of computability in finite precision by setting in a unified framework techniques that belong to areas traditionally kept far apart, such as functional analysis, familiar to mathematicians, and numerical software, more familiar to engineers. The presentation combines the use of three principles:

  i) the Lax principle of equicontinuity to prove convergence when, ideally, the number of digits in the arithmetic tends to infinity,
 ii) the Wilkinson principle of backward error analysis to grade the quality of algorithms and numerical methods with respect to the available machine precision and/or the level of data uncertainty, and
iii) the principle of robust convergence with respect to perturbations in the data.

The fact that numerical stability in exact arithmetic can become conditional to finite precision arithmetic is illustrated on a variety of examples that represent a cross section of applied numerical analysis. An in-depth treatment is given for the most basic problems in scientific computing. The unified survey of normwise and componentwise error analysis for linear algebra (systems, eigenvalues, least squares) and roots of polynomials that is presented appears in a book for the first time. Special attention is given to the influence of spectral instability on the robustness of the convergence of methods, with emphasis on nonnormality. The treatment takes advantage of modern programming environments (graphical facilities and numerical software tools) to perform experimental mathematics near a singularity by means of the toolbox PRECISE developed under MATLAB, which is available electronically.

By bridging the traditional gap between applied mathematicians and software developers, this book will provide a better understanding of the mathematical principles that underlie the stability of computations on a computer and, in particular, a better understanding of the role of rounding errors. The book will help to disseminate the essential knowledge about backward error analysis beyond the circle of software developers.

The book is intended for applied mathematicians involved in intensive numerical computations, especially those working on extreme problems at the edge of chaos. It is also designed for engineers dealing with numerical simulations, who must assess the quality of their software. Although concise, the text is written in an informal, nonintimidating style that is enhanced by a variety of illustrative computer plots.

The book has been used as a text for advanced undergraduate and beginning graduate students at the University of Paris IX Dauphine. It has also served as a written support for several advanced training courses for engineers organized by CERFACS.

Even though a book is a singularity in itself, like any human enterprise, it is a pleasant duty to acknowledge our numerous debts. We learned a lot from the founding fathers of modern scientific computing, Turing and von Neumann, and from two children of theirs, Wilkinson and Henrici. As for our loans from their innumerable descendants, they are too many to cite them all. Out of friendship, we would like to single out the names of Serguei Godunov, Gene Golub, Velvel Kahan, Beresford Parlett, Pete Stewart, and, in the younger generation, Mario Arioli, Jim Demmel, Nick Higham, and Nick Trefethen.

The congenial environment provided by CERFACS made the writing of this book truly enjoyable. We benefited beyond reward from the skills in round-off and numerical software that are gathered into the Parallel Algorithms Project; Iain Duff deserves our deepest thanks for providing the necessary synergism.

We were taught about software practice in industry by many engineers. We wish to thank in particular Jean-Claude Bergès from CNES, Jean-Claude Dunyach from Aerospatiale, and Pascal Trouvé from Thomson–CSF.

Finally, we realise that the writing of these Lectures has been made possible by the skillful and friendly support of the Qualitative Computing Group at CERFACS. Maria Bennani, Serge Gratton, and Vincent Toumazou share our warmest thanks with Thierry Braconnier. Thierry's intimate knowledge of eigensolvers was essential, more than once, to the design of the eigenvalue experiments.

Françoise Chaitin-Chatelin and Valérie Frayssé
Toulouse, January 1995

Notation

$\mathbb{C}$	the field of complex numbers.
$\mathbb{R}$	the field of real numbers.
$\mathbb{F}$	the set of floating-point numbers.
$\bar{z}$	the complex conjugate scalar of z in $\mathbb{C}$.
A	a complex or real matrix.
A^T	the transpose of the matrix A.
$A^* = A^H$	the conjugate transpose of the matrix A.
x^T	the transpose of the vector x.
$x^* = x^H$	the conjugate transpose of the vector x.
δ_{ij}	the Kronecker symbol ($\delta_{ij} = 1$ if $i = j$ and $\delta_{ij} = 0$ if $i \neq j$).
$\| \cdot \|_*$	the dual norm of $\| \cdot \|$: $\|y\|_* = \max_{\|x\|=1} |y^*x|$.
$\|x\|_p$	the Hölder vector norm: $\|x\|_p = \left(\sum_{i=1}^n |x_i|^p\right)^{1/p}$, $1 \leq p \leq \infty$.
$\|A\|_p$	the Hölder matrix norm: $\|A\|_p = \sup_{\|x\|_p=1} \|Ax\|_p$
$\|A\|_F$	the Frobenius norm of A: $\|A\|_F = \left(\sum_{i,j=1}^n |a_{ij}|^2\right)^{1/2}$.
Ψ	the machine precision $\Psi = 1^+ - 1$, where 1^+ is the successor of 1 in the computer arithmetic. If p is the number of digits of the mantissa and β is the basis, then $\Psi = \beta^{-p+1}$.
$\mathbf{u}$	the unit round-off, $\mathbf{u} = \max\{u;\ \mathrm{fl}(1+u) = 1\}$.

Finite precision computations
at a glance

I. Computability

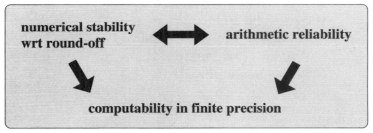

numerical stability wrt round-off ⬌ **arithmetic reliability**

computability in finite precision

II. Quality of reliable software

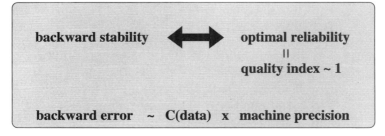

backward stability ⬌ **optimal reliability**

||

quality index ~ 1

backward error ~ C(data) x machine precision

III. Robustness

behaviour of the constant C(data)

under perturbations on the data

Chapter 1

General Presentation

Attractive mathematics does not protect one from the rigors of digital computation.

J. H. Wilkinson, von Neumann Lecture,
Society for Industrial and Applied Mathematics
Meeting, Boston, Fall 1970

The fast evolution of techniques and performance in scientific computing modifies how one approaches high-technology problems. The models are more complex and can take into account the complete phenomenon in its environment (nonlinear equations, unsteady behaviour, coupling between several physical and chemical aspects, for example). Often, research and development give rise to documented software that is part of the deliverables. Engineering practice also evolves. Parametric studies allow the integration of a large number of parameters, and this reduces significantly the number of prototypes.

Since scientific computing is at the heart of the development of high technologies in industry, the problem of assessing the robustness of numerical methods becomes increasingly important today.

1.1 Coupling

Taking into account more and more detailed phenomena closer to physical reality leads to an evolution of modelling techniques. This evolution is twofold: first, taking into account a much larger number of degrees of freedom at the lowest level of the description and, second, increasing the complexity of the description, that is, the number of levels that have to be integrated. This evolution is made possible by the increasing availability of software that realizes the coupling of different physical phenomena, often on parallel platforms. However, the overall behaviour of a complete system is sometimes hard to predict. It is in the interaction zone between two strongly coupled models

1

that new phenomena that require a qualitative study before any attempt at computation can occur.

1.2   Chaotic computations

Until the 1970s, the classical approach of proving the numerical convergence of approximation methods in exact arithmetic was sufficient in most cases to assess the validity of the computer simulations in finite precision. The global stability of the equations of computational physics at that time was, in general, strong enough to accept the perturbation induced by finite precision. However, in the past two decades and through extensive computer experiments, scientists and engineers became aware of the theoretical role of chaos (i.e., extreme sensitivity to initial conditions) in evolution phenomena ruled by certain nonlinear equations.

Nowadays, the new problems at the edge of instability that are encountered more often in physics and high technology challenge the classical approach. To assess the validity of chaotic computations, it is necessary to study the robustness with respect to machine precision of the stability conditions for numerical methods that have been proven convergent in exact arithmetic. This robustness can be derived from the stability properties of the physical phenomenon under study.

1.3   Computability in finite precision

A rigorous theory of computability in finite precision is presented. The key feature is the introduction of the quantity known as "machine precision," that is, $1^+ - 1$, where 1^+ is the successor of 1 in the computer arithmetic, as a parameter ε that tends to zero. This corresponds to a mantissa of increasing length for the computer representation of numbers. Then the embedding of the floating-point computations into the field of mathematical real numbers allows the use of the powerful tools of classical analysis to prove the convergence toward the exact result of the results of an *algorithm* (finite number of steps) computed in an arithmetic with precision ε as $\varepsilon \to 0$. The Lax principle of equicontinuity in ε is the tool of choice. More generally, the convergence analysis of *numerical methods* in finite precision requires the *coupling* of the arithmetic with all the convergence parameters. Therefore, the numerical stability proved in exact arithmetic can become *conditional to finite precision*.

1.4   Numerical quality of computations

It is important to distinguish in a computer result the amount of error due to the arithmetic instability (curable) from the amount due to a possible mathematical or physical instability (unavoidable) but that can be studied by theoretical means. Wilkinson establishes the *optimal quality* of a reliable algorithm with respect to machine precision, or to the level of inaccuracy in the data, by means of a backward error analysis. We show how Wilkinson's principle can be extended to assess the optimal reliability of a numerical method with respect to the numerical and arithmetic parameters. This allows the user to choose the methods that are guaranteed to make the best use of the finite precision of the computer and to match the quality of the algorithm with the level of uncertainty in the data.

1.5   Role of singularities

Singularities correspond to cases where the solution has no continuous derivatives in some parameter. The singularities of a general differentiable map can be very complex, but they are a set of measure zero. However, their computational influence can be devastating, because when a computation takes place in the neighbourhood of a singularity, the results obtained in finite precision can vastly differ from their exact counterparts. Because singularities are rare, they are not preserved under general perturbations: a double root is computed as two close simple roots in finite precision. Therefore, there has been a tendency to underestimate their role in practice, but, indeed, they play an essential role in the area of theoretical physics concerned with the reduction of theory (Berry (1991)). Often enough, a general theory based on elementary principles is reduced to a particular theory when some dimensionless parameter (say, δ) tends to zero, for example. Then the key question is the nature of the limit as δ tends to zero, and very often it is *highly singular*. The type of singularity is important, and the existence of singularities is directly connected to the emergence of new phenomena. For example, statistical mechanics reduces to thermodynamics when $\delta = \frac{1}{N}$ tends to zero, N being the number of particles. The pressure $P(v, t)$ as a function of volume v and temperature t can be derived from the principles of statistical mechanics by large N asymptotics. But the reduction runs into difficulty near a critical point (v_c, t_c), where the compressibility $k = [-v(\partial P/\partial v)_t]^{-1}$ is infinite. The nature of the divergence of k as $t \to t_c$ is a power law, which determines the critical exponents. Thermodynamics is a continuous theory, except at critical points, which correspond to a new state of matter. Other areas in physics where singularities underlie some of the most difficult and intensively studied problems today include the limit wave optics $\to$ geometrical optics and quantum mechanics $\to$ classical mechanics.

The computational drift in the neighbourhood of a singularity depends on its type but also, for singularities of the same mathematical nature, on their individual strength for diffusion into the regularity domain.

1.6   Spectral instability and nonnormality

Nonnormal matrices ($AA^* \neq A^*A$) are prone to spectral instability. If the conditions for numerical stability are not robust enough to spectral perturbations, the numerical stability in exact arithmetic is at risk. The spectral instability is often inherited from physics. High nonnormality can occur in physics and technology whenever there exists a strong coupling between different phenomena, giving rise to physical instabilities.

Such extreme situations can be encountered when the spectrum of a family of operators depending on a parameter exhibits a *severe discontinuity* as the parameter varies. However, it is possible that the pseudospectra remain continuous. The continuity of pseudospectra allows the use of Trefethen's principle to guarantee the convergence of numerical methods in exact arithmetic under conditions on the pseudospectra, which are robust with respect to nonnormality.

1.7   Influence on numerical software

In finite precision, the computation necessarily creates perturbations. Therefore, the numerical stability may be guaranteed only under restrictive conditions coupling machine precision to discretization parameters such as time and space mesh sizes. Reliable software reflects the instability in the equations; it does not create it. Under the influence of certain parameters of the problem, such as the departure from normality for a matrix, the Reynolds number in computational fluid dynamics, or the resistivity in magnetohydrodynamics, singularities that are isolated in exact arithmetic can be *coupled by the computation*. This coupling, which is at first local, can gradually become global as the relevant parameters evolve. This results in the emergence of new collective phenomena that mimic physical reality at the edge of chaos.

However, there exists another potential danger for numerical software that cannot happen in exact computation: the quality of the convergence may be seriously reduced by nonnormality. The danger is present for iterative solvers as well as finite algorithms. This should be a matter of serious concern for software developers.

1.8   Qualitative computing

In ill-posed situations, the mathematical or numerical instability is so high that we cannot hope for a conventional control of the computational error, as was possible in less ill conditioned situations. Classical computation seems meaningless at first because none of the digits in the results are correct. However, there may exist a broad spectrum of intermediate situations between right and wrong on the computer. In qualitative computing, the aim is no longer to control the computing error (it does not tend to zero) but rather to extract meaning from wrong results. When the computation cannot deliver full information on the exact solution because the problem is singular, then the computation—by means of a reliable method—can still deliver relevant *partial information* about the singularity.

1.9 Experimental mathematics

The presentation of the theory of computability in finite precision is complemented by a software toolbox PRECISE (PRecision Estimation and Control In Scientific and Engineering computing) to help the user set up computer experiments to explore the impact of finite precision on the computation at regular points and in the neighbourhood of singularities. This tool has a good explicative power and can often be used predictively. It provides an estimate of the distance to the nearest singularity viewed by the computer, together with the order of this singularity. It is available electronically.

1.10 Sense of errors: For a rehabilitation of finite precision computations

Round-off errors are often considered negatively as a severe limitation on the purity of exact mathematics. However, we wish to argue, by means of two examples, that computation in exact arithmetic is not always the most appropriate choice to describe the mathematical or physical reality. The first example deals with the Lanczos or Arnoldi method, which could not compute multiple eigenvalues if they were run in exact arithmetic. The second example concerns the logistic. The gradual divergence of (2.27) to solve the logistic equation (2.25) presented in Chapter 2 disappears if the computation is exact. (One gets essentially the various fixed points of $x = f^k(x)$.) However, the experimental diagram for CO_2 lasers (Glorieux (1988)) reproduces the computed logistic and not the family of fixed-point solutions. Finite precision has the property to make visible the zone of gradual divergence that has physical meaning.

Exact computation in simulations is a sensible aim, but only if it is exact with respect to the appropriate reference, the reference that makes sense for the simulation. It may not be useful to compute exactly a transient solution with no physical existence because its instability is too high.

As every physicist knows, no equation is exact; therefore, we believe that finite precision computation can be closer to physical reality than exact computation. Thus, it appears possible to *transform the limitations of the computer arithmetic into an asset*. Finite precision computation in the neighbourhood of a singularity can be put into remarkable correspondence with physical phenomena at critical points. Because finite precision necessarily introduces perturbations into the computation, the computer results follow *laws of computation* that might shed some light on certain critical phenomena. To close this introduction on a poetic note, one can cite rainbows in the sky or the glittering of the sea under the sun, which can be explained by perturbations of the caustics that appear in the limit of wave optics when the wavelength tends to zero (Berry (1978)).

Chapter 2

Computability in Finite Precision

We consider the mathematical problem (P), which consists of solving the equation

$$F(x) = y. \tag{2.1}$$

We assume that there is a solution $x = F^{-1}(y)$ that is locally unique, for which we wish to compute an approximation.

F is a map, nonlinear in general, from X to Y, which are, for instance, normed vector spaces on $\mathbb{R}$ or $\mathbb{C}$. In the next two sections, we recall the fundamental analysis tools about *stability* and *convergence* that we shall use heavily throughout these lectures.

2.1 Well-posed problems

We suppose that F (resp., F^{-1}) is continuous in the neighbourhood of x (resp., y). The problem (P) is then *well posed* in the sense of Hadamard: the solution x exists and is unique, and F^{-1} is continuous. The continuity of F^{-1} is often referred to as a *stability* property for (P), since a small variation in the datum y induces a small variation in the solution x. We shall introduce in Chapter 3 stronger notions of stability, based on Fréchet derivatives, together with norms suited for the analysis of computations.

In the following, we shall use the term *stability* as an equivalent to the continuity of F^{-1}. Since it was assumed that the equation (2.1) has a solution $x = F^{-1}(y)$, we can write it formally as

$$x = G(y) \tag{2.2}$$

with $G = F^{-1}$. However, (2.1) is usually not solvable in closed form, and even if it were, the relation (2.2) might not be easily computable. This is why the equation (2.1) or the relation (2.2) are often approximated to be computed.

2.2 Approximations

Let θ be a real parameter, $0 \le \theta < 1$, which will tend to zero. We introduce
the family of approximate equations

$$F_\theta(x_\theta) = y_\theta \tag{2.3}$$

or, equivalently, the family of approximate relations, with $F_\theta^{-1} = G_\theta$,

$$x_\theta = G_\theta(y_\theta). \tag{2.4}$$

We are interested in the general conditions on F_θ, F or G_θ, G that ensure
that $x_\theta \to x$ as $\theta \to 0$ under the assumption that (P) is well posed (F and F^{-1}
continuous). We recall the following definition.

Definition 2.1 *The family* $\{F_\theta, \ 0 \le \theta < 1\}$ *is equicontinuous at* x *if* $\forall \varepsilon > 0$,
$\exists \delta > 0$ *independent of* θ *such that* $\|x' - x\| \le \delta$ *implies* $\|F_\theta(x') - F_\theta(x)\| \le \varepsilon$
for all θ, $0 \le \theta < 1$.

2.3 Convergence in exact arithmetic

We study the general conditions that ensure that $x_\theta \to x$ as $\theta \to 0$. The
convergence $x_\theta \to x$ that occurs generally in practice falls into one of the two
categories of increasing generality:

    i) convergence under a condition independent of θ, that is, with a condition
        on F (resp., G) in the neighbourhood of x (resp., y);

    ii) convergence under a condition that depends on θ, that is, on F_θ (resp.,
        G_θ) in a neighbourhood of x (resp., y).

For the sake of completeness, one should add the case where the convergence
condition is trivially satisfied, that is, when the problem can be solved by
an explicit finite *algorithm* $x = G(y)$. Typically, *direct methods* to solve
$Ax = b$, for example, fall into this category, but there are also some infinite
algorithms that can converge without any condition. One such example of
fundamental importance is the shifted QR algorithm, which cannot be proved
always convergent (Batterson (1990)).[1] Despite this theoretical gap, we will
give indications in Chapter 10 that confirm that QR can safely be considered
as converging in practice. We now turn to the study of the most frequent
situation: the conditional convergence.

2.3.1 Convergence condition independent of θ

We use the identity $G - G_\theta = F^{-1} - F^{-1} \circ F \circ G_\theta$ and derive the formulae for
the errors:

    i) *direct* error:

$$x - x_\theta = G(y) - G_\theta(y_\theta) = F^{-1}(y) - F^{-1} \circ F(x_\theta),$$

---

[1] An open region of nonconvergence for HQR has been discovered in exact and floating-
point arithmetic (communication from an anonymous referee).

ii) *residual* error:

$$y - F(x_\theta) = y - F \circ G_\theta(y_\theta).$$

Proposition 2.1 $x_\theta \to x$ as $\theta \to 0 \iff F(x_\theta) \to y$.

Proof: The proof is clear since F and F^{-1} are continuous. □

It is possible for certain equations $F(x) = y$ to show directly the convergence $x_\theta \to x$ by proving that the residual error $F(x_\theta) - y$ tends to 0 as $\theta \to 0$.

Example 2.1

Consider the linear equation $x = Ax + b$, which we wish to solve by *successive iterations*

$$x_0 = u, \quad x_k = Ax_{k-1} + b, \quad k = 1, 2, \ldots, \tag{2.5}$$

whenever $B = I - A$ is regular. We translate the problem in our general framework with $\theta = 1/k$. $F(x) = y$ corresponds to $Bx = (I - A)x = b$, and $x_\theta = G_\theta(y)$ corresponds to $x_k = A^k x_0 + (I + A + \cdots + A^{k-1})b$. The residual at x_k is $Bx_k - b = A^k(Bx_0 - b)$. A fundamental theorem in linear algebra establishes the following equivalences:

$\lim_{k\to\infty} A^k = 0 \iff \lim_{k\to\infty} A^k u = 0$ for any $u \iff$ spectral radius[2] $\rho(A) < 1 \iff \sum_{k=0}^{\infty} A^k$ converges to $(I - A)^{-1} \iff$ there exists a subordinate norm $\| \cdot \|$ such that $\|A\| < 1 \iff$ for any subordinate norm, there exists k such that $\|A^k\| < 1$.

The convergence of (2.5) is therefore established for any right-hand-side vector b and any starting vector u under the necessary and sufficient condition $\rho(A) < 1$ on the iteration matrix A. The key point is that the matrix $H_k = I + A + \cdots + A^k$ is *an approximate inverse* for $B = (I - A)$ iff $\rho(A) < 1$. Indeed $(I + A + \cdots + A^k)(I - A) = (I - A)(I + A + \cdots + A^k) = I - A^{k+1}$, with A^k small for k large enough. △

Many methods of iterative refinement in numerical analysis are amenable to this framework (see Chatelin (1988c, 1993a)). They involve an approximate inverse G_θ such that $U_\theta = \mathbf{1} - G_\theta \circ F$ is small in some sense, where $\mathbf{1}$ denotes the identity map. The condition put on U_θ often requires that the form U_θ is a *local contraction* in some norm.

In Example 2.1 (with $\theta = 1/k$), the maps F and G_θ are affine and the spaces are finite dimensional. This explains why we can get a necessary and sufficient condition for convergence as $k \to \infty$ that does not involve k. The choice for G_k amounts to

$$U_k = I - H_k(I - A) = A^{k+1},$$

which is a contraction for some norm iff $\rho(A) < 1$.

2.3.2   Convergence condition dependent on θ

We now describe the most common situation. We use the following identities:

$$G - G_\theta = G_\theta \circ F_\theta \circ F^{-1} - G_\theta \circ F \circ F^{-1} \tag{2.6}$$

---

[2]The *spectral radius* $\rho(A)$ denotes $\max|\lambda|$ for all eigenvalues λ of A.

and

$$F \circ G - F \circ G_\theta = F \circ G_\theta \circ F_\theta \circ F^{-1} - F \circ G_\theta \circ F \circ F^{-1}.$$

From (2.6) we derive the formulae for the errors:

  i) *direct* error:

$$
\begin{aligned}
x - x_\theta &= G(y) - G_\theta(y_\theta) \\
&= G_\theta \circ F_\theta(x) - G_\theta \circ F(x) + G_\theta(y) - G_\theta(y_\theta),
\end{aligned}
\tag{2.7}
$$

  ii) *residual* error:

$$
\begin{aligned}
y - F(x_\theta) &= y - F \circ G_\theta(y_\theta) \\
&= F \circ G_\theta \circ F_\theta(x) - F \circ G_\theta \circ F(x) \\
&\quad + F \circ G_\theta(y) - F \circ G_\theta(y_\theta).
\end{aligned}
\tag{2.8}
$$

Definition 2.2 G_θ *is an* approximate inverse *of F iff the* consistency *condition*

$$y_\theta \to y \text{ and } F_\theta(z) \to F(z) \text{ as } \theta \to 0 \tag{2.9}$$

holds for all z in a neighbourhood of x.

Theorem 2.1 *Under the consistency assumption (2.9), the equicontinuity of G_θ or $F \circ G_\theta$ for $0 \le \theta < 1$ is a sufficient condition for convergence.*

Proof: If the family G_θ (resp., $F \circ G_\theta$) is equicontinuous for $0 \le \theta < 1$, apply (2.7) (resp., (2.8)) to show that $F_\theta(x) \to F(x)$ and $y_\theta \to y$ imply $x_\theta \to x$ (resp., $F(x_\theta) \to y$). $\quad \square$

Definition 2.3 *The approximation method F_θ (or, equivalently, the approximate inverse G_θ) is said to be* stable *(with respect to θ) whenever G_θ is equicontinuous for $0 \le \theta < 1$.*

Theorem 2.1 shows that the convergence can be proved by looking at the direct error (2.7) (resp., at the residual error (2.8)) and using the stability of G_θ (resp., $F \circ G_\theta$).

Theorem 2.1 states that, under the natural consistency assumption for the approximation method F_θ, stability of F_θ is a *sufficient condition* for convergence: it is known among numerical analysts as the *Lax principle*.

Consistency + stability $\Longrightarrow$ convergence.

Stability of F_θ (or G_θ) with respect to θ is usually referred to in theoretical numerical analysis as *numerical stability* for the approximate method F_θ (or G_θ).

Whenever the maps F and F_θ are *linear*, then under the consistency assumption, stability is a *necessary* as well as a *sufficient* condition for convergence. We show in the following section that the Lax principle provides an appropriate theoretical framework for the analysis of the convergence of algorithms executed with a computer. In that case, the parameter θ will be associated with the finite precision arithmetic of the computer.

It is traditional in theoretical numerical analysis and functional analysis to prove convergence by inspecting the *direct* error (2.7) (Aubin (1972), Chatelin (1983)). On the contrary, in applied numerical analysis or numerical software, it is often the *residual* error (2.8) that plays the fundamental role (Wilkinson (1961)). This difference in attitude reveals much more than a matter of taste or tradition. As we have proved, the two attitudes are mathematically equivalent in exact arithmetic. But we shall see in Chapter 5 why they are not anymore equivalent *in finite precision*.

We have looked earlier at the convergence of x_θ, the solution of $F_\theta(x_\theta) = y_\theta$, toward x, which is the solution of $F(x) = y$. If, instead of solving an equation like (2.1), the computational problem consists of evaluating the relation (2.2) $x = G(y)$, then F and F_θ may not be available. It is also possible that it is easier to deal with G and G_θ than with F and F_θ, even if the latter are available. It is therefore natural to introduce the following definition.

Definition 2.4 *The direct and residual consistency errors are defined respectively as*

   i) direct *consistency error at t:* $G_\theta(t) - G(t)$,

   ii) residual *consistency error at z:* $F_\theta(z) - F(z)$.

Theorem 2.2 *Theorem 2.1 remains valid when the residual consistency condition (2.9) is replaced by the analogous direct consistency condition*

$$y_\theta \to y \quad and \quad G_\theta(t) \to G(t) \text{ as } \theta \to 0$$

for all t in a neighbourhood of y.

Proof: The proof is easy with the following formulae for the errors:

   i) $x - x_\theta = G(y) - G_\theta(y) + G_\theta(y) - G_\theta(y_\theta)$,

   ii) $y - F(x_\theta) = F \circ G(y) - F \circ G_\theta(y) + F \circ G_\theta(y) - F \circ G_\theta(y_\theta)$.   □

2.4 Computability in finite precision

In this section we focus on the basic situation where $x = G(y)$ is exactly computable in a finite number of steps in exact arithmetic: G is an *algorithm* according to the following definition.

Definition 2.5 *An* algorithm *is a finite sequence of elementary operations that prescribes how to calculate the solution x from the data y.*

In other words, an algorithm is what is realized by a finite computer program, which is supposed always to halt. Such an assumption is stringent from a theoretical computer science point of view but is common practice in numerical software and scientific computing, where limits are always set by programmers to the maximum number of iterations allowed in each conditional loop. However, an algorithm is a notion that is too restrictive for numerical analysis and that covers only the simplest cases of *direct methods* in linear algebra. The theory will be extended in § 2.9 to cover iterative and approximate methods.

We suppose that the arithmetic of the computer has p digits in base β. Therefore, the *machine precision*[3] is $\Psi = 1^+ - 1 = \beta^{-p+1}$, where 1^+ is the successor of 1 in the computer arithmetic. Modern computers use the floating-point representation to code real numbers on the computer after rounding. We denote by $\mathrm{fl}(x)$ the floating-point number that represents the real x in the computer arithmetic. The *unit rounding* $\mathbf{u} = \max_{x \neq 0} |(\mathrm{fl}(x) - x)/x|$ is also important. It depends on the type of rounding. For example, $\mathbf{u} = \Psi$ for chopping and $\mathbf{u} = \frac{1}{2}\Psi$ for rounding to the nearest floating-point number.[4]

Clearly, if one could let the number p of digits tend to infinity, both Ψ and $\mathbf{u}$ would tend to zero. We shall look at the asymptotic properties of computations on such an ideal computer as a parameter ε (which may represent Ψ or $\mathbf{u}$) tends to zero. Therefore, we denote by $I\!\!F_\epsilon$ the set of floating-point numbers in a computer arithmetic associated with $0 < \varepsilon < 1$.

The exact algorithm G run on a computer (with machine precision Ψ) becomes $\mathcal{G}_\varepsilon$ and delivers the computed solution $X_\varepsilon = \mathcal{G}_\varepsilon(Y_\varepsilon)$, computed in the set of floating-point numbers $I\!\!F_\epsilon$. The floating-point solution X_ε solves the discrete problem $(\mathcal{P}_\varepsilon)$ characterized by the equation

$$\mathcal{F}_\varepsilon(X_\varepsilon) = Y_\varepsilon \longleftrightarrow X_\varepsilon = \mathcal{G}_\varepsilon(Y_\varepsilon) \tag{2.10}$$

defined on sets in $I\!\!F_\epsilon$: X_ε and Y_ε are lists of floating-point numbers that can also trivially be considered as vectors x_ε and y_ε in the original vector spaces on $I\!\!R$ or $\mathcal{C}$. This defines a *canonical embedding* of vectors of floating-point numbers into vectors of real numbers. To compare x_ε to x, one may further *embed* $(\mathcal{P}_\varepsilon)$ into the original real or complex vector space by considering x_ε the exact solution of (P_ε), a slightly perturbed problem of the same type as (P), that is,

$$F_\varepsilon(x_\varepsilon) = y_\varepsilon \iff x_\varepsilon = G_\varepsilon(y_\varepsilon). \tag{2.11}$$

In this formalism, $\mathcal{G}_\varepsilon$ represents the algorithm actually performed on floating-point numbers when one runs the exact algorithm G on the computer. It is fully dependent on the computer arithmetic. On the other hand, $G_\varepsilon = F_\varepsilon^{-1}$ exists in $I\!\!R$ or $\mathcal{C}$.

We are now ready to define the key notion of computability in finite precision by means of an algorithm.

Definition 2.6 x is computable *in finite precision by the algorithm G if and only if $x_\varepsilon \to x$ as $\varepsilon \to 0$.*

The Lax principle expressed by Theorem 2.1 applies readily to provide a sufficient condition for computability. Residual (resp., direct) consistency corresponds to $y_\varepsilon \to y$ and $F_\varepsilon(z) \to F(z)$ (resp., $G_\varepsilon(t) \to G(t)$) as $\varepsilon \to 0$ in a

---

[3]According to the definition in Cody (1973).

[4]This is an overly simplified account for computer arithmetic. For a more comprehensive treatment, the reader is referred to Goldberg (1991).

neighbourhood of x (resp., y). The stability, with respect to ε, of F_ε or G_ε is by definition the equicontinuity of G_ε or $F \circ G_\varepsilon$ for $\varepsilon < 1$.

> An algorithm always computes the exact solution x in exact arithmetic in a finite number of steps. However, in finite precision arithmetic, the computability $x_\varepsilon \to x$ as $\varepsilon \to 0$ is ruled by the *Lax principle*, with machine precision ε as the convergence parameter.

We remark that the Lax principle is the tool of choice to prove the convergence of methods that depend on *one* parameter θ only. This is why, when machine precision ε plays the role of θ, this approach enables only the analysis of algorithms, according to Definition 2.3. The more general situation of several parameters will be looked at later (§§ 2.8–2.11). We now give the simplest example of noncomputability in finite precision.

Example 2.2 "Catastrophic" cancellation (Chatelin (1989b)).

We wish to evaluate $x = \frac{(1+y)-1}{y}$ for various values of y, small but not 0, on a computer. The results with IEEE arithmetic (round to nearest, $\Psi \sim 10^{-15}$) are plotted in Figure 2.1. In the left (resp., right) graph, y varies in $[10^{-16}, 10^{-14}]$ (resp., $[5\ 10^{-17}, 5\ 10^{-16}]$). Mathematically, $x = G(y) = \frac{(1+y)-1}{y} = 1$ for all $y \neq 0$. As y tends to 0, one has the indeterminacy $\frac{0}{0}$, which can be resolved by $\lim_{y \to 0} \frac{(1+y)-1}{y} = 1$. But the computed value $x_\varepsilon = G_\varepsilon(y)$ is 0 for y small enough ($y < \Psi(\varepsilon)$, $\Psi(\varepsilon) \sim \Psi = 1^+ - 1$): this happens when the floating-point representations of $1 + y$ and of 1 do not differ. This phenomenon is due to an *arithmetic cancellation*: $(1 + y)$ and 1 are seen as identical by the computer. The numerator, and hence the quotient, are computed at the value 0 (see Figure 2.1). For $\Psi(\varepsilon) < y < \Phi(\varepsilon)$, $G_\varepsilon(y)$ oscillates between 0 and 2 (when the rounding is chosen to be rounded to nearest).

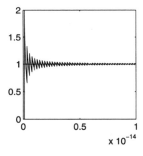 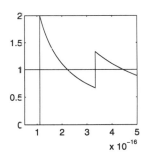

FIG. 2.1. *Arithmetic cancellation: finite precision computation of* $\frac{(1+y)-1}{y}$ *as* $y \to 0$.

This example exposes the *large relative error* that can happen in computer subtraction. For this reason, the phenomenon has been nicknamed "catastrophic" cancellation.

Figure 2.1 shows that $G_\varepsilon(y)$ is discontinuous for certain values of y and hence displays a *convergence condition that is conditional to the arithmetic*: $\lim_{\varepsilon \to 0, y \to 0} G_\varepsilon(y) = 1$ only if $y > \Phi(\varepsilon)$. The formula $x = \frac{(1+y)-1}{y}$ cannot therefore be *computed with finite precision* ($\varepsilon > 0$) for nonzero values of y smaller than $\Psi(\varepsilon)$. $\triangle$

Despite its name, there is nothing pathologic about this arithmetic cancellation from the computer arithmetic point of view: all the arithmetic operations are performed exactly, given the data available to the computer. This cancellation property is even essential to some high-precision algorithms.

Another way to put it in better perspective is to interpret the computation $x = G(y)$ as the finite difference approximation of the derivative of the identity map $t \longmapsto t$ at $t = 1$. We consider, more generally, the derivation $f(t) \longmapsto g(t) = f'(t)$, which maps the C^1 function $f(t)$ into its derivative $f'(t)$. The problem defined by the integral equation

$$\int_0^t g(s)ds = f(t) \Longleftrightarrow f'(t) = g(t)$$

is ill posed: the map $f \longmapsto f'$ is not continuous in f. Indeed, a variation $\Delta f = \varepsilon \sin \omega t$ induces $\Delta g = \varepsilon \omega \cos \omega t$. With the choice $\omega = 1/\varepsilon^2$, $\|\Delta g\|_\infty = 1/\varepsilon$ can be arbitrarily large when $\|\Delta f\|_\infty = \varepsilon$ tends to 0.

The role of finite precision arithmetic in Example 2.2 is merely to expose the mathematical ill-posedness of the derivation. It does not create the problem.

Remarks:

1. *Warning:* The notion of computability in finite precision is *very different* from the computability on a universal Turing machine used in logic and theoretical computer science (recursive functions), after Turing in the 1930s. This latter view of computability is suited to development of a general theory of complexity in terms of the number of *exact* arithmetic operations (see also Blum, Shub, and Smale (1989), Smale (1990)). With our version of computational computability, on the other hand, we propose a theoretical framework for an analysis of stability and convergence that takes round-off errors very naturally into account.

2. The embedding of $(\mathcal{P}_\varepsilon)$ from $I\!F_\epsilon$ into $I\!R$ is similar to that realized in *theoretical* numerical analysis from $I\!R^n$ into functional spaces (by means of prolongation operators) to study the convergence of the finite differences method for partial differential equations (see, for example, Chatelin (1983)).

3. The comparison of F and F_ε is known in *applied* numerical analysis or numerical software as a *backward error analysis*, introduced in the late 1950s by Givens and Wilkinson. The comparison of G and G_ε is a *forward error analysis*.

   The presentation adopted here is a somewhat simplified version of the computation reality, because G_ε and F_ε are not easily accessible since they heavily depend on the properties of the computer arithmetic. A more detailed presentation will be given in Chapter 5.

4. The notion of a family of algorithms that is equicontinuous with respect to ε has been only implicit so far in the vast literature on the assessment of numerical software. The situation is strikingly reminiscent of the state in the 1950s of the literature about the use of the finite elements method in civil engineering. Letting the size of an element tend to zero in theory

was as foreign to civil engineers at that time as the idea of letting the
machine precision ideally tend to zero is now for software developers.

5. To study the convergence $x_\varepsilon \to x$ when ε tends to zero, it is natural
   to consider the embedded problem (P_ε). But for the analysis of the
   quality of the solution on a given computer (ε fixed) it may be interesting
   to consider the discrete problem ($\mathcal{P}_\varepsilon$) defined on sets of floating-point
   numbers $\mathbb{F}_\epsilon$. This is essentially done in Robert (1986), who introduces a
   notion of discrete derivative for that purpose . Similarly, finite difference
   methods are often studied in discrete spaces (Aubin (1972)).

When F and F_ε are *linear*, there are simplifications to the above theory:

1. stability for F_ε with respect to ε is a *necessary* as well as a sufficient
   condition for the convergence $x_\varepsilon \to x$ as $\varepsilon \to 0$;
2. moreover, in *finite* dimensional spaces, the pointwise convergence
   $F_\varepsilon(z) \to F(z)$ as $\varepsilon \to 0$ implies the *normwise* convergence $\|F_\varepsilon - F\| \to 0$,
   which is uniform with respect to z.

2.5   Gaussian elimination

It is almost a matter of folklore that two *different* but mathematically
equivalent methods $(a+b)+c$ and $a+(b+c)$ for evaluating the same expression
$a + b + c$ may lead to different results in finite precision. For algorithmic
purposes, it is therefore important to distinguish between different evaluation
schemes even if they are mathematically equivalent because some schemes may
behave better with respect to computer arithmetic than others.

This necessity is illustrated by the problem (P), which consists of solving
the regular linear system $Ax = b$ of order n by Gaussian elimination (GE).
This is the basic problem in linear algebra, and GE will serve as a prototype
algorithm in these lectures.

Let $A = LU$ be the exact Gaussian factorization[5] of A. L_ε and U_ε are
the computed factors. The computed solution x_ε is obtained by successively
solving the corresponding triangular systems in finite precision. The essential
step for the analysis is to consider x_ε as the *exact* solution in $\mathbb{R}^n$ of a nearby
linear system, which we write as $A_\varepsilon x_\varepsilon = b_\varepsilon$. In general, such a system exactly
solved by x_ε may not be uniquely defined. All what matters for the analysis
is the existence of a system close enough to the original one.

To study the stability of GE for $Ax = b$, Wilkinson (1961) proved that

$$\|A - A_\varepsilon\|_\infty \leq 8n^3 \rho_n \|A\|_\infty \mathbf{u} + O(\mathbf{u}^2), \tag{2.12}$$

where n is the order of A and ρ_n is the growth factor[6] of the elements of U.
For matrices A of a fixed order n, inequality (2.12) entails residual consistency

---

[5]The Gaussian factorization $A = LU$ is one of many factorizations of A that are used in
numerical software. One can cite also the Gram–Schmidt (resp., polar) factorization $A = QR$
(resp., $A = QH$), where Q is a unitary matrix and R (resp., H) is upper triangular (resp.,
Hermitian (semi) definite positive).

[6]See Golub and Van Loan (1989, p. 115) for a precise definition of ρ_n.

$(A_\varepsilon \to A$ as $\varepsilon \to 0)$ as well as the stability of A_ε with respect to ε, as we show with $\| \, . \, \| = \| \, . \, \|_\infty$.

Let $E_\varepsilon = A - A_\varepsilon$, $A_\varepsilon = (I - E_\varepsilon A^{-1})A$ and $A_\varepsilon^{-1} = A^{-1}(I - E_\varepsilon A^{-1})^{-1}$. If the system $Ax = b$ is *far enough from singularity*, then for ε small enough so that $\|E_\varepsilon\| \le (2\|A^{-1}\|)^{-1}$, i.e., $\|E_\varepsilon\|\|A^{-1}\| \le 1/2$, one gets the uniform bound $\sup_\varepsilon \|A_\varepsilon^{-1}\| \le 2\|A^{-1}\|$. The convergence of $x_\varepsilon \to x$ as $\varepsilon \to 0$ follows. One also gets the residual stability $\sup_\varepsilon \|AA_\varepsilon^{-1}\| \le 2$.

This analysis requires rigorously that the growth factor ρ_n can be bounded by a continuous function of n. But there are cases when ρ_n can be infinite for a finite n because of a zero pivot. In order to overcome this artificial instability of GE compared with A^{-1}, one can use two variants of GE, either with partial pivoting (GEPP) or with complete pivoting (GECP).

With complete pivoting, a bound in $O(n^{\log n})$ can be proved for ρ_n. The same is true in general for GEPP, although examples for which $\rho_n = 2^n$ can be constructed. Such an example is given by the system of order 50, $W_{50}x = b$, with

$$W_{50} = \begin{pmatrix} 1 & 0 & \dots & 0 & 1 \\ -1 & \ddots & \ddots & 0 & \vdots \\ -1 & \ddots & \ddots & 0 & \vdots \\ \vdots & \ddots & \ddots & 1 & 1 \\ -1 & \dots & -1 & -1 & 0.9 \end{pmatrix}, \qquad b = (1, \dots, 1)^T.$$

The residual $W_{50}x_\varepsilon - b$ (where x_ε has been computed by GEPP) has all its components equal to zero at machine precision, except the 50th, which is of order 0.025. This indicates the so-called *backward* instability (see Chapter 5) of GEPP in this example. Indeed $\|x - x_\varepsilon\|$ is large, but W_{50} is well conditioned: the large error comes from the algorithm, not from the problem.

In practice, the growth factor is almost always much smaller than what is predicted by the theory. It is interesting to note that, despite 40 years of efforts, GE still resists a complete stability analysis. It is all the more surprising that GE is an algorithm designed to solve what is considered the simplest set of equations that one can conceive: a set of n *linear* equations in n unknowns. Perhaps one finds here an indication that the analysis of finite precision computations is truly a difficult subject!

This example can be set in the general framework of § 2.3 in the following manner. $Ax = b$ corresponds to (P) : $F(x) = y$. The exact computation of x by GE corresponds to $x = G(y)$. Similarly $A_\varepsilon x_\varepsilon = b_\varepsilon$ corresponds to $(P_\varepsilon) : F_\varepsilon(x_\varepsilon) = y_\varepsilon \Longleftrightarrow x_\varepsilon = G_\varepsilon(y_\varepsilon)$.

Note that G is a *representation of F^{-1} different* from A^{-1}. Only the exact result x is identical, but the computational routes are different. Indeed the mathematical calculation for $x = A^{-1}b$ is through Cramer determinants, and x exists and is unique iff A is regular. In contradistinction, when x is computed by GE, one has the supplementary condition for existence that the pivots are nonzero. In this case, the problem and the algorithm have *different* stabilities. The continuity of A^{-1} defines the mathematical stability, whereas the continuity of G expresses the algorithmic stability of GE.

2.6 Forward error analysis

The analysis of the error $\Delta x = x - \tilde{x}$ in the computation of x by an algorithm $x = G(y)$ is a key question in numerical software. The computed output $\tilde{x}$ is the result of perturbations of various origins in the computation (computer arithmetic, uncertainty on data, and the like). Traditionally, the error analysis done on $x = G(y)$ is called *forward*, and the analysis performed by means of the equation $F(x) = y$ is called *backward*.

2.6.1 Sensitivity analysis at a regular point

We suppose that F is a map from $X = I\!R^n$ into $Y = I\!R^m$; that is, we solve a set of m nonlinear equations into n unknowns. We suppose that the solution $x = G(y)$ is defined by the map G from $Y = I\!R^m$ into $X = I\!R^n$:

$$x_i = g_i(y_1, \ldots, y_m), \qquad i = 1, \ldots, n. \tag{2.13}$$

The error propagation through the computation can be studied by means of a *differential sensitivity analysis* if we assume that the n components g_i of G have continuous first derivatives.

Definition 2.7 *A solution x such that its n components g_i have continuous first derivatives (at least) at y is said to be* regular. *It is called* singular *otherwise.*

We suppose that x is regular. Let $\tilde{y}$ be an approximate value for y, generating the absolute errors $\Delta y_j = \tilde{y}_j - y_j$ and relative errors $\varepsilon_{y_j} = \frac{\Delta y_j}{y_j}$, if $y_j \neq 0$, on the data y_j, $j = 1, \ldots, m$. Replacing y with $\tilde{y}$ in $x = G(y)$ leads to the result $\tilde{x} = G(\tilde{y})$ instead of x. The first-order term in the Taylor expansion gives

$$\Delta x_i = g_i(\tilde{y}) - g_i(y) \sim \sum_{j=1}^{m} \frac{\partial g_i(y)}{\partial y_j} \Delta y_j, \qquad i = 1, \ldots, n,$$

that is,

$$\Delta x \sim DG(y)\Delta y, \tag{2.14}$$

where $DG(y)$ denotes the $n \times m$ Jacobian matrix $(\frac{\partial g_i}{\partial y_j}(y))$. The partial derivative $\frac{\partial g_i}{\partial y_j}$ represents the sensitivity with which the ith component x_i reacts to the absolute perturbation Δy_j. If $y_j \neq 0$, $j = 1, \ldots, m$, and $x_i \neq 0$, $i = 1, \ldots, n$, a similar error propagation formula holds for relative errors:

$$\varepsilon_{x_i} = \sum_{j=1}^{n} \frac{y_j}{g_i(y)} \frac{\partial g_i(y)}{\partial y_j} \varepsilon_{y_j}. \tag{2.15}$$

Again the factor $k_{ij} = \frac{y_j}{g_i}\frac{\partial g_i}{\partial y_j}$ indicates how strongly a relative error in y_j affects the resulting relative error in x_i. The amplification factors k_{ij} for relative errors have the advantage of not depending on the scales of x_i and y_j. Such amplification factors, properly quantified, are often called *condition numbers* (see Chapter 3). If any k_{ij} that has a large absolute value is present, then one speaks of an ill-conditioned problem. Otherwise, this is a well-conditioned problem. Such a detailed analysis of G could be heavy in practice since the condition of G is described by mn numbers. This is why the condition of special classes of problems are often described in a more global fashion. Chapter 3 will be devoted to that topic.

2.6.2   The particular case of elementary arithmetic operations

For the arithmetic operations, (2.13) specializes to ($y_1 \neq 0$, $y_2 \neq 0$):

i) $G(y_1, y_2) = y_1 y_2 :\ \varepsilon_{y_1 y_2} = \varepsilon_{y_1} + \varepsilon_{y_2}$,

ii) $G(y_1, y_2) = y_1/y_2 :\ \varepsilon_{y_1/y_2} = \varepsilon_{y_1} - \varepsilon_{y_2}$,

iii) $G(y_1, y_2) = y_1 + y_2 :\ \varepsilon_{y_1 + y_2} = \frac{y_1}{y_1 + y_2}\varepsilon_{y_1} + \frac{y_2}{y_1 + y_2}\varepsilon_{y_2}$ if $y_1 + y_2 \neq 0$,

iv) $G(y_1) = \sqrt{y_1} :\ \varepsilon_{\sqrt{y_1}} = \frac{1}{2}\varepsilon_{y_1}$.

It follows that multiplication, division, and square root are not dangerous. This is also the case for the addition, provided that the operands y_1 and y_2 have *the same sign* ($y_1 y_2 > 0$). In that case, the condition numbers $\frac{y_1}{y_1 + y_2}$ and $\frac{y_2}{y_1 + y_2}$ lie between 0 and 1; therefore,

$$|\varepsilon_{y_1 + y_2}| \leq \max(|\varepsilon_{y_1}|, |\varepsilon_{y_2}|).$$

If, for example, y_2 is small compared to y_1 but carries a large ε_{y_2}, the result $y_1 + y_2$ can have a small relative error if ε_{y_1} is small. This shows how *error damping* can occur.

However, if y_1 and y_2 are of different signs ($y_1 y_2 < 0$), then at least one of the condition numbers $|\frac{y_1}{y_1 + y_2}|$ and $|\frac{y_2}{y_1 + y_2}|$ is larger than 1 so that at least one of the relative errors ε_{y_1}, ε_{y_2} will be amplified. This amplification is drastic when $y_1 \approx y_2$, and catastrophic cancellation can occur (see § 2.4, Example 2.2).

2.6.3   Forward analysis of round-off error propagation in an algorithm

We now focus on the first-order propagation of a particular type of errors— namely, the round-off errors—resulting from the finite precision arithmetic of the computer. Given an *algorithm* to compute x, its sequence of elementary operations gives rise to a decomposition of G into a sequence of $r+1$ elementary maps $G^{(i)}, i = 0, \ldots, r$, such that $G = G^{(r)} \circ \cdots \circ G^{(0)}$: such a factorization of G is specific to the given algorithm to compute x_i by (2.13). The decomposition of G according to the chosen algorithm leads from $y^{(0)} = y$, via the chain of intermediate results

$$y^{(0)} = y \rightarrow G^{(0)}(y^{(0)}) = y^{(1)} \rightarrow \ \cdots\ \rightarrow G^{(r)}(y^{(r)}) = y^{(r+1)} = x,$$

to the result x. Again we assume that each $G^{(i)}$ has continuous partial derivatives for $i = 0, \ldots, r$.

We now define the *remainder maps* by

$$\psi^{(i)} = G^{(r)} \circ G^{(r-1)} \circ \cdots \circ G^{(i)}, \qquad i = 0, \ldots, r.$$

Clearly, $\psi^{(0)} = G$. Let $DG^{(i)}$ (resp., $D\psi^{(i)}$) denote the Jacobian of the map $G^{(i)}$ (resp., $\psi^{(i)}$). Then apply $D(f \circ g) = Df(g)Dg$ to write

$$\begin{aligned}
DG(y) &= DG^{(r)}(y^{(r)})DG^{(r-1)}(y^{(r-1)}) \ldots DG^{(0)}(y), \\
D\psi^{(i)}(y^{(i)}) &= DG^{(r)}(y^{(r)})DG^{(r-1)}(y^{(r-1)}) \ldots DG^{(i)}(y^{(i)})
\end{aligned} \qquad (2.16)$$

for $i = 0, \ldots, r$.

With floating-point arithmetic, input and round-off errors will perturb the exact intermediate result $y^{(i)}$ into the approximate value $\tilde{y}^{(i)}$ according to the rule

$$\tilde{y}^{(i+1)} = \mathrm{fl}(G^{(i)}(\tilde{y}^{(i)})), \qquad i = 0, \ldots r.$$

Therefore, the absolute errors $\Delta y^{(i)} = \tilde{y}^{(i)} - y^{(i)}$ satisfy

$$\Delta y^{(i+1)} = \left[\mathrm{fl}(G^{(i)}(\tilde{y}^{(i)})) - G^{(i)}(\tilde{y}^{(i)}) \right] + \left[G^{(i)}(\tilde{y}^{(i)}) - G^{(i)}(y^{(i)}) \right] = [A] + [B],$$

where $B = DG^{(i)}(y^{(i)})\Delta y^{(i)}$, and in A, for the jth component of $G^{(i)}$,

$$\mathrm{fl}(g_j^{(i)}(z)) = (1 + \delta_j)g_j^{(i)}(z) \text{ with } |\delta_j| \leq \mathbf{u},$$

since $G^{(i)}$ involves only independent elementary operations by definition. That is, in matrix notation,

$$\mathrm{fl}(G^{(i)}(z) = (I + \Delta_{i+1})G^{(i)}(z),$$

where Δ_{i+1} is the diagonal error matrix $\mathrm{diag}(\delta_j)$. Therefore, $A = \Delta_{i+1}G^{(i)}(\tilde{y}^{(i)})$. Moreover, $\Delta_{i+1}G^{(i)}(\tilde{y}^{(i)}) = \Delta_{i+1}G^{(i)}(y^{(i)})$ to first order. Consequently,

$$A = \Delta_{i+1}G^{(i)}(y^{(i)}) = \Delta_{i+1}(y^{(i+1)}) = \alpha_{i+1}.$$

The quantity α_{i+1} can be interpreted as the absolute round-off error created when $G^{(i)}$ is evaluated in floating-point arithmetic. The diagonal of Δ_{i+1} is the corresponding relative round-off errors.

Finally $\Delta y^{(i+1)} = \alpha_{i+1} + DG^{(i)}y^{(i)}\Delta y^{(i)}$, $i = 0, \ldots, r$. Starting from $\Delta y^{(0)} = \Delta y$, the iteration yields for $i = 0, \ldots, r$

$$\begin{aligned}
\Delta y^{(1)} &= DG^{(0)}(y)\Delta y + \alpha_1, \\
\Delta y^{(2)} &= DG^{(1)}(y^{(1)})[DG^{(0)}(y)\Delta y + \alpha_1] + \alpha_2, \\
&\vdots \\
\Delta x = \Delta y^{(r+1)} &= DG^{(r)} \ldots DG^{(0)}\Delta y + DG^{(r)} \ldots DG^{(1)}\alpha_1 + \cdots + \alpha_{r+1}.
\end{aligned}$$

2.6.4 Numerical stability with respect to round-off

By means of (2.16), Δx can be rewritten as

$$
\begin{aligned}
\Delta x &= DG(y)\Delta y + \left[D\psi^{(1)}(y^{(1)})\alpha_1 + \cdots + D\psi^{(r)}(y^{(r)})\alpha_r \right] + \alpha_{r+1} \\
&= A + [B] + C. \tag{2.17}
\end{aligned}
$$

The resulting error Δx is decomposed into three parts:

i) $A = DG(y)\Delta y$ depends only on the Jacobian of G at y.

ii) $[B]$ describes the part of the propagation of intermediate round-off errors that depends on the specific computational route chosen, i.e., on the factorization $G = \prod G^{(i)}$. Indeed, in the contribution of $[B]$ to the error, it is the regularity of the Jacobian matrix $D\psi^{(i)}$ of the remainder map $\psi^{(i)}$ that is critical for the effect of the intermediate round-off error $\alpha_i = \Delta_i y^{(i)}$ on the final result, for $i = 1, \ldots, r$.

iii) $C = \alpha_{r+1} = \Delta_{r+1} x$.

Thanks to the decomposition (2.17), two different algorithms for computing the same result $x = G(y)$ can be compared. If, for a given set of data y, the total effect of rounding $([B] + C)$ is smaller with a certain algorithm, this algorithm is arithmetically more trustworthy for the computation of $x = G(y)$.

In the error formula (2.17), the last term C (which is a vector in $\mathbb{R}^n$) can be bounded componentwise by $|\alpha_{r+1}| = |\Delta_{r+1} x| \leq |x|\mathbf{u}$ *independently* of the algorithm that has been used to compute $x = G(y)$. An error Δx of magnitude at least $|x|\mathbf{u}$ has to be expected for any algorithm. Moreover, the rounding of the data y will cause in general an input error $\Delta y^{(0)}$ with

$$
|\Delta y^{(0)}| = |\Delta y| \leq |y|\mathbf{u}.
$$

Consequently, any algorithm for computing $x = G(y)$ will have to be assumed to create at least the error

$$
DG(y)\Delta y + \alpha_{r+1} = A + C
$$

of magnitude bounded by $(|DG(y)||y| + |x|)\mathbf{u} = \Delta_0 x$.

This unavoidable part $\Delta_0 x$ of the global computational error $|\Delta x|$ is called the *inherent error* of x: it is of the order of machine precision Ψ.

It is therefore desirable to design algorithms for which the contribution B to the error Δx in (2.17) will also be of the order of machine precision Ψ, that is,

$$
|B| = \mathrm{O}(\Psi). \tag{2.18}
$$

The property for an algorithm to satisfy (2.18) is traditionally called *numerical stability* in the numerical software community (Wilkinson (1963), Bauer (1966), Dahlquist and Björck (1980)).

> This particular notion of "stability with respect to *round-off*" should not be confused with the more classical notion of "numerical stability," which is broadly used in theoretical numerical analysis for the convergence analysis of numerical methods in *exact* arithmetic, as was recalled in § 2.3.

In the next paragraph, we explicit the differences, by reinterpreting (2.18) in the limit $\varepsilon \to 0$. However, at this point, it is essential to realize that condition (2.18) is not enough to guarantee a small computing error. Looking at (2.17), one sees that the contribution of A to Δx should not be forgotten, as we illustrate now.

Example 2.3 (Forsythe, Malcom, and Moler (1977)).
We want to compute the term I_{50} of the sequence of integrals

$$I_n = \int_0^1 x^n e^{-x} dx, \quad n \geq 0.$$

1) Forward recurrence. Integration by parts yields the recurrence formula

$$I_0 = 1 - 1/e, \quad I_n = nI_{n-1} - 1/e, \quad n \geq 1. \tag{2.19}$$

However, in finite precision, the formula (2.19) yields a wrong computed result for $n = 50$, because (2.19) is highly sensitive to perturbations.

Let ΔI_0 be an inaccuracy in $I_0 = 1 - 1/e$, and suppose that the subsequent calculations are exact. The resulting error ΔI_n in I_n satisfies $\Delta I_n = n\Delta I_{n-1} = n!\Delta I_0$. Therefore (2.19) amplifies exponentially any error made on the datum e.

2) Backward recurrence. The recurrence (2.19) can be rewritten

$$I_{n-1} = \frac{1}{n}\left(I_n + \frac{1}{e}\right), \tag{2.20}$$

which can be used to compute I_n from a known I_p for $p > n$. The problem is that we do not know I_p. However, the sensitivity of (2.20) to perturbations is now small for p large enough: an initial error ΔI_p is propagated by exact calculations as $\Delta I_n = (n!/p!)\Delta I_p$.

For example, with $p = 60$ and the approximate value $\tilde{I}_{60} = 1$, $|\Delta \tilde{I}_{60}| < 1$; therefore, $|\Delta I_{50}| \sim (50!/60!) \sim 3 \times 10^{-18}$. Indeed, $I_{50} = 7.355 \times 10^{-3}$ and the computed value obtained with the recurrence (2.19) is $\tilde{I}_{50} = 1.9 \times 10^{48}$, whereas that obtained with (2.20) differs from the exact value only in the last two digits in double precision. $\triangle$

2.6.5 Arithmetic reliability

Let us change notation to make explicit the dependence of Δx on the arithmetic parameter ε. In the previous paragraph, we have analysed $\Delta x = x - \tilde{x}$, where $\tilde{x} = \widetilde{G}(\tilde{y})$ represents the result of the algorithm $G = \Pi G^{(i)}$ modified by round-off into $\widetilde{G}$ applied to the rounded data $\tilde{y}$. With the general notation of § 2.4, $\tilde{x}$, $\widetilde{G}$, $\tilde{y}$, and $\Delta x = x - \tilde{x}$ identify with x_ε, G_ε, y_ε, and $x - x_\varepsilon$, respectively. Therefore, the computation error

$$x - x_\varepsilon = G(y) - G_\varepsilon(y_\varepsilon) = [G(y) - G(y_\varepsilon)] + [G(y_\varepsilon) - G_\varepsilon(y_\varepsilon)]$$

has two sources (see Figure 2.2):

1. $E_1 = G(y) - G(y_\varepsilon) = DG(y)(y - y_\varepsilon) + O(\varepsilon^2)$, which depends on the mathematical stability of G at y;
2. $E_2 = G_\varepsilon(y_\varepsilon) - G(y_\varepsilon)$, which represents the direct consistency error at y_ε.

In the expression (2.17) for Δx, the quantity E_1 is represented by A, and the quantity E_2 by $[B] + C$. The bound $|C| \le \varepsilon|x|$ shows that the direct consistency error is *at least of the order of* ε.

Because of the inherent error due to machine representation of data, the consistency error is at best of order 1 in ε.

Condition (2.18) can be rewritten

$$|G_\varepsilon(y_\varepsilon) - G(y_\varepsilon)| \le C(y, G)\varepsilon. \tag{2.21}$$

This ensures that the direct consistency error at y_ε is indeed of the order of ε, which is the best order that can be achieved. From (2.21), the convergence $x_\varepsilon \to x$ as $\varepsilon \to 0$ follows at once. But the consistency of G_ε in a whole neighbourhood of y is not guaranteed. Equations (2.18) and (2.21) express merely that, at $y_\varepsilon = \mathrm{fl}(y)$, the ratio of the consistency error to the rounding error ε is bounded componentwise by a constant in ε. Therefore, the condition (2.21) can be interpreted as a specific convergence condition for the algorithm $G = \Pi G^{(i)}$ *with respect to round-off*.

Example 2.4 GE on $Ax = b$.

In the case where G_ε and G are *linear*, consistency at y_ε implies consistency at an arbitrary point z. With the notations of §2.4, $G_\varepsilon(z) - G(z)$ is rewritten $A_\varepsilon^{-1}z - A^{-1}z = A_\varepsilon^{-1}(A - A_\varepsilon)A^{-1}z$. The conclusion follows by (2.12).   △

By specializing the parameter $\theta = \varepsilon$ in Definition 2.3, we say that the algorithm G is *arithmetically* stable whenever G_ε is equicontinuous with respect to ε in a neighbourhood of y. The arithmetic stability of GE has been analysed in §2.5.

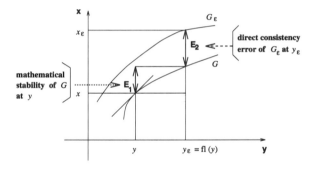

FIG. 2.2. *Decomposition of the computation error $x - x_\varepsilon$ for the algorithm G.*

Now the interpretation of the condition (2.21) becomes evident: (2.21) ensures that G_ε is an *arithmetic approximation of order* 1 for $F(x) = y$ at $y_\varepsilon = \mathrm{fl}(y)$.

Definition 2.8 *The algorithm G to compute the solution of $F(x) = y$ is arithmetically reliable whenever the perturbation $(G_\varepsilon - G,\ y_\varepsilon - y)$ generated on $x = G(y)$ at a regular point, by the computer arithmetic, induces a direct consistency error $G_\varepsilon(y_\varepsilon) - G(y_\varepsilon)$ of order 1 in ε.*

Definition 2.8 is an alternative way to express that G_ε is numerically stable with respect to round-off, which avoids the possible confusion with the numerical stability in exact arithmetic. If we recall the assumption that the n components g_i of G have continuous first derivatives, then the crucial notion of *arithmetic reliability* can be summarized as follows:

Arithmetic reliability $\iff$	direct consistency error of order 1 in ε, at regular points.

Strictly speaking, the arithmetic reliability defined by (2.21) is valid only for the specific perturbation $(G_\varepsilon - G, y_\varepsilon - y)$ generated by round-off. It will soon become apparent that, in practice, the property of reliability at y_ε is too narrow whenever one wants to vary a parameter in the algorithm $G : y \longmapsto x = G(y)$, such as y, for example.

This will lead to a *more generic* notion of reliability, that is, a reliability with a constant $C(y, G)$ in (2.21) bounded when the data y, G are allowed to vary in some specified way.

What we have just described is the essence of a *forward error analysis*. It allows a very detailed analysis of algorithms but can be very tedious. Unless the algorithm is so specific that its analysis requires such a detailed treatment, it is often possible to avoid a full forward analysis at the expense of a possible increase in the error bounds. When the algorithm G is meant to solve the equation $F(x) = y$, this can be achieved, for example, by means of the *backward error analysis* proposed by Wilkinson and Givens. In this approach, the more global view of G_ε stems from the fact that one allows the perturbations $\Delta G = G_\varepsilon - G$ and $\Delta y = y - y_\varepsilon$ to vary in a prescribed class (τ) of perturbations. The detailed analysis of the associated *backward stability* notion is deferred until Chapter 5. For the time being, it is sufficient to realize that the property of arithmetic reliability that is restricted to one specific perturbation cannot be extended to a larger class of perturbations without caution.

Remark: One can now clearly see an important difference between the convergence of approximate methods in exact arithmetic and the computability for algorithms in finite precision. It concerns the orders of convergence that can be achieved, which follow from the orders of consistency.

At a regular point, it is desirable that a numerical scheme has an order of convergence with respect to mesh size—for example, larger than 1—whereas for an algorithm, the order of convergence with respect to ε is *at best* 1.

2.6.6 Limits of the differential analysis

This forward sensitivity analysis is valid under the assumption that G and its factors $G^{(i)}$ have continuous partial derivatives. Such an assumption is not valid as soon as the map $G : \mathbb{R}^m \to \mathbb{R}^n$ is not C^1 in the neighbourhood of y, that is, when x is a singular point. Such a case, where the analysis given earlier no longer applies, is the topic of the next section.

2.7 The influence of singularities

Regular and singular points were defined in Definition 2.7.

Example 2.5 (see Chapters 3 and 4 for more examples).

a) Consider the linear system $Ax = b$, where the matrix A is regular. Then $x = A^{-1}b$ is a regular point of the linear equation. At a singular point for $A \longmapsto x$, the matrix A is singular, and solving the linear system is an *ill-posed* problem. The eigenvalues of A are the singular points of the family of linear equations $(A - zI)x = b$ for $z \in \mathbb{C}$.

b) Consider the problem $Ax = \lambda x$, $x \neq 0$. The nonlinear map $A \longmapsto \lambda$ is regular at any simple eigenvalue. It is singular at any multiple eigenvalue. Note that, at such a singularity, the map $A \longmapsto \lambda$ remains C^0; it is either Lipschitzian if λ is semi-simple or Hölder-continuous (see Definition 2.9 below) if λ is defective.[7] Therefore, the computation of a multiple eigenvalue remains *well posed* in the sense of Hadamard. Computing a multiple eigenvalue is a severely ill conditioned problem (the condition number tends to infinity) that is well posed. $\triangle$

Example 2.6

The multiple roots of a polynomial are another example of singular points, where the problem remains well posed. $\triangle$

Example 2.7

We consider the equation (2.1) $F(x) = y$ with $F : X = \mathbb{R}^n \longmapsto Y = \mathbb{R}^m$, which is assumed to be differentiable. The existence of x is ruled by a fundamental theorem in calculus, called the *implicit function theorem*, which requires that the $m \times n$ Jacobian matrix $DF = \left(\frac{\partial f_i}{\partial x_j}\right)$ be of maximal rank $\min(m, n)$ at x. The following two definitions are then very natural.

1. A point $x \in X$ is *regular* iff the Jacobian matrix DF has maximal rank $\min(m, n)$ at x.
2. A point x is called *singular* (or critical) iff it is not regular. The image $y = F(x)$ is called a singular (or critical) value accordingly.

When $m = n$, the regular points/values of F and G are related through the identity on regular Jacobians $DG = (DF)^{-1}$. Let the map F be linear: it is defined by a matrix A. The point $x = A^{-1}b$ is a regular point of the map A when A is regular. The eigenvalues of A are the singular points of the family of linear maps $A - zI$, $z \in \mathbb{C}$. $\triangle$

Example 2.8

Let $m = n = 1$ and consider the single equation in one unknown x given by $f(x) = y$. At a regular point x , f' is defined and nonzero. At a singular point x, either $f' = 0$

---

[7] A *defective* eigenvalue is an eigenvalue of algebraic multiplicity m that admits less than m independent eigenvectors.

or f' is not defined. If we define $x = g(y)$, then $g' = 1/f'$ and the singular/regular points of g are defined similarly (see Figure 2.3). △

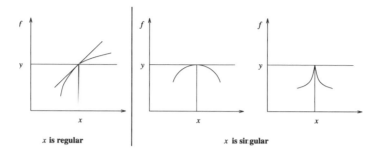

x is regular   x is singular

FIG. 2.3. *Regular versus singular points for* $f(x) = y$.

Mathematically, the singularities of a general map F can be very complex but they are *necessarily rare* according to the following theorem.

Theorem 2.3 (Sard (1942)) *The set of singular values of* F *is of measure zero in* X. *Therefore the set of regular values is dense in* Y.

In view of this theorem, one could be tempted to overlook the role of singularities in finite precision computations, with the excuse that singularities are not generic: they disappear under the influence of perturbations.

On the contrary, these lectures intend to show why singularities are to be taken seriously, according to the rule that

> singularities are rare, but their computational influence can be fatal.

In exact arithmetic, the main borderline for computability of nonlinear problems is that of the class of *well-posed* problems. Since x is a continuous function of y, a small perturbation Δy on y (such as that induced by numerical approximation) induces a small perturbation Δx on the solution. Therefore, it is reasonable to look for numerical methods that converge in exact arithmetic ($\Delta x \to 0$ as $\Delta y \to 0$). But in finite precision arithmetic, we have seen that the borderline is drawn closer to enclose only the subset of the well-posed problems consisting of those problems that are *regular* enough compared to machine precision. As a result, the borderline is fuzzy and depends on the machine precision of the available computer.

Problems in area II (see Figure 2.4) are increasingly singular and increasingly difficult to solve on a computer. These lecture notes will focus on the computer solution of some problems in this area.

It is interesting to note that the presence of this intermediate area II between regular (area I) and ill-posed (area III) problems is specific to *nonlinear* problems. Indeed, a linear problem such as $Ax = b$ can be only either regular or ill posed.

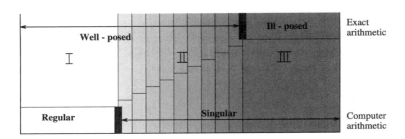

FIG. 2.4. *Classification of nonlinear problems with respect to computability in exact versus inexact arithmetic.*

In these lectures, we shall study a particular class of singularities that we call *algebraic* and that correspond to any of the two categories often encountered in scientific computing:

i) (P) is a particular case of well-posed nonlinear problems with a *multiple* solution of multiplicity m: multiple root of a polynomial or multiple eigenvalue of a matrix.

ii) (P) is a particular case of ill-posed linear problems: solving a *linear* system $Ax = b$ when A is singular.

Definition 2.9 *The continuous map* $G : Y \to X$ *is* Hölder-continuous *of order* $h \leq 1$ *in the neighbourhood* V *in* Y *iff there exists a constant* L *such that*

$$\|G(y) - G(y')\|_X = \|x - x'\|_X \leq L\|y - y'\|_Y^h$$

for any y, y' *in* V.

The particular case $h = 1$ corresponds to a map G, which is Lipschitz-continuous.

Example 2.9 Multiple roots.

a) Let ξ be a root of multiplicity m, $1 < m < q$, of the polynomial $p(x) = \sum_{i=0}^{q} a_i x^i$, that is, $p(\xi) = p'(\xi) = \cdots = p^{(m-1)}(\xi) = 0$, $p^{(m)}(\xi) \neq 0$. Then the map $a = (a_i) \longmapsto \xi$ is Hölder-continuous of order $h = 1/m$.

b) Let λ be a defective eigenvalue of A of multiplicity m and ascent[8] l, $1 < l \leq m$. Then the map $A \longmapsto \lambda$ is Hölder-continuous of order $h = 1/l$. If λ is a semisimple eigenvalue—that is, if $l = 1$—then $A \longmapsto \lambda$ is Lipschitz-continuous. $\triangle$

Clearly, multiple roots define a *hierarchy* of increasing singularities: simple, double, triple, ..., which is a hierarchy of decreasing regularities. Indeed a double root is singular when compared with simple roots (more regular points) but regular when compared with a triple root (more singular points). The notions regular and singular are context dependent: they depend on the chosen point of view.

Definition 2.10 *The* order γ *of a Hölder-continuous regular or singular point is defined by* $\gamma = 1/h$, *where* h *is the order of its Hölder continuity.*

In Example 2.9, $\gamma = m$ in case a) and $\gamma = l$ in case b).

---

[8]The *ascent* l is the order of the largest Jordan block associated with λ.

Definition 2.11 *An algebraic singularity that is Hölder-continuous of order* γ *is also called a* Hölderian singularity *of Hölderian order* γ.

2.8 Numerical stability in exact arithmetic

As we have already pointed out, the Lax principle is the basic tool to prove the convergence of numerical methods depending on one parameter. When there are several parameters, the uniform stability may not hold anymore without restriction, which results in a coupling of the parameters. The phenomenon of the necessary coupling between parameters is often present in many areas of theoretical numerical analysis. For example, in the analysis of approximation methods for *evolution* equations, the *coupling between time and space* is ubiquitous, as illustrated here.

Example 2.10 Fully discrete spectral method (Trefethen and Trummer (1987)). Consider the first-order hyperbolic mixed initial-boundary value problem

$$\begin{cases} \dfrac{\partial u}{\partial t} = \dfrac{\partial u}{\partial x}, & -1 < x < 1,\ t > 0, \\ u(x,0) = f(x)m, & -1 < x < 1, \\ u(1,t) = 0, & t \geq 0, \end{cases}$$

fully discretized in space and in time. The question arises of the numerical stability of the discretization in space *coupled* with the discretization in time. The chosen discretization in space corresponds to the Chebyshev collocation method, and we denote by D_N the $N \times N$–associated differentiation matrix $\Delta x = \mathrm{O}(1/N)$. In time, we choose the Adams–Bashforth formula of third order at each time step Δt and call Σ the associated stability region in $\mathbb{C}$. The condition that the eigenvalues of $\Delta t D_N$ are in Σ was known to be a necessary condition only when D_N is nonnormal. It is only recently that Reddy and Trefethen (1990, 1992) proposed a necessary and sufficient criterion. Consider the family of matrices $A = \Delta t D_N$, which depend on the two parameters Δx and Δt, together with the sets $S_\varepsilon = \{z \in \mathbb{C};\ z \text{ is an eigenvalue of } A + \Delta A,\ \|\Delta A\| \leq \varepsilon\}$. The necessary and sufficient condition proposed by Reddy and Trefethen imposes that S_ε lies within a distance at most $\mathrm{O}(\varepsilon)$ of Σ as $\varepsilon \to 0$ and for all Δt small enough.

This is a very natural condition that one should replace the spectrum of A by the sets S_ε of points that represent approximate eigenvalues in the sense that for any λ in S_ε, there exists x, $\|x\| = 1$, such that the residual vector $r = Ax - \lambda x$ satisfies $\|r\| \leq \|\Delta A\| \leq \varepsilon$. S_ϵ is called the *ε-pseudospectrum* of A. Its importance stems from the fact that its size reflects the possible nonnormality of A, a property that is not shared by the spectrum of A. It turns out that the Chebyshev collocation method leads to a differentiation matrix D_N, which gets increasingly nonnormal as $N \to \infty$ (Trefethen and Trummer (1987)). The phenomenon is illustrated in Figure 2.5, where the border of Σ and the computed spectra of samples of size 10 of randomly perturbed matrices $A + tE$ for $t = 2^{-p}$, $p = 45$ to 53 by steps of 2 (with $2^{-45} \sim 3\ 10^{-14}$ and $2^{-53} \sim 10^{-16}$), are plotted. The (pseudo) random matrices E have entries equal to ± 1 with probability $1/2$. Figure 2.5 gives the perturbed spectra for $N = 14$, 28, 56, and 100. The matrix D_N is given by $x_k = \cos \frac{k\pi}{N}$, $k = 1, \ldots, N$, $D_{ij} = (-1)^{i+j+1}/(x_i - x_j)$ for $i \neq j$, $d_{ii} = -x_i/(2(1 - x_i^2))$, and $D_{NN} = -(1 + 2N^2)/6$. Also, $A = \Delta t D_N = (1/N) D_N$. Part of the computed spectra lie outside Σ for $N = 28$,

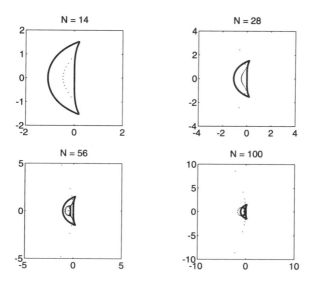

FIG. 2.5. *Perturbed spectra for the matrices* $A = (1/N)D_N$.

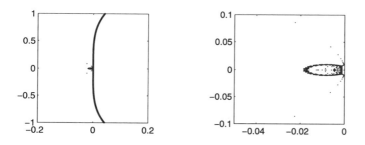

FIG. 2.6. *Perturbed spectra for the matrix* $A' = (1/N^2)D_N$, $N = 100$.

56, and 100. By comparison, Figure 2.6 gives the perturbed spectra for the matrix $A' = (1/N^2)D_N$ with $N = 100$. On the left plot, a portion of the border of Σ can be seen.

These results suggest the time-step restriction $\Delta t = O(1/N^2)$ for the Chebyshev spectral method. Note that in this example the nonnormality is not in the equation but results from the choice of the space discretization method. $\triangle$

2.9   Computability in finite precision for iterative and approximate methods

The general situation where x is not exactly computable in a finite number of steps can be divided into two main cases (in exact arithmetic):

    i) G is an iterative method such that x is obtained asymptotically in the limit $k \to \infty$ of an infinite number of steps; that is, $x_k \to x$ as $k \to \infty$.

ii) G_h is associated with a numerical method (where $h \to 0$ is a parameter related to the discretization mesh) such that $F_h(x_h) = y_h$ and $x_h = G_h(y_h)$ is obtained in the limit of an infinite number of steps. The solution x would be obtained only in the limit $x_h \to x$ when $h \to 0$.

In case i), the computed solution is $x_{l\varepsilon} = G_{l\varepsilon}(y_\varepsilon)$, where l is a parameter associated with the finite number K of steps performed in practice (for example $l = 1/K \to 0$). In case ii), the computed solution is similarly $x_{hl\varepsilon} = G_{hl\varepsilon}(y_{h\varepsilon})$.

We can fit these two cases into the unique formalism of § 2.3: $x_\theta = G_\theta(y_\theta)$, where the parameter θ is now a *vector* of dimension ≥ 2. In case i), $\theta = (l, \varepsilon)$, and in case ii), $\theta = (h, l, \varepsilon)$.

Clearly, the formalism can describe more general cases where, for example, there is a time step $\tau = \Delta t$ associated with a time variable t for evolution equations. The uniform stability, which is a sufficient condition for the convergence $x_\theta \to x$, becomes a uniform stability condition with respect to *several* parameters. These parameters may include data, as is the case in Example 2.10.

Therefore, proving the convergence of computations in finite precision arithmetic requires addition of the parameter ε of the computer arithmetic to the list θ of parameters for which it is sufficient to prove a numerical stability. When x is not exactly computable by an algorithm, the computation requires an approximate method G_θ, where θ is a vector of dimension at least 1 in exact arithmetic and at least 2 in finite precision.

If, for example, $\theta = (h, \varepsilon)$, then stability for $\bar{F}_{h\varepsilon}$ with respect to h *and* ε is a sufficient condition for convergence of the computed solution: $x_{h\varepsilon} \to x$ when both h and ε tend to zero. Such a stability with respect to two parameters is not always satisfied for all h and ε in $\mathbb{R}_+^2$. One often gets a *domain of stability* K for (h, ε) in the positive orthant. This means that the stability is uniform for $(h, \varepsilon) \in K$ only. Such a stability is a *conditional stability*.

Example 2.11 Numerical cancellation (Kulisch and Miranker (1986)).
Consider the function
$$f(t) = \frac{4970t - 4923}{4970t^2 - 9799t + 4830},$$

and compute $x = f''(1) = 94$ by finite differences for $t = 1$: $x_h = \frac{f(1+h) - 2f(1) + f(1-h)}{h^2} = G_h(1)$. Computed values $x_{h\varepsilon} = G_{h\varepsilon}(1)$ for decreasing h are given in Figure 2.7. The computation is convergent; that is, $x_{h\varepsilon}$ as h and $\varepsilon \to 0$ if h is not too small with respect to machine precision: there exists a *conditional stability* only, that is, stability for (h, ε) such that $h \geq h_0(\varepsilon)$.

What happens? A *numerical* catastrophic cancellation, similar to the previous arithmetic one (see Example 2.2). There is a severe loss of numerical significance, which takes place when the computed values for $f(1 + h) - f(1)$ and $f(1) - f(1 - h)$ differ only by digits that are *wrong*. In double precision ($\Psi \sim 10^{-16}$), $f(1) = 47$ is exact, but $f(1 + h)$ and $f(1 - h)$ have about 12 correct digits only, because of the instability of the evaluation $t \longmapsto f(t)$ around 1. Numerical cancellation occurs for $h \sim 10^{-5}$. It is useless to decrease h further. The computed value is 94.415, and the arithmetic operations are correct. Figure 2.7 shows very large oscillations around

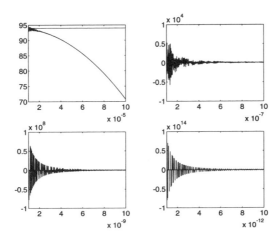

FIG. 2.7. *Numerical cancellation: computer approximation of $f''(1)$ by finite differences.*

the value 94 for small enough h. The four cases displayed correspond to a decreasing scale in the variation of h: $h \in [h_i, 10h_i]$, $i = 1, 2, 3, 4$, with $h_1 = 10^{-5}$, $h_2 = 10^{-7}$, $h_3 = 10^{-9}$, and $h_4 = 10^{-12}$. The vertical scale for $x_{h\varepsilon}$ varies widely also. In the three last graphs, the amplitude of the oscillations is so large that the line $x = 94$ does not appear and seems to be merged with $x = 0$. The oscillations in $G_{h\varepsilon}(1)$ increase as h decreases so that $G_{h\varepsilon}$ cannot be uniformly continuous in h and ε in an arbitrary neighbourhood of $(0, 0)$. The stability of this finite difference scheme is conditional to the arithmetic: the mesh size h should be larger than a threshold depending on the arithmetic precision ε. $\triangle$

2.10   The limit of numerical stability in finite precision

In theoretical numerical analysis, the convergence of numerical methods in exact arithmetic is often shown by means of the Lax principle, by involving the *numerical stability* with respect to θ, the list of all the computation parameters.

Is the proof of numerical stability in exact arithmetic sufficient to ensure computability in finite precision?

The answer obviously is *not always*, as Example 2.11 has already shown. And the answer depends on the uniform stability with respect to the augmented vector $\theta_\varepsilon = (\theta, \varepsilon)$, where the arithmetic parameter ε has been added to the previous list θ. The usual theoretical tools consist of the two classical partial stabilities, which are

i) the *numerical stability in exact arithmetic*, which is proven for $\theta_0 = (\theta, 0)$, that is, a uniform stability with respect to $\theta \to 0$ and for $\varepsilon = 0$ fixed;

ii) the *arithmetic stability in finite precision*, which corresponds to $\bar{\theta}_\varepsilon = (\bar{\theta}, \varepsilon)$, that is, a uniform stability with respect to $\varepsilon \to 0$ and for a fixed value $\bar{\theta}$ of the parameter vector θ.

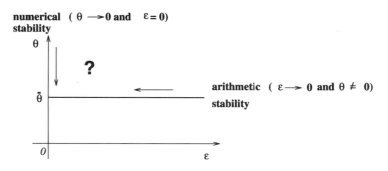

FIG. 2.8. *The two particular stabilities in* $\mathbb{R}^2_+$ *with respect to* θ *and* ε.

Clearly these two partial stabilities may fail to ensure the uniform stability with respect to θ_ε (see Figure 2.8).

> Technically, the convergence analysis of a numerical method in finite precision arithmetic requires the *coupling* of the arithmetic precision with all the previous computation parameters θ, including data.

Example 2.12 Multiple defective eigenvalues (Chatelin (1970, 1984)).
Consider the spectral problem $Tx = \lambda x$, λ multiple *defective*, set in a functional space. The notion of *strong stability* (expressed in terms of the reduced resolvent) of T_h was introduced by Chatelin (1970) to ensure the convergence of spectral approximation methods $T_h x_h = \lambda_h x_h$ in exact arithmetic. But in finite precision arithmetic, one needs the stronger notion of stability for the *block-reduced resolvent* (see Chatelin (1984, 1993a)) to prove the global convergence $\lambda_{h\varepsilon} \to \lambda$, when h and ε tend to zero, where $\lambda_{h\varepsilon}$ are the computed eigenvalues of T_h. $\triangle$

This example illustrates the reason why the classical approach taken in theoretical numerical analysis may not be sufficient to ensure the uniform stability in θ *and* ε, required in general for finite precision computation.

Numerical stability in exact arithmetic may become conditional to the arithmetic in finite precision.

2.11   Arithmetically robust convergence

So far, the necessity of dealing with the coupling between the arithmetic and the method parameter θ has been established only when the convergence condition depends on θ. The hurried reader might then conclude that such a coupling does not occur for convergence conditions independent of θ. However, the reality is more subtle as we see by taking another look at Example 2.1. The matrix iteration with A converges in exact arithmetic for all matrices A whose spectrum lies in $\Delta = \{z \in \mathbb{C}; \ |z| < 1\}$. This is a convergence condition, or equivalently by linearity, a stability condition. In finite precision ε, one deals with a family of matrices A_ε for which the condition should hold *uniformly with respect to* ε. Whenever A is normal, this is satisfied, but when A is far from normal, this may not be the case anymore. Example 2.10 illustrates such a phenomenon (where Δ is replaced by Σ).

At this point, we wish to point out that the computational difficulties that may arise from nonnormality are *not created* by the finite precision. Highly nonnormal matrices have a high spectral sensitivity; the computer arithmetic merely exposes it by introducing perturbations on the exact problem, implicitly or explicitly. It is important to bear this in mind, especially that in scientific computing the matrices are often associated with the modelling of a physical phenomenon so that the nonnormality of matrices can be inherited from the physics.

We now show by way of a simple example that the robustness of convergence conditions with respect to arithmetic perturbations can sometimes be delicate to analyse.

Example 2.13 (Francois and Muller (1990)).
The second-order nonlinear recursion

$$x_0 = 11/2, \quad x_1 = 61/11,$$
$$x_{k+1} = 111 - \frac{1130}{x_k} + \frac{3000}{x_k x_{k-1}}, \qquad k \geq 3, \qquad (2.22)$$

converges always very rapidly in finite precision toward 100. However, the exact limit is 6, which is never computable in finite precision.

What happens? The sequence defined by (2.22) converges to one of the three roots of the polynomial $p(x) = x^3 - 111x^2 + 1130x - 3000$, which are 5, 6, and 100 (see Figure 2.9).

There are nearby singular polynomials with a double root, at 5.5, for example: $q(x) = x^3 - 111x^2 - 1130.25x - 3025 = (x - 5.5)^2(x - 100)$. The relative variation in the coefficients is less than 10^{-2}.

The mathematical convergence of (2.22) depends on the initial conditions x_0, x_1:

i)   convergence to 100 for almost all (x_0, x_1),

ii) convergence to 6 $\Longleftrightarrow x_0(11 - x_1) = 30$,   (2.23)

iii) convergence to 5 $\Longleftrightarrow x_0 = x_1 = 5$.   (2.24)

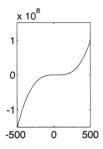 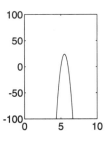 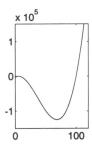

FIG. 2.9. *Graph for $p(x)$.*

This can be easily verified on the third-order linear recurrence $y_{k+2} = 111y_{k+1} - 1130y_k + 3000y_{k-1}$, equivalent to (2.22) by the change of variable $x_k = y_{k+1}/y_k$.

Conditions (2.23) and (2.24) are unstable under arbitrary perturbations. This explains why on any computer with $x_0 = 11/2$ and $x_1 = 61/11$, the sequence actually converges to 100 very rapidly. But with an arithmetic with base 2, the sequence $\{x_0 = x_1 = 5, \ x_k\}$ remains stationary. This is because 5 satisfies the identity

$$5 = 111 - \frac{1130}{5} + \frac{3000}{25}$$

exactly in machine representation. There is no perturbation induced by the floating-point representation. This is a very rare situation that explains why, on any binary computer, the iteration $\{x_k\}$ is stationary for $x_0 = x_1 = 5$. $\triangle$

There remains only the case of unconditional convergence to examine under finite precision. In that case at least, there should be no reason to fear any coupling between the arithmetic of the computer and the mathematics in exact arithmetic. However, the dependence on n of the constants which occur in the stability of GE given earlier (see § 2.5) has indicated to the reader a possible source of difficulties when n is implicitly allowed to grow without bound. More generally, Chapter 5 will look at the *arithmetic quality* of the solution delivered by a reliable algorithm.

We can summarize this section by stating the principle that

> computability in finite precision is achieved with numerical methods that are proved convergent in exact arithmetic under *arithmetically robust conditions.*

Convergence conditions that are arithmetically robust are conditions that remain satisfied under special types of perturbations on the parameters (including data) generated by the finite precision arithmetic. This leads to the property of *robust convergence*, which will be developed in Chapters 5, 6, and 10.

2.12   The computed logistic[9]

We end this chapter with the stability analysis of a simple yet highly complex example of iteration with a *nonlinear* map f. The map is a simple *quadratic* function in one variable $f_r(x) = rx(1 - x)$, and we associate the fixed-point equation

$$x = f_r(x) = rx(1 - x), \tag{2.25}$$

where x is a real unknown and r is a real parameter. The index r in f is dropped for simplicity.

---

[9]The term *logistic* comes from economics and population dynamics, where a fixed-point equation of the type (2.25) is used to model the evolution of a prey-predator population under limited allocation of resources.

2.12.1 Solving (2.25)

The quadratic equation $rx(1-x) - x = 0$ yields the two solutions $x^* = 0$ for all r and $x^* = 1 - 1/r$ for $r \neq 0$. Equation (2.25) can be rewritten as $g(x) = (1-f)(x) = 0$ so that $x = g^{-1}(0) = h(0)$. The derivative of the map h in the neighbourhood of 0 is $h' = 1/g' = 1/(1-f')$. The map h' is not defined if $f' = 1$, where $f'(x) = r(1-2x)$. This happens for $r = 1$ at the solution $x^* = 0$, which is *double*: the equation has only one singular point, for $r = 1$. As r varies, $r \neq 1$, the stability of h can be measured by the condition number

$$|h'(x,r)| = \frac{1}{|1 - r(1-2x)|}, \tag{2.26}$$

which varies between 0 and ∞. It is best for $x = 1/2$, for which it takes the optimal value $h' = 1$. Figure 2.10 displays the stability map $r \longmapsto |h'(x,r)|$ for $-3 \le r \le 5$, where x is constrained to be equal to the solution $x^* = 0$ on $[-3, 1]$ and $x^* = 1 - 1/r$ on $[1, 5]$. It is not defined at the singularity $(r = 1, x = 0)$.

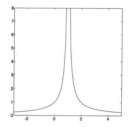

FIG. 2.10. *Stability map for the solutions $x^* = 0$ and $x^* = 1 - 1/r$.*

2.12.2 Computing the solutions of (2.25) by a fixed-point iteration

We consider the iteration

$$x_0, \quad x_{k+1} = f(x_k), \qquad k \ge 0, \tag{2.27}$$

for a fixed value of the parameter r. Let x^* be one of the two solutions of (2.25). For x_0 close enough to x^*, the iteration converges toward x^* if $|f'(x^*)| < 1$.

i) For $x^* = 0$, $f' = r$, so $|f'| < 1$ for $-1 < r < 1$. Divergence occurs for $r = -1^-$ with $f' = -1$ and for $r = 1^+$ with $f' = +1$. Note that the convergence on $[0, 1[$ (resp., $]-1, 0]$) is monotone ($f' > 0$) (resp., alternate ($f' < 0$)).

ii) For $x^* = 1 - 1/r$, $r \neq 0$, $f' = 2 - r$ so that $|f'| < 1$ for $1 < r < 3$. Similarly, $f' = +1$ for $r = 1$ and $f' = -1$ for $r = 3$.

The convergence (or stability) intervals for the iteration with f are therefore $]-1, 1[$ and $]1, 3[$. At the two end points $r = -1$ and $r = 3$, however, the *divergence is mild*: it is only a bifurcation and not a divergence to infinity. What happens can be now explained in terms of the map $f \circ f$.

2.12.3 Fixed-point iteration with $f^2 = f \circ f$

The iteration (2.27) can also be interpreted as an iteration with $f^2 = f \circ f$ if one sorts the odd and even iterates:

$$\begin{cases} x_0, \ x_2 = f^2(x_0), \ \dots : & \text{even iterates,} \\ x_1 = f(x_0), \ x_3 = f^2(x_1), \ \dots : & \text{odd iterates.} \end{cases}$$

The associated fixed-point equation

$$x = f^2(x) = f(f(x)) \tag{2.28}$$

has, in addition to the two solutions of (2.25) ($x = 0$ and $x = 1 - 1/r$ for $r \neq 0$), the two new solutions $x = \frac{1}{2r}(1 + r \pm \sqrt{(r+1)(r-3)})$ for $r < -1$ or $r > 3$. With the identity $[f(f(x))]' = f'(f(x))f'(x)$, it is easy to check that (2.28) has two singular (triple) points: $r = 3$, $x = 2/3$ and $r = -1$, $x = 0$.

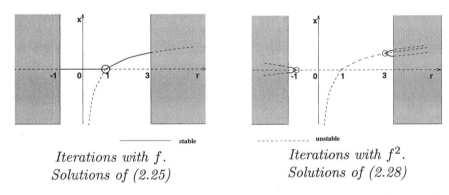

Iterations with f.	*Iterations with f^2.*
Solutions of (2.25)	*Solutions of (2.28)*

FIG. 2.11. *Stability analysis for the fixed-point iteration on f and on $f \circ f$.*

The iteration with the map $f \circ f$ has the two convergence (or stability) intervals $]1 - \sqrt{6}, -1[$ and $]3, 1 + \sqrt{6}[$ (see Figure 2.11). The values $r'_1 = 1 - \sqrt{6}$ and $r_1 = 1 + \sqrt{6}$ correspond to four new bifurcations, which can be analysed with f^4. This stability analysis can be iterated on f^{2^i}, $i \geq 0$. It can be proved that each of the two sequences of bifurcation values r_i (r'_i) converges to a limit r_∞ (r'_∞). For $r > r_\infty$ (or $r < r'_\infty$) the convergence of subsequences of x_k is not guaranteed anymore for all values of r. This corresponds to the *chaotic regime* for the iteration (2.27) interpreted as a discrete dynamical system with a discrete time variable $k = 0, \ 1, \ 2, \ \dots$ (Schuster (1989)). For $r > 4$ (or $r < -2$), a complete divergence to infinity occurs for almost all x_0.

2.12.4 The iteration (2.27) in finite precision

Figure 2.12 displays the computed logistic on the complete stability interval $[-2, 4]$. Figure 2.13 displays an enlargement of the interval $[3.5, 4]$. The starting point is $x_0 = 0.5$, and for values of r in $[3.5, 4]$, the computed iterates $\tilde{x}_k$

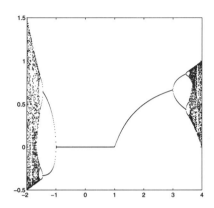

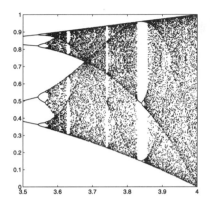

FIG. 2.12.　*The logistic on* $[-2, 4]$.　　　FIG. 2.13.　*Zoom on* $[3.5, 4]$.

for $k = 201$ to 250 are plotted. As expected, only the stable solutions for the iterated map $f, f^2, \ldots, f^3$ appear on the plot. Figure 2.14 displays the computed iterates for f^2; that is, only the even iterates of (2.27) have been plotted.

The computed logistic displays, with each window of periodicity p, the corresponding stability interval for f^p. (See in Figure 2.15 a zoom in the window of periodicity 3.) Once more, we repeat that the finite precision on such a simple calculation reveals the intricate stability pattern of the iteration (2.27) without adding to its inherent mathematical instability. A backward stability result for (2.27) will be given in Chapter 6. The parameter r unfolds the complete variety of stabilities for the computational scheme (2.27), ranging from full stability on $] - 1, 3[$, $r \neq 1$ (convergence $x_k \to x^*$ as $k \to \infty$), to no stability outside $[-2, 4]$ (divergence $x_k \to \pm\infty$ as $k \to \infty$ for almost all x_0). In the intermediate zones $[-2, -1[$ and $] - 3, 4]$, patterns of convergence are observed for subsequences extracted from $\{x_k\}_{I\!N}$. They can be interpreted as convergence toward the stable solutions of the equation $x = f^p(x)$: they correspond to the convergence of the p subsequences of $\{x_k\}$ starting from the p values x_0, $x_1 = f(x_0)$, $\ldots, x_{p-1} = f^{p-1}(x_0)$.

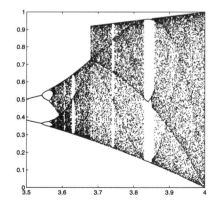

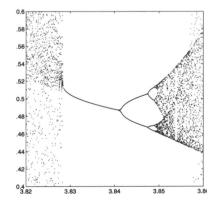

FIG. 2.14.　*Computed iterates*　　　FIG. 2.15.　*Zoom on* $[3.82, 3.86]$
for f^2 *on* $[3.5, 4]$.　　　　　　*for* f.

The logistic graph illustrates dramatically the fuzzy zone II between regular and ill-posed problems, which was presented in §2.7 (Figure 2.4). This zone consists of the set of problems $x = f^p(x)$ at singular (multiple) points. As p increases, the domain of stability in r for the fixed-point iteration with f_r^p decreases. Alternatively, the zone of gradual divergence for the sequence $\{x_k\}_{I\!N}$ that occurs outside $]-1, 3[$ can be viewed as the unfolding by r of the variability of the computational stability of the iteration by f_r to compute a fixed point for $x = f_r(x)$.

The gradual divergence of (2.27) is displayed in Figure 2.16 by means of the graph of the residual values $y_k = rx_k^2 + (1 - r)x_k$, which shows by how much x_k fails to satisfy (2.25), that is, $x - f(x) = 0$.

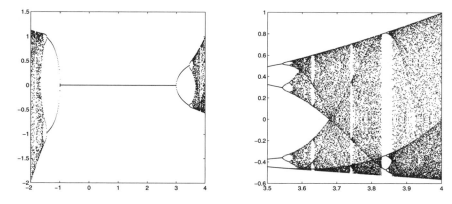

FIG. 2.16. *Residual values* $(1 - f)(x_k)$.

The variability of stability is generated by the computational bifurcation at the unique singular point (double root) of the equation $x = f(x)$, which occurs for $r = 1$ and is reflected for $r > 3$ (resp., $r < -1$) on the computation of the solution $x^* = 1 - 1/r$ (resp., $x^* = 0$). This is the unfolding of stability for the *iteration with* f_r as a computational process to solve the equation $x = f_r(x)$. The unfolding shows how the *algebraic singularity of order* 2 at $r = 1$ is reflected as a *bifurcation in the stability* of the computation process. For $r > 3$ (resp., $r < -1$), convergence does not occur anymore for the complete sequence. However, divergence does not occur abruptly. Subsequences may still converge, and divergence is bounded for $3 < r \leq 4$ (resp., $-2 \leq r < -1$) until full divergence to $-\infty$ (resp., $+\infty$) occurs for $r > 4$ (resp., $r < -1$).

The bifurcation by computation at $r = 3$ and -1 expresses, through the dynamics of the computation (iteration with f), the mathematical singularity of order 2 for the underlying equation at $r = 1$.

2.13 Bibliographical comments

The theoretical framework for a rigorous theory of computability in finite precision, which has been presented, is taken from Chatelin (1988a, 1989b). The forward error analysis presentation is adapted from Stoer and Bulirsch (1980). The traditional notion of *numerical stability* of an algorithm *with respect to round-off* is interpreted as a direct consistency error of order 1 in the arithmetic parameter ε for regular problems (Chaitin-Chatelin (1994b)). Such a notion is ubiquitous in numerical software; its name is often shortened to numerical stability or even only stability, thus creating a possible confusion with the mathematical notion of numerical stability (in exact arithmetic). This is why it has been renamed arithmetic reliability.

Our definition of singular points and singular problems follows the mathematical use. It departs from the custom in numerical analysis, where problems that are not regular are often called (numerically) ill posed (Kahan (1972), Demmel (1987)). The notion of robust convergence is borrowed from control theory.

Chapter 3

Measures of Stability for Regular Problems

We devote this chapter to the quantification of stability for the problem (P) at a *regular* point $x = F^{-1}(y) = G(y)$. For small enough perturbations of the data y, the induced first-order variation Δx on x can be written

$$\Delta x = DG(y)\Delta y, \tag{3.1}$$

where $DG(y)$ represents the derivative of G at y. Of course, the formula (3.1) is in general too detailed and may not be easy to interpret. Therefore, it is tempting to use the straightforward bound

$$\|\Delta x\| \leq \|DG(y)\|\|\Delta y\| \tag{3.2}$$

to analyse the sensitivity of $x = G(y)$ to the variation Δy on the data y. The difficulties that we are facing to get a useful bound for the forward error $\|\Delta x\|$ are twofold:

  i) to find tractable expressions for $DG(y)$,

  ii) to find a working compromise between the simplicity stemming from a large overestimation and the complexity of a myopic description of the reality of floating-point computation.

This quantification of stability assumes that the computation is *exact*. The aim is to understand how perturbations on the data are reflected on the exact solution. The first application that comes to mind is the case where the data are known with a certain level of uncertainty. However, our main application will be *finite precision* computation, thanks to the backward error analysis of Wilkinson, which will be presented in Chapter 5.

As we have seen, choosing an algorithm to compute $x = G(y)$ amounts to specifying a factorization $G = \prod_{i=0}^{r} G^{(i)}$. Whenever necessary, one should distinguish clearly between $G = F^{-1}$ and $G_{alg} = \prod_{i=0}^{r} G^{(i)}$, as they may have different stabilities.

3.1   Choice of data and class of perturbations

Any stability analysis requires that the *data to be perturbed* have been prescribed. For example, in the case of an equation $F(x) = y$, the data which specify the equation consist of the map F and the right-hand side y.

Let Z be the space of data to be perturbed (parameter space). Z is a subspace of $Y \times M$, where M is some space of maps $X \to Y$, and we define the solution $x = G(y)$ as a function g at the point $z \in Z$:

$$g : \quad Z \quad \to \quad X,$$
$$z \quad \longmapsto \quad x = g(z),$$

where x solves $F(x) = y$.

Examples:

- For a general nonlinear equation $F(x) = y$, one often considers the stability of $y \longmapsto x = F^{-1}(y) = G(y)$, which means that y represents the chosen data and is allowed to vary, whereas F remains fixed.

- For the solution of a linear system $Ax = b$, one may consider a variety of data ranging from one element in A or b to the complete set (A, b).

- To solve $Ax = b$, one can use an algorithm based on one of the classical factorizations $A = LU$, $A = QR$, or $A = QH$ (see §3.5). The corresponding algorithms may have different stability properties.

- A Vandermonde matrix (a_{ij}) of order n depends on n distinct parameters $\{\alpha_i\}_1^n$ only: $(a_{ij} = \alpha_i^{j-1}, \ i, j = 1, \ldots, n)$. it is clear that its stability with respect to a change in the α_i only (that is, $A + \Delta A$ remains a Vandermonde matrix) can be stronger than its stability when the elements a_{ij} are allowed to vary arbitrarily. It is known that, in this latter case, the usual condition number can grow exponentially with n.

Any stability analysis is relative to the choice of parameters and to the class of perturbations. One of the difficulties in the arithmetic analysis of algorithms or methods consists in the characterization of the class of perturbations generated by the finite precision arithmetic. It is one of the main tasks of software developers (see LAPACK). And despite more than four decades of efforts, the last word has not been said on GE, the most basic algorithm of all.

3.2   Choice of norms: Scaling

Once the data to be perturbed have been selected, one has to choose a metric in the spaces Z and X to quantify the size of the perturbations on data and solution. In X or Z (assumed to be of finite dimension) we generally consider a metric or a distance deriving from a norm.

Example 3.1

For $x \neq 0 \in \mathbb{C}^n$, $\|\Delta x\|$ represents an absolute measure of the variation $\Delta x = x - \tilde{x}$. Most commonly used norms include the Euclidean norm $\|x\|_2 = \sqrt{\sum_{i=1}^n |x_i|^2}$ and the max norm $\| \cdot \|_\infty = \max_i |x_i|$.   △

Mathematically, convergence is characterized by the condition $\|\Delta x\| \to 0$ for some norm. But in numerical analysis and physics, an absolute criterion such as "$\|\Delta x\|$ small enough" is not quantitative enough. One wants, if possible, to satisfy a relative criterion such as "$\|\Delta x\|/\|x\|$ small" with respect to some threshold. The threshold can be chosen as machine precision or the level of uncertainty in the data. Such a strategy for measuring relative variations has been systematically developed in numerical analysis under the generic name of *scaling*.

3.2.1   Scaling and scaled norms

Scaling consists in applying some linear transformation on the data and the solution. For example, one considers the transformed data $\hat{z} = S_1 z$ and the transformed solution $\hat{x} = S_2 x$, where S_1 and S_2 are linear transformations. So $x = g(z)$ becomes $\hat{x} = S_2 \circ g \circ S_1^{-1}(\hat{z})$ if we assume that S_1 is invertible: the nonlinear map g is transformed into $\hat{g} = S_2 \circ g \circ S_1^{-1}$.

In linear algebra, one often considers *diagonal scaling*.

Example 3.2 Normwise and componentwise scalings.

Let $f \neq 0$ be a given vector with positive components $f_i > 0$, $i = 1, \ldots, n$. Introduce the diagonal matrices $D_{1f} = \|f\| I$ and $D_{2f} = \mathrm{diag}(f_i)$.

Definition 3.1 *The vector f defines a*

   i) *normwise scaling by setting* $S_f^{\mathcal{N}} = D_{1f}^{-1}$;

   ii) *componentwise scaling by setting* $S_f^{\mathcal{C}} = D_{2f}^{-1}$.

Then $\hat{x} = S_f^{\mathcal{N}} x = x/\|f\|$ or $\hat{x} = S_f^{\mathcal{C}} x = (x_i/f_i)_{i=1,\ldots,n}$. Moreover $\|\hat{x}\| = \|S_f x\|$ yields $\|S_f^{\mathcal{N}} x\| = \|x\|/\|f\|$ denoted by $\|x\|^{\mathcal{N}}$ or $\|S_f^{\mathcal{C}} x\| = \max_i |x_i/f_i|$ denoted by $\|x\|^{\mathcal{C}}$. The measures $\|\,.\,\|^{\mathcal{N}}$ and $\|\,.\,\|^{\mathcal{C}}$ represent weighted norms of the vector x defined by means of f. A choice often made is $f = |x|$ so that the associated *scaled norms* for $\Delta x = x - \tilde{x}$ are $|\Delta x\|^{\mathcal{N}} = \|\Delta x\|/\|x\|$ and $\|\Delta x\|^{\mathcal{C}} = \max_i |\Delta x_i/x_i|$ defined for $x_i \neq 0$. $\triangle$

Example 3.3

When the objects to be measured are matrices, a similar approach can be taken. Let be given a matrix E with positive elements $e_{ij} > 0$, $i, j = 1, \ldots, n$. The associated scaled norms for $\Delta A = A - \tilde{A}$ are $\|\Delta A\|^{\mathcal{N}} = \|\Delta A\|/\|E\|$ and $\|\Delta A\|^{\mathcal{C}} = \max_{i,j} |\Delta a_{ij}/e_{ij}|$. Clearly, $\|\Delta A\|^{\mathcal{N}}$ remains an operator norm on $\mathbb{C}^{n \times n}$ if $\|\,.\,\|$ is itself an operator norm, but $\|\Delta A\|^{\mathcal{C}}$ is a weighted max norm on $\mathbb{C}^{n^2}$. $\triangle$

Example 3.4 Sparsity pattern.

Let the data to be perturbed be a sparse matrix A. It may be interesting to consider perturbations ΔA of A that preserve the sparsity pattern; i.e., if $a_{ij} = 0$, then it remains zero under perturbation. This can be achieved by choosing $E = |A|$, which has nonnegative elements $|a_{ij}| \geq 0$; $\max_{ij} |\Delta a_{ij}/a_{ij}|$ is defined if $|a_{ij}| > 0$. The definition can be extended to the case $a_{ij} = 0$ by the following rule: $0/0$ is taken as 0 and $\xi/0$ is interpreted as ∞ when $\xi \neq 0$.

Therefore, the choice $E = |A|$ allows definition of the norm $\|\Delta A\|^{\mathcal{C}}$ in Z (that is, when A is a *datum*). $\triangle$

We define below the scaled norms on Z and X that are basic for linear algebra. They will be used throughout the lectures and are divided into two main classes:

i) For the normwise analysis (indexed by $\mathcal{N}$), α and β are given positive constants and $\|\,.\,\|$ represents an arbitrary vector norm. The norm of the matrices is the associated operator norm or subordinate norm.

ii) For the componentwise analysis (indexed by $\mathcal{C}$), one is given a matrix E with nonnegative entries $e_{ij} \geq 0$ and a vector f with nonnegative components $f_i \geq 0$.

The norms for the space Z of parameters are given in Table 3.1. Table 3.2 gives the norms used for the solution space X, which again can be a space of vectors x or of matrices B. The normwise case corresponds to the choice of constants $\|x\|$ and $\|B\|$. Similarly, the componentwise case corresponds to the choice $|x|$ and $|B|$.

Analysis Data (space Z)	normwise $\mathcal{N}$	componentwise $\mathcal{C}$
matrix A in $Z_1 = \mathbb{C}^{n \times n}$ $\|\,.\,\|$ subordinate	$\|\Delta A\|^{\mathcal{N}} = \dfrac{\|\Delta A\|}{\alpha}$	$\|A\|^{\mathcal{C}} = \max\limits_{ij,\ e_{ij} \neq 0} \dfrac{|\Delta a_{ij}|}{e_{ij}}$
vector b in $Z_2 = \mathbb{C}^n$	$\|\Delta b\|^{\mathcal{N}} = \dfrac{\|\Delta b\|}{\beta}$	$\|\Delta b\|^{\mathcal{C}} = \max\limits_{i,\ f_i \neq 0} \dfrac{|\Delta b_i|}{f_i}$
(A,b) in $Z_1 \times Z_2$	product norm	product norm
frequent choice	$\alpha = \|A\|,\ \beta = \|b\|$	$E = |A|,\ f = |b|$

TABLE 3.1
Basic scaled norms for data in linear algebra

Note that in the choice of $\|\,.\,\|^{\mathcal{C}}$ for matrices, as either data or solutions, their structure as linear operator is *not preserved*: they are considered only as vectors in $\mathbb{C}^{n^2}$.

Example 3.5 Linear control.
In linear control theory, the system $\mathcal{S}$ defined by

$$\begin{cases} \lambda x = Ax + Bu, \\ y = Cx + Du \end{cases}$$

plays a fundamental role, where λ is a complex parameter; A, B, C, and D are complex matrices of sizes $n \times n$, $n \times l$, $m \times n$, and $m \times l$, respectively; and $x \in \mathbb{C}^n$, $u \in \mathbb{C}^l$, $y \in \mathbb{C}^m$. In particular, $y = \left[C(\lambda I_n - A)^{-1}B + D\right]u$, where the matrix in brackets is the transfer function of $\mathcal{S}$: it gives the output y in terms of the input or control u. If

Analysis Solution (space X)	normwise $\mathcal{N}$	componentwise $\mathcal{C}$
vector x in $X = \mathbb{C}^n$	$\|\Delta x\|^{\mathcal{N}} = \dfrac{\|\Delta x\|}{\|x\|}$	$\|x\|^{\mathcal{C}} = \max_i \dfrac{\|\Delta x_i\|}{\|x_i\|}$ defined if $x_i \neq 0$
matrix B $\begin{cases} \text{in } X = \mathbb{C}^{n \times n} \\ \|\,.\,\| \text{ subordinate} \\[2pt] \text{in } X = \mathbb{C}^{n^2} \end{cases}$	$\|\Delta B\|^{\mathcal{N}} = \dfrac{\|\Delta B\|}{\|B\|}$	—— $\|\Delta B\|^{\mathcal{C}} = \max_{i,j} \dfrac{\|\Delta b_{ij}\|}{\|b_{ij}\|}$ defined if $b_{ij} \neq 0$

TABLE 3.2
Scaled norms for solutions in linear algebra

$m = l$, the transfer matrix is square and satisfies the identity

$$\left(C(\lambda I_n - A)^{-1}B + D\right)^{-1} = -D^{-1}C(\lambda I_n - A + BD^{-1}C)^{-1}BD^{-1} + D^{-1}.$$

This explains why, in robustness analysis, the perturbations ΔA on the matrix A have the particular structure $\Delta A = BEC$, where E is of size $l \times m$ in general and B and C play the role of scaling matrices (Lancaster and Tismenetsky (1985, p. 70), Hinrichsen and Kelb (1993)).   △

3.3   Conditioning of regular problems

The stability of $g(z)$ is a qualitative property of the sensitivity of $x = g(z)$ to perturbations of the selected data z, which is described by the Jacobian $Dg(z) = (\frac{\partial g_i}{\partial z_j})$ (see § 2.6).

With scaled norms $\|\,.\,\|_X$ and $\|\,.\,\|_Z$ defined on X and Z, one may quantify the stability by what is traditionally called a *condition number* in numerical analysis. Such a quantity is clearly *relative to* the choice of data, the norms put on X and Z, and the associated class of perturbations defined as $(\tau)_\delta = \{z \in Z, \|z' - z\|_Z \leq \delta\}$. For *structured* perturbations, z may be constrained to stay in a subset $K \subset Z$ (see § 3.8.1).

3.3.1   Definitions

The condition number of the map $g : z \longmapsto x = g(z)$ assumed to be C^1 at z can be defined as follows for *unstructured* perturbations.

Definition 3.2   a. *The δ-condition number for g at z is*

$$C_\delta = \sup_{z',0<\|z'-z\|_Z\leq\delta} \frac{\|g(z') - g(z)\|_X}{\|z' - z\|_Z}. \tag{3.3}$$

b. *The asymptotic condition number for g at z is*

$$C = \lim_{\delta\to 0} C_\delta.$$

C_δ is a local Lipschitz constant, while the limit C as $\delta \to 0$ is the norm of the first *derivative* at z and, as such, can be called the *linear condition number*.
Theorem 3.1 *If $g: Z \to X$ is C^1 at z, then*

$$C = \lim_{\delta\to 0} C_\delta = \|g'\|,$$

where Z and X are equipped with norms $\|\,.\,\|_Z$ and $\|\,.\,\|_X$.
Proof: The proof follows readily from (3.3) with $g'(z) = Dg(z)$.   □
Example 3.6
In the study of the mathematical stability of the equation $F(x) = y$ at a regular point, one may define $y \longmapsto x = F^{-1}(y) = G(y)$. We suppose $x \neq 0$. With the choice of a norm $\|\,.\,\|^{\mathcal{N}}$ on the input and output spaces, and if $DF^{-1}(y)$ denotes the Fréchet derivative of F^{-1} at y, then $C = \|DF^{-1}(y)\|\|y\|/\|x\|$. C represents the relative normwise condition number denoted $C^{\mathcal{N}}$. It provides an error bound for computing $x = G(y)$ corresponding to the *worst case* over all possible perturbations of y: $\frac{\|\Delta x\|}{\|x\|} \approx C^{\mathcal{N}} \frac{\|\Delta y\|}{\|y\|}$ in a neighbourhood of y.   △
Corollary 3.2 *Under scalings S_1 in Z and S_2 in X, the condition number C becomes*

$$\|S_2 g' S_1^{-1}\|.$$

Proof: The proof follows readily from $\hat{g}' = S_2 g' S_1^{-1}$.   □

In general, depending on whether $\|\,.\,\|_X$ and $\|\,.\,\|_Z$ correspond to absolute (resp., relative) measures, the associated condition number is called absolute (resp., relative). In finite precision computation, where the relative error on the data is at least of the order of $\mathbf{u}$, a regular problem is declared *ill conditioned* when its relative condition number is too large compared with $1/\mathbf{u}$.

3.3.2   Types of conditioning

As we have already indicated, two types of error analysis are interesting for algorithms: normwise and componentwise analyses. This freedom of choice induces a variety of condition numbers, which are qualified according to the Table 3.3.   For the mixed conditioning, the vector norm on $X = \mathbb{C}^n$ is $\|\,.\,\|_\infty^{\mathcal{N}} = \|\Delta x\|_\infty/\|x\|_\infty$, the matrix norm on $X = \mathbb{C}^{n\times n}$ is subordinate to $\|\,.\,\|_\infty$. However, one can also consider $X = \mathbb{C}^{n^2}$ with the $\|\,.\,\|_\infty$ vector norm.

$\overset{\displaystyle Z}{X}$	$\mathcal{N}$	$\mathcal{C}$
$\mathcal{N}$	normwise (k)	mixed (m)
$\mathcal{C}$	———	componentwise(c)

TABLE 3.3
Menu for conditioning

Example 3.7

We suppose that $g : Z = \mathbb{C}^p \to X = \mathbb{C}^n$ is at least C^1 at z in Z and denote its derivative by $Dg(z) = (\frac{\partial g_i}{\partial z_j}) = g'$. Let be given the vector f in data space Z and the vector x in solution space X. Then, with the notation introduced in Definition 3.1,

$$S_x^{\mathcal{N}} g'(S_f^{\mathcal{N}})^{-1} = D_{1x}^{-1} g' D_{1f},$$
$$S_x^{\mathcal{C}} g'(S_f^{\mathcal{C}})^{-1} = D_{2x}^{-1} g' D_{2f}.$$

Let the norms on X and Z be the scaled norms defined in Tables 3.1 and 3.2. All matrix norms that appear in k, m, and c are subordinate. The resulting formulae for the normwise, mixed, and componentwise relative condition numbers are given in Table 3.4, when $D_f = D_{2f} = \mathrm{diag}(f_i)$ and $D_x = D_{2x} = \mathrm{diag}(x_i)$. D_x is invertible only if all components of x are nonzero. It is easy to check that $m \le k^\infty$ when the subordinate norm for k is chosen as $\| \cdot \|_\infty$. We shall illustrate these formulae on several important examples in linear algebra. $\triangle$

Normwise	Mixed	Componentwise
$k = \dfrac{\|Dg(z)\|\|z\|}{\|x\|}$	$m = \dfrac{\|Dg(z)D_f\|_\infty}{\|x\|_\infty}$	$c = \|D_x^{-1}[Dg(z)]D_f\|_\infty$ defined if $x_i \ne 0,\ i = 1, \ldots, n$

TABLE 3.4
Relative condition numbers for $g : z \longmapsto x = g(z)$

3.4   Simple roots of polynomials

Finding roots of polynomials is one of the most ancient computational problems in calculus. It can be traced back to the Babylonians. The question of defining a condition number for roots of polynomials in connection with computers seems to have been studied first by Wilkinson (1963), who examined the influence of perturbations in all the coefficients of the polynomial on one root.

We consider here a simple root; the case of multiple roots will be treated in Chapter 4. We define $p(x) = \sum_{k=0}^{n} a_k x^k$ to be a polynomial of degree $\leq n$ and consider the map

$$\phi: \quad Z = \mathbb{C}^{n+1} \quad \rightarrow \quad X = \mathbb{C},$$
$$a = (a_0, \ldots, a_n)^T \quad \longmapsto \quad \xi \text{ such that } p(\xi) = 0, \ \xi \text{ simple}.$$

The derivative of ϕ at a is $\phi'(a) = -\frac{1}{p'(\xi)}\underline{\xi}^T$, with $\underline{\xi} = (1 \ \xi \ \xi^2 \ \ldots \ \xi^n)^T$. The associated first-order error formula is $\Delta\xi = -\frac{1}{p'(\xi)}\underline{\xi}^T\Delta a$.

The norm on $X = \mathbb{C}$ is $\|\Delta\xi\|_X = |\xi - \xi'|/|\xi|$ for $\xi \neq 0$. With the norm on Z defined in Table 3.1, one gets the condition numbers given in Table 3.5 for $\xi \neq 0$. The subscript W refers to Wilkinson (1965), and G to Geurts (1982).

Proof: Using the first-order error development given previously, it is easy to show that the formulae given in Table 3.5 are upper bounds. Particular perturbations that realize the supremum are

i) normwise: $\Delta a = -\delta\beta v$, where v is such that $\|v\| = 1$ and $\underline{\xi}^T v = \|\underline{\xi}\|_*$;

ii) componentwise: the elements of Δa are taken as

$$\Delta a_i = -\delta \frac{\overline{\xi_i}}{|\underline{\xi}_i|} f_i,$$

where $0/0$ has to be taken as 0. $\quad\square$

For a monic polynomial $p(x) = x^n + \sum_{k=0}^{n-1} a_k x^k$, the formulae are formally the same, with a and $\underline{\xi}$ replaced by $(a_0, \ldots, a_{n-1})^T$ and $(1, \ldots, \xi^{n-1})^T$.

Normwise $K_W(\xi)$	Componentwise $K_G(\xi)$
$\dfrac{\beta\|\underline{\xi}\|_*}{\|\xi p'(\xi)\|}$	$\dfrac{f^T|\underline{\xi}|}{\|\xi p'(\xi)\|}$

TABLE 3.5
Relative condition numbers for the simple root $\xi \neq 0$ of a polynomial p

Example 3.8

Toh and Trefethen (1994) choose the particular norm on Z denoted by $\| \cdot \|_d$, which is the weighted 2-norm defined by $\|a\|_d = \left(\sum_{i=0}^{n} |d_i|^2 |a_i|^2\right)^{1/2}$, with $d = (d_0, \ldots, d_n)^T$, $d_i \neq 0$. Since $(\|a\|_d)_* = \|a\|_{d^{-1}}$ with $d^{-1} = (1/d_0, \ldots, 1/d_n)^T$, this leads to the normwise condition number $K(\xi, a; d) = \|a\|_d \|\underline{\xi}\|_{d^{-1}}/|\xi p'(\xi)|$. $\quad\triangle$

Eigenvalues of a matrix represent an important example of roots of polynomials. We define the eigenvalue problem

$$Z = \mathbb{C}^{n \times n} \rightarrow X = \mathbb{C},$$
$$A \longmapsto \lambda$$

and consider on Z the relative norm $\| . \|^{\mathcal{N}}$ or $\| . \|^{\mathcal{C}}$ and on X the relative modulus. Condition numbers are given in Table 3.6 for $\lambda \neq 0$, where x (resp., x_*) represents the right (resp., left) eigenvector associated with λ.

Normwise $K_W(\lambda)$	Componentwise $K_G(\lambda)$
$\dfrac{\alpha \|x_*\|_* \|x\|}{\|x_*^* x\| |\lambda|}$	$\dfrac{|x_*|^* E |x|}{|x_*^* x| |\lambda|}$

TABLE 3.6
Relative condition numbers for the simple eigenvalue $\lambda \neq 0$

Proof: It is easy to establish that $K_W(\lambda)$ and $K_G(\lambda)$ are upper bounds for the condition number. It remains to prove that they can be achieved. Particular perturbations that realize the supremum are

   i) normwise: $\Delta A = \alpha \delta w v^*$, where v and w are two vectors such that $v^* x = \|x\|$, $\|v\|_* = 1$, and $x_*^* w = \|x_*\|_*$, $\|w\| = 1$;

   ii) componentwise: the entries of ΔA are

$$\Delta a_{ij} = \delta \frac{x_{*i}}{|x_{*i}|} e_{ij} \frac{\overline{x}_j}{|x_j|},$$

where $0/0$ has to be taken as 0. $\square$

Example 3.9

Let A be a companion matrix associated with the monic polynomial $p(x) = x^n + \sum_{i=0}^{n-1} a_i x^i$ of degree n; we represent A under the Hessenberg form

$$A = \text{Comp}(p) = \begin{pmatrix} 0 & & & & -a_0 \\ 1 & \ddots & & & -a_1 \\ & \ddots & \ddots & & \vdots \\ & & \ddots & 0 & -a_{n-2} \\ & & & 1 & -a_{n-1} \end{pmatrix}.$$

The zeroes of p are the eigenvalues of $\text{Comp}(p)$. Let λ be a simple eigenvalue. The right eigenvector associated with the root λ is $b = (b_0 \ b_1 \ \dots b_{n-1})$, where $(b_i)_{i=0,\dots,n-1}$

are the coefficients of the monic polynomial $(p(z) - p(\lambda))/(z - \lambda) = \sum_{i=0}^{n-1} b_i z^i$. The left eigenvector is $\underline{\lambda} = (1 \ \lambda \ \dots \ \lambda^{n-1})^*$. Moreover, a simple calculation shows that $\underline{\lambda}^* b = p'(\lambda)$ and the condition numbers of λ zero of p, considered as an eigenvalue of $A = \mathrm{Comp}(p)$, are

$$K_W(\lambda) = \alpha \frac{\|\underline{\lambda}\|_*\|b\|}{|\lambda p'(\lambda)|}, \qquad K_G(\lambda) = \frac{|\underline{\lambda}|^* E |b|}{|\lambda p'(\lambda)|},$$

which are proportional to the reciprocal of the derivative of the polynomial p (compare with Tables 3.5 and 3.6). $\triangle$

The rest of this chapter is devoted to regular problems in linear algebra. In the next chapter, we shall treat eigenvalues under an alternative light as *singular* points for $A - zI$ as z varies in $\mathbb{C}$. Similarly, eigenvectors x will be treated as nonzero solutions of the singular system $(A - \lambda I)x = 0$.

3.5 Factorizations of a complex matrix

Stewart (1993b) and Largillier (1994) have computed the normwise stability of certain matrix factorizations that play an important role in a variety of matrix computations. The matrix A has n rows and m columns, $n \geq m$, and has full rank m. Let A^+ be its pseudoinverse, and we define $K_2^+(A) = \|A\|_2\|A^+\|_2$. If $m = n$, then $K_2^+(A)$ identifies with the classical condition number of A, that is, $K_2(A) = \|A\|_2\|A^{-1}\|_2$. The space of data is $Z = \mathbb{C}^{n \times m}$ equipped with the Frobenius norm. The space of solution $X = \mathbb{C}^{n \times m}$ is also equipped with the same norm.

3.5.1 Orthogonal factorizations

We consider two such factorizations, where Q is an $n \times m$ orthogonal matrix such that $Q^*Q = I_m$:

    i) the Gram–Schmidt factorization $A = QR$, where R is upper triangular with positive diagonal elements $(K_2^+(A) = K_2(R))$. When $m = n$ and A is Hermitian positive definite, this leads to the Cholesky factorization $A = R^*R$.

    ii) the polar factorization $A = QH$, where H is Hermitian positive definite $(K_2^+(A) = K_2(H))$.

The upper bounds proposed by Stewart (1993b) and Largillier (1994) are summarized in Table 3.7. See Gratton (1995b) for exact formulae.

3.5.2 Triangular factorization

The analysis of the derivative of the left and right factors in $A = LU$ leads to the upper bound (Stewart (1993b)):

$$\max\left(\frac{\|\Delta L\|}{\|L\|}, \frac{\|\Delta U\|}{\|U\|}\right) \leq \left(\|L^{-1}\|\|U^{-1}\|\|A\|\right)\frac{\|\Delta A\|}{\|A\|},$$

where $\| . \|$ is any absolute consistent matrix norm.

Factorization	$A \longmapsto Q$	$A \longmapsto$ right factor R or H
$A = QR$	$\leq K_2^+(A) \times \begin{cases} \sqrt{2} \text{ if } m = n \\ \sqrt{3} \text{ if } m < n \end{cases}$	$\leq \sqrt{2} K_2^+(A)$
$A = R^*R,\ m = n$	——	$\leq \dfrac{1}{\sqrt{2}} K_2(A)$
$A = QH$	$\leq K_2^+(A) \times \begin{cases} 1 \text{ if } m = n \\ \sqrt{2} \text{ if } m < n \end{cases}$	$\leq \sqrt{2}$

TABLE 3.7
Stability of orthogonal factorizations of a matrix A of size $n \times m$, $m \leq n$

3.6 Solving linear systems

The stability of solutions of linear systems on computers was studied first by
Turing in 1948, using the Frobenius norm of a matrix on the input space and a
vector norm on the output space (*normwise analysis*). This path was followed
in the 1950s by Givens and Wilkinson, who derived condition numbers that
were sometimes found too pessimistic when compared with the reality of the
computation. It was subsequently realized that normwise perturbations are
not always a good model for the perturbations generated by the floating-point
arithmetic. In the 1960s, Bauer (1966) introduced a relative componentwise
metric that is better suited for the analysis of certain algorithms. The use of
this metric for the parameter space Z has been developed by Skeel (1979) in the
context of iterative refinement for linear systems. The resulting *componentwise
analysis* is now incorporated into the software LAPACK (Anderson, et al.
(1992)).

3.6.1 Solving $Ax = b$, A regular

The metrics on $Z_1 \times Z_2$ with $Z_1 = \mathbb{C}^{n \times n}$, $Z_2 = \mathbb{C}^n$ have been defined
in Table 3.1. The derivative of $(A, b) \longmapsto x = A^{-1}b$ is the linear map
$(U, u) \longmapsto A^{-1}(u - Ux)$. This leads directly to Table 3.8, where the subscripts
T, S, and R refer respectively to Turing (1948), Skeel (1979), and Rohn (1989).
Alternative proof: It is easy to establish that K_T, K_S, and K_R are upper
bounds for the condition numbers. It remains to be proven that they can be
achieved. Particular perturbations that realize the supremum are defined as
follows:

i) Turing: $\Delta A = -\delta \alpha a v^*$, $\Delta b = \delta \beta a$, where a is a unit vector such that
$\|A^{-1}a\| = \|A\|$ and v is such that $v^*x = \|x\|$ with $\|v\|_* = 1$.

Data	Normwise K_T	Mixed K_S	Componentwise $K_R{}^1$
(A,b)	$\dfrac{\|A^{-1}\|(\alpha\|x\|+\beta)}{\|x\|}$	$\dfrac{\|\,\|A^{-1}\|\,(E\|x\|+f)\|_\infty}{\|x\|_\infty}$	$\max_i \dfrac{(\|A^{-1}\|(E\|x\|+f))_i}{\|x_i\|}$
A	$\alpha\|A^{-1}\|$	$\dfrac{\|\,\|A^{-1}\|E\|x\|\,\|_\infty}{\|x\|_\infty}$	$\max_i \dfrac{(\|A^{-1}\|E\|x\|)_i}{\|x_i\|}$
b	$\dfrac{\beta\|A^{-1}\|}{\|x\|}$	$\dfrac{\|\,\|A^{-1}\|f\|_\infty}{\|x\|_\infty}$	$\max_i \dfrac{(\|A^{-1}\|f)_i}{\|x_i\|}$

TABLE 3.8
Relative condition numbers for the linear system $Ax = b$

ii) Skeel: let $A^{-1} = (\alpha_{ij})$ and k be the subscript of the maximum component of the vector $|A^{-1}|(E|x| + f)$. Then, with the convention $0/0 = 0$, the upper bound is achieved with the choice

$$\Delta a_{ij} = -\delta \frac{\overline{\alpha}_{ki}}{|\alpha_{ki}|} \frac{\overline{x}_j}{|x_j|} e_{ij} \text{ and } \Delta b_i = \delta \frac{\overline{\alpha}_{ki}}{|\alpha_{ki}|} f_i,$$

where k is the subscript of the maximum component of the vector $|A^{-1}|(E|x| + f)$.

iii) Rohn: the same choice as above applies, but k is now the subscript of the maximum component of $\{|A^{-1}|(E|x| + f)\}_i / |x_i|$.

Often one chooses $E = |A|$, $f = |b|$. Other choices include

1. $E = \|A\|_\infty ee^T, f = \|b\|_\infty e$ with $e = (1,\ldots,1)^T$. In this case, the componentwise analysis is identical to the normwise analysis in infinite norm with the particular choice $\alpha = \|A\|_\infty \|ee^T\|_\infty = n\|A\|_\infty$ and $\beta = \|b\|_\infty$ (Arioli, Duff, and Ruiz (1992)).

2. special choices of E and f suited for sparse matrices (Arioli, Demmel, and Duff (1989)).

3.6.2   Other condition numbers

A variety of condition numbers can be obtained if one varies the metric and the classes of perturbations. If necessary, one can quantify the stability by

---

[1]Condition number defined if $x_i \neq 0$, $i = 1,\ldots,n$.

means of several numbers rather than a single one. For example, one can define a condition number for each component of the solution. This permits individual exhibition of the ill-conditioned components of the solution, which may possibly have a poor accuracy, whereas other components can be well conditioned. This approach was initiated by Wilkinson (1963).

3.6.3 Solving $Ax = b$ by least squares when A is $m \times n$, $m > n$

In this section, we assume that A is full rank, i.e., $\text{rank}(A) = n$. The solution x is defined by $x = A^+ b$, where A^+ is the pseudoinverse of A. The norms on the data space $Z_1 \times Z_2$ with $Z_1 = \mathbb{C}^{n \times m}$, $Z_2 = \mathbb{C}^n$ have been defined in Table 3.1. The normwise (resp., mixed) analysis is realized with the relative Euclidean norm (resp., infinite norm) on the solution space X. Bounds for the condition number are gathered in Table 3.9. The derivative of the map $(A, b) \longmapsto x = A^+ b$ is defined by the linear map $(U, u) \longmapsto -A^+ U x + (A^* A)^{-1} U^* \rho + A^+ u$, where $\rho = Ax - b$ is the *exact* residual at the least-squares solution x. We denote $\kappa^+ = \alpha \| A^+ \|_2$. The subscripts We and Bj refer respectively to Wedin (1973) and Björck (1991).

Proof: i) For the normwise condition number, the upper bound M is obtained by directly bounding the norm of the derivative (Wedin (1973)). The lower

Data	Normwise K_{We}	Mixed K_{Bj}
(A, b)	$\dfrac{1}{\sqrt{2}} M \leq K_{We} \leq M$ $M = \kappa^+ \left[1 + \kappa^+ \dfrac{\|\rho\|_2}{\alpha \|x\|_2} + \dfrac{\beta}{\alpha \|x\|_2} \right]$	$\leq \dfrac{\| \, |A^+|(E|x| + f) + |(A^* A)^{-1}| E^* |\rho| \, \|_\infty}{\|x\|_\infty}$
A	$\dfrac{1}{\sqrt{2}} M \leq K_{We} \leq M$ $M = \kappa^+ \left[1 + \kappa^+ \dfrac{\|\rho\|_2}{\alpha \|x\|_2} \right]$	$\leq \dfrac{\| \, |A^+| E |x| + |(A^* A)^{-1}| E^* |\rho| \, \|_\infty}{\|x\|_\infty}$
b	$\dfrac{\beta \| A^+ \|_2}{\|x\|_2}$	$\dfrac{\| A^+ |f| \|_\infty}{\|x\|_\infty}$

TABLE 3.9
Bounds for the relative condition numbers for the linear least-squares problem

bound $\frac{1}{\sqrt{2}}M$ is obtained from a specific choice of ΔA that can be found in Geurts (1979). The particular choice for Δb is always $\Delta b = \delta\beta a$, where a is such that $\|A^+\|_2 = \|A^+a\|_2$ with $\|a\|_2 = 1$.

ii) The upper bound of the mixed condition number can be either deduced from the derivative or obtained by reformulating the least-squares problem as an augmented linear system and applying Skeel's results directly. When b is perturbed, the specific perturbation for obtaining the maximum is

$$\Delta b_i = \frac{\overline{\alpha_{ki}}}{|\alpha_{ki}|}\delta f_i,$$

where $A^+ = (\alpha_{ij})$ with the convention that $0/0$ is zero. The subscript k is the one of the maximal elements in $|A^+|f$. $\square$

3.7   Functions of a square matrix

We review in this section various examples of condition numbers for the function $\mathbf{F}$ of a matrix $A \longmapsto B = \mathbf{F}(A)$, where $\mathbf{F}$ is a smooth (or regular) function on the set $Z = \mathbb{C}^{n \times n}$ of square matrices of order n. Let $\mathbf{F}'(A)$ represent the derivative of $\mathbf{F}$ at A; then up to the first order, $\Delta B = \mathbf{F}'(A)\Delta A$, and we suppose that $\mathbf{F}'(A)$ is invertible at A.

3.7.1   Algebraic structure of the derivative $\mathbf{F}'(A)$

We define the scalar function $z \longmapsto F(z) = \sum_{n=0}^{\infty} a_n z^n$, where the series is absolutely convergent for $|z| < r$ for some $r > 0$. We also consider the matrix function $\mathbf{F} : \quad A \longmapsto F(A)$ and its derivative $\mathbf{F}'(A)$.

Example 3.10

For $A \longmapsto A^2$, the derivative is defined by $\mathbf{F}'(A) : \quad U \longmapsto AU + UA$. For the exponential $A \longmapsto e^A$, then $\mathbf{F}'(A)$ is given by $U \longmapsto \int_0^1 e^{A(1-t)}U e^{At}\mathrm{d}t$. $\triangle$

In general, it is easy to check that $\mathbf{F}'(A)$ is given by

$$\mathbf{F}'(A) : \quad U \longmapsto \sum_{n=1}^{\infty} a_n \sum_{k=0}^{n-1} A^k U A^{n-1-k}. \tag{3.4}$$

To obtain a matrix representation $\mathcal{F}'$ of $\mathbf{F}'(A)$, we use the isomorphism between $\mathbb{C}^{n \times n}$ and $\mathbb{C}^{n^2}$, denoted vec (Chatelin (1988c)):

$$U = [z_1, z_2, \ldots, z_n] \longmapsto \mathrm{vec}U = \begin{bmatrix} z_1 \\ z_2 \\ \vdots \\ z_n \end{bmatrix}.$$

Let $\otimes$ denotes the tensor (or Kronecker) product of matrices: $A \otimes B = (a_{ij}B)$. Because $\mathrm{vec}(AUB) = (B^T \otimes A)\mathrm{vec}U$, one easily gets the formula

$$\mathcal{F}'(A) = \sum_{n=1}^{\infty} a_n \sum_{k=0}^{n-1} (A^T)^{n-k-1} \otimes A^k. \tag{3.5}$$

Example 3.11

For $A \longmapsto A^p$, then

$$\mathcal{F}'(A) = \sum_{k=0}^{p-1} (A^T)^{p-1-k} \otimes A^k.$$

Such a map occurs in matrix iterations of the type discussed in Example 2.1. $\triangle$

Example 3.12 (Gratton (1995b)).

Let A be a *real* matrix in $\mathbb{R}^{m \times n}$ of maximal rank $n < m$ and b be a *real* vector in $\mathbb{R}^m$. The absolute normwise condition number (with $\| . \|_F$) for $(A, b) \longmapsto x = A^+ b$ has the *explicit* formulation

$$K_{Gr} = \|A^+ \left[-x^T \otimes I_m - (A^+\rho)^T L_T, I_m \right] \|_2,$$

where $L_T = (l_{ij})$ is a square matrix of order nm such that $l_{ij} = 1$ for $(i, j) = (m(k-1) + l, n(l-1) + k)$, $l = 1, \ldots, m$, $k = 1, \ldots, n$, and $l_{ij} = 0$ otherwise. L_T is a matrix such that $\text{vec} A^T = L_T \text{vec} A$. The subscript Gr refers to Gratton (1995b).
$\triangle$

3.7.2   Inversion $A \longmapsto B = A^{-1}$, A regular

The inversion represents one of the most basic operations on matrices. With $\mathbf{F}'(A)$ defined as $U \longmapsto -A^{-1}UA^{-1}$, one obtains Table 3.10.

Since the solution space $X = \mathbb{C}^{n \times n}$ is a space of matrices, one has the choice in the mixed analysis to preserve this structure with the norm subordinate to $\| . \|_\infty$ or to consider X as the vector space $\mathbb{C}^{n^2}$ with $| . \|_\infty$. In this latter case, we use the notation $\|A\|_\nu = \max_{ij} |a_{ij}|$ to avoid possible confusion with the subordinate norm.

The subscripts B and GK refer to Bauer (1966) and Gohberg and Koltracht (1993), respectively. These formulae can also be obtained by elementary matrix algebra. The only nontrivial part is to show that the upper bounds can be achieved for certain perturbations.

  i) K_T is achieved for $\Delta A = \delta \alpha a v^*$, where a is a unit vector such that $\|A^{-1}a\| = \|A^{-1}\|$ and v satisfies $\|v^* A^{-1}\| = \|A^{-1}\|$ and $\|v\|_* = 1$.

 ii) In general, $K_B < L_B$. However, Geurts (1982) proved that equality can be obtained for certain matrices: if there exist two diagonal matrices D_1 and D_2 with diagonal entries ± 1 (signature matrices) such that $|A^{-1}| = D_1 A^{-1} D_2$, then $L_B = K_B$. Examples of such matrices are all matrices showing a checkerboard sign pattern.

The existence of two signature matrices such that $|A^{-1}| = D_1 A^{-1} D_2$ is not a necessary condition for $K_B = L_B$ to hold. The following is a counterexample proposed by Geurts (1992). Let

$$A = \begin{bmatrix} 1 & -1 & -2/a \\ & 1 & 1/a \\ & & 1/a \end{bmatrix} \text{ and } B = A^{-1} = \begin{bmatrix} 1 & 1 & 1 \\ & 1 & -1 \\ & & a \end{bmatrix},$$

Normwise	Mixed		Componentwise
K_T	K_B	K_{GK}	$K_R{}^2$
$\alpha\|A^{-1}\|$	$\leq L_B = \dfrac{\| \|A^{-1}\|E\|A\| \|_\infty}{\|A^{-1}\|_\infty}$	$\dfrac{\| \|A^{-1}\|E\|A^{-1}\| \|_\nu}{\|A^{-1}\|_\nu}$	$\max_{ij} \dfrac{(\|A^{-1}\|E\|A^{-1}\|)_{ij}}{\|A^{-1}\|_{ij}}$

TABLE 3.10
Relative condition numbers for matrix inversion $A \longmapsto A^{-1}$

where $a \geq 11$. One can easily compute $L_B = 1$, and if one chooses $\Delta A = \delta A$, then $|\Delta A| = \delta |A|$ and

$$\frac{\|\Delta B\|_\infty}{\|B\|_\infty} = \delta \times 1 = \delta L_B.$$

Therefore, $K_B = L_B = 1$, but a simple calculation shows that it is not possible to find two signature matrices such that $|A^{-1}| = D_1 A^{-1} D_2$.

Another upper bound for K_B, easier to compute than L_B, is $M_B = \| |A^{-1}| E \|_\infty$: $K_B \leq L_B \leq M_B$.

iii) Let $A^{-1} = (\alpha_{ij})$. The choice

$$\Delta a_{ij} = -\delta \frac{\overline{\alpha_{ki}}}{|\alpha_{ki}|} \frac{\overline{\alpha_{jp}}}{|\alpha_{jp}|} e_{ij},$$

where (k, p) are the subscripts of the maximum component in $|A^{-1}|E|A^{-1}|$, allows us to show that K_{GK} is also a lower bound. Therefore, K_{GK} is the condition number.

iv) To show that K_R is also a lower bound, the same choice for ΔA as in iii) applies, with (k, p) now the subscripts of the maximum component over i and j in

$$\frac{(|A^{-1}|E|A^{-1}|)_{ij}}{|A^{-1}|_{ij}}.$$

The formula for the normwise condition number also holds for singular matrices if one restricts the class of perturbations appropriately.

Example 3.13 The pseudoinverse A^+ (Kahan (1972), Wedin (1973)).

The stability of the computation of the pseudoinverse (or Moore–Penrose inverse) A^+ of a rectangular $m \times n$ matrix A of rank k, with $k \leq n \leq m$, is that of the map $A \longmapsto B = A^+$. The perturbations ΔA on A are allowed in the class $(\tau)_{r,k}$ of normwise perturbations that *preserve the rank* k: $(\tau)_{r,k} = \{\Delta A; \|\Delta A\| \leq r$ and $A + \Delta A$ has rank $k\}$. Under this assumption, the absolute condition number of $A \longmapsto A^+$ (using the Frobenius norm on data and solution) is

$$\kappa_F(A^+) = \lim_{r \to 0} \sup_{\Delta A \in (\tau)_r^k} \frac{\|\Delta B\|_F}{\|\Delta A\|_F} = \|A^+\|_2^2.$$

---

[2]Condition number defined only if all entries of A^{-1} are nonzero.

Note the analogy between this condition number and the absolute normwise condition number $\|A^{-1}\|^2$ for matrix inversion $A \longmapsto A^{-1}$, which also corresponds to perturbations preserving the rank, here equal to $n = m$. $\triangle$

3.7.3   Projection $A \longmapsto B = Q^*AQ$ on an invariant subspace

The projection of a matrix A on an invariant subspace M (of dimension m) plays an important role in eigencomputations. Let Q be an orthonomal basis for M; then the $m \times m$ matrix $B = Q^*AQ$ represents the map $A_{\lceil M}$ in the basis Q. Let X_* represent the basis of the left invariant subspace M_*, normalized by $Q^*X_* = I_m$; then $P = QX_*^*$ is the spectral projection for A on M.

The derivative of $A \longmapsto B$ is given by $U \longmapsto X_*^*UQ$, which can be represented, via the vec representation, by the matrix $Q^* \otimes X_*^*$.
Example 3.14 The arithmetic mean $\hat{\lambda}$.
The above result can be applied to compute the condition (in the Frobenius norm) of the map $A \longmapsto \hat{\lambda} = \frac{1}{m}\mathrm{tr}B$, which is shown to be equal to

$$\mathrm{cond}_F(\hat{\lambda}) = \frac{1}{m}\|X_*\|_F \leq \|X_*\|_2$$

by the technique used in Gratton (1995b). $\triangle$

3.8   Concluding remarks

The condition numbers that we have introduced express the *worst case amplification factor* for perturbations on the data that belong to the chosen class (τ). They are relative to the choice of data and of perturbations. Therefore, a bound of the type (3.2) for the computing error $\Delta x = x - \tilde{x}$ may be a large overestimation of the actual computing error if the chosen class of perturbations is much larger than the perturbations actually generated by finite precision computation.

In some cases, one gets computed results that are much more accurate than predicted by the general theory, because the potential instability of the mathematical problem is not excited by the actual computation. This may happen for matrices with special structure and will be a topic of further investigation in Chapter 5.

3.8.1   Structured condition numbers

Several types of matrices of order n, such as Vandermonde, Cauchy, and Toeplitz, can be defined by prescribing a number of parameters smaller than n^2, the number of elements. As a result, their condition number associated with a perturbation of these parameters only may be much smaller than their condition number when subjected to arbitrary perturbations. An elegant derivation of such condition numbers can be found in Gohberg and Koltracht (1990, 1993).

3.8.2 A is Hermitian or normal

There are a number of well-known simplifications in the theory when A is Hermitian ($A = A^*$) or normal ($AA^* = A^*A$). They can be summarized as follows:

    i) the singular values are given by the moduli, or absolute values, of the eigenvalues of A, depending whether the eigenvalues are complex or real;

    ii) there is no spectral instability.

3.8.3 Worst-case versus average condition numbers

The condition numbers C and C_δ describe the worst possible amplification of the error that can happen when the computation of $x = g(z)$ is subject to a perturbation on z. It may be of interest to analyse the average condition number. This is done by Weiss, et al. (1986) for a fixed linear system $Ax = b$, assuming a uniform distribution for the perturbation ΔA. They then compare the average and worst-case loss of precision (i.e., log of the condition number), proving that the ratio is of the order of $\log n$.

3.9 Bibliographical comments

This chapter presents in a unified framework the essential stability tools, such as Fréchet derivatives and condition numbers, that have appeared scattered in the literature on matrix computations for the past 40 years. Many recent results by Rohn, Geurts, and Gohberg and Koltracht, for example, appear in a book for the first time. The name condition number is attributed to Turing, although the notion of ill-conditioning was used much earlier.

The general definition 3.2 was given by Rice (1966). Bauer (1966) was the first to consider the effect of componentwise perturbations rather than normwise perturbations to analyse $Ax = b$. The idea flourished in the 1980s (Skeel (1979)), and the corresponding software is now incorporated into LAPACK. Important additional references about condition numbers for $Ax = b$ are Chan and Foulser (1988), Higham (1987a, 1987b, 1989, 1990, 1991b) and Higham and Higham (1992a, 1992b). Interesting new results on condition numbers are presented in Gratton (1995a, 1995b).

Chapter 4

Computation in the Neighbourhood of a Singularity

Well-posed problems that are so smooth that the solution is at least a C^1 function of the data have been defined as *regular* problems. Solving such problems presents no computational difficulty, and their solutions computed in finite precision arithmetic with a reliable algorithm are generally good approximations of the exact ones, provided that the problems are not too ill conditioned.

Any problem that is not regular is called *singular*. It is in the neighbourhood of such singularities that computational difficulties arise. Singular problems are not generic: under perturbations (such as the one induced by finite precision arithmetic), they are usually transformed into regular problems that then appear as classically ill conditioned (their linear condition number tends to be infinite).

4.1 Singular problems that are well posed

If one wants to compute a multiple root of multiplicity m, it is perturbed by finite precision computation into a set of m (often distinct) approximate roots. Each individual root is ill conditioned: its linear condition number tends to be infinite. Any method which is stable at a regular point becomes unstable with respect to a *linear* analysis at a singular point. In order to recover some stability, one has to consider the Hölder continuity of order $h = 1/m$: the error $\|\Delta x\|$ on the solution is proportional to $\|\Delta z\|^h$, the hth power of the size of the perturbation on the data (see Chapter 2).

If one is not primarily interested in each individual approximation, one can recover a linear stability by grouping the m approximate roots, that is, by taking the computed arithmetic mean as an approximation to the multiple root.

4.2   Condition numbers of Hölder singularities

The linear condition number (which corresponds to some measure of the Fréchet derivative) is a measure of stability for a regular problem. It tends to infinity whenever the problem approaches a singularity. For Hölder singularities of well-posed problems, we can likewise define normwise Hölderian condition numbers. It measures the intrinsic difficulty of computing a multiple root, knowing its order h, and taking into account the fact that the error $\|\Delta x\|$ is now proportional to the hth power of the size of the perturbation on the data (see Wilkinson (1963) for roots of polynomials and Chatelin (1986) for eigenvalues).

4.2.1   Definitions

Let $g : z \longmapsto x = g(z)$ be Hölder-continuous of order $h \leq 1$ in the neighbourhood of z:
$$\|x' - x\| \leq C\|z' - z\|^h.$$
We introduce definitions similar to Definition 3.2 (Chapter 3).
Definition 4.1   a. *The δ-Hölderian condition number for g is*

$$C_{\delta(h)} = \sup_{z', \; 0<\|z'-z\|\leq\delta} \frac{\|g(z') - g(z)\|}{\|z' - z\|^h}. \tag{4.1}$$

     b. *The asymptotic Hölderian condition number for g is*

$$C_{(h)} = \lim_{\delta \to 0} C_{\delta(h)}.$$

$C_{\delta(h)}$ is a local Hölderian constant, while $C_{(h)}$ (if it exists) is the asymptotic one. The classical condition numbers C_δ, C correspond to $h = 1$.

4.2.2   Examples

We treat successively the case of a multiple defective eigenvalue and then the multiple root of a polynomial.
i) Multiple eigenvalues
Suppose λ is a multiple eigenvalue of A of ascent l. When $l = 1$, λ is a semisimple eigenvalue; otherwise λ is a defective eigenvalue: λ is Hölder-continuous of order $h = 1/l$. We denote by M the invariant subspace of dimension m associated with λ; Q is an orthonormal basis of M. The matrix X_* is a basis of the left invariant subspace, normalised by $Q^*X_* = I$, and V is a Jordan basis of Q^*AQ.
Theorem 4.1 (Chatelin (1986)) *If $A' = A + \Delta A$ for any eigenvalue λ' of A', there exists an eigenvalue λ of A of ascent $l \geq 1$ such that*

$$|\lambda' - \lambda| \leq 2 \left(\mathrm{cond}_2(V)\|X_*\|_2\right)^{1/l} \|\Delta A\|_2^{1/l},$$

provided that $\|\Delta A\|_2$ is small enough.

We use the notation $\text{cond}_2(V) = \|V\|_2 \|V^{-1}\|_2$. From this theorem it follows that if $K_{1/l}$ is the absolute Hölder condition number of order $1/l$ for a multiple eigenvalue λ of ascent l, then necessarily

$$K_{1/l}^{\mathcal{N}} \leq 2 \left(\text{cond}_2(V) \|X_*\|_2 \right)^{1/l}.$$

We have here implicitly assumed that we use the Euclidean norm on the input space and the modulus on the output space. We notice that the error on the approximate eigenvalue does not depend linearly on the matrix perturbation $\|\Delta A\|_2$, as was the case for a simple eigenvalue, but grows as $\|\Delta A\|_2^{1/l}$.

Remarks:

1) In case of a multiple root λ, it may be interesting from a computational point of view to consider the approximation of λ by the arithmetic mean $\hat{\lambda}' = \frac{1}{m} \sum_{i=1}^{m} \lambda'_i$ of the m approximate eigenvalues λ'_i in the neighbourhood of λ. The bound (Chatelin (1993a, pp. 155–156) and Example 3.14)

$$|\hat{\lambda}' - \lambda| \leq \|X_*\|_2 \|\Delta A\|_2,$$

valid for $\|\Delta A\|_2$ small enough, shows that we recover a linear behaviour.

2) If λ is a semisimple eigenvalue, then $l = 1$ and $K_1^{\mathcal{N}} \leq \|X_*\|_2$. In such a case, the error on the eigenvalue is proportional to the matrix perturbation. This is due to the property of Lipschitz continuity of the mapping $A \longmapsto \lambda$ for $l = 1$.

3) The property of Lipschitz continuity does not hold for multiple roots of polynomials: seen as eigenvalues of the associated companion matrix, they are fully defective and their ascent l always equals their multiplicity m.

ii) Multiple roots of polynomials

We use the same notation and the same choice of data and measures as in § 3.4 and suppose that the polynomial p admits ξ as a root of multiplicity m.

Theorem 4.2 (Wilkinson (1963)) *The relative Hölder condition number of order $1/m$ for the nonzero root ξ of multiplicity m of the polynomial $p(\xi) = 0$ is*

$$K_{1/m}^{\mathcal{C}} = \frac{1}{|\xi|} \left(\frac{m!}{|p^{(m)}(\xi)|} f^T \underline{\xi} \right)^{1/m}.$$

A similar formula for the normwise condition number has been recently established (Gratton (1995a)):

$$K_{1/m}^{\mathcal{N}} = \frac{1}{|\xi|} \left(\frac{m!}{|p^{(m)}(\xi)|} \beta \|\underline{\xi}\|_* \right)^{1/m}.$$

As for eigenvalues, one can recover a linear behaviour by considering the arithmetic mean of the m perturbed roots. However, for polynomials, many methods, such as Newton's iteration, deliver usually one approximate root and not the complete cluster of m approximate solutions known to lie in the neighbourhood of a root of multiplicity m.

4.2.3   The influence zone of a Hölder singularity

Let x be a *regular* point and ξ a *Hölder singular* point of order $1/h > 1$.[1]
Mathematically, the problem should be regarded as regular as long as $x \neq \xi$.
But in practice the dual view is more useful to interpret finite precision
computations: x should be regarded as singular in a small neighbourhood
of ξ, which is the zone of influence of ξ. It can be metaphorically said that
a singularity "diffuses" in its neighbourhood consisting of regular points. At
singularities of equal order γ, the importance of this diffusion is proportional
to the respective Hölderian condition number.

When $x \to \xi$, $\lim_{x \to \xi} C_{(1)}(x) = \infty$ and $\lim_{x \to \xi} C_{\delta(h)}(x) = C_{\delta(h)}(\xi) < \infty$.
As a result, even if $x \neq \xi$, it behaves, in the influence zone of ξ, as a singular
point and obeys the corresponding *power law of error*:

$$\|\Delta x\| \leq C_{\delta(h)}(\xi) \|\Delta y\|^h.$$

A quantification of this qualitative statement will be given by the method
PRECISE in Chapter 8.

4.3   Computability of ill-posed problems

Well-posed problems are, in principle, computable in the traditional sense,
since the perturbation on the solution tends to zero when the perturbation on
the data tends to zero. The only computational difficulty is that they may be
ill conditioned; that is, their condition number (linear or Hölderian) may be
too large with respect with the available machine precision.

But ill-posed problems are no longer computable in the traditional sense:
the computing error does not tend to zero. A classical example of an ill-
posed problem is solving $Ax = b$ with A singular: it admits either 0 or
an infinite number of solutions, depending on whether b belongs to ImA or
not. Many ways around this difficulty have been developed. One can think,
for example, of solving this problem by a least-squares approach or by the
Tikhonov regularisation. When $b = 0$, one can interpret the equation as an
eigenvector computation of the form $Ax = 0$, $x \neq 0$ (see below). Another
familiar example of ill-posed problem is the computation of the Jordan form
of a matrix (see Chapter 11). The general treatment of ill-posed problems is
beyond the scope of this study. We shall only consider the particular class of
such problems consisting of singular *linear* systems, because they arise in the
context of the distance of a regular linear system to a singular one.

4.4   Singularities of $z \longmapsto A - zI$

Zero is a singular point of the linear map A, where A is a singular matrix.
Any associated linear system is ill posed. However, one can also define the

---

[1]We recall that if $h < 1$ is the order of Hölder continuity, then $\gamma = 1/h > 1$ is the order
of the Hölder singularity.

condition number of the singularity (see Chatelin (1993b)). It turns out to be identical to that of 0 as an eigenvalue of A. This is not surprising since the eigenvalues of A are indeed the singular points, or poles, of the resolvent map $z \in \mathbb{C} \longmapsto (A - zI)^{-1}$ (Chatelin (1988c)).

4.4.1 Condition number of a singular point

For an ill-posed problem involving a singular matrix, the difficulty in defining a condition number is that there exists no natural *forward* distance to singularity: at the singularity, the solution either does not exist or is not unique. One way to resolve this difficulty is to represent the forward distance by means of the *spectral* distance: $\min(|\mu|, \ \mu \in \operatorname{sp}(A)) = \operatorname{dist}(\operatorname{sp}(A), 0)$. The matrix $B = A + \Delta A$ is exactly singular; that is, B admits the eigenvalue $\lambda = 0$. If λ is a simple eigenvalue of B, then $|\Delta \lambda| = |\mu - 0|$ represents a variation of λ under the variation ΔA of B; it is proportional to $\|\Delta A\|$ for $\|\Delta A\|$ small enough. The quantity $C(\lambda) = \lim_{\|\Delta A\| \to 0} \frac{|\Delta \lambda|}{\|\Delta A\|}$ measures the ratio of the forward to the backward distance to the singularity. It is also the classical condition number of λ as an eigenvalue of B. It defines the region $\{z \in \mathbb{C}; |z - \lambda| \le C(\lambda)\|\Delta A\|\}$ of $\mathbb{C}$, which is affected by the singularity λ at the level $\|\Delta A\|$ of perturbation amplitude on A to the first order. The larger $C(\lambda)$, the stronger the influence of the singularity. If λ is a multiple eigenvalue with ascent l, then $|\Delta \lambda|$ is proportional to $\|\Delta A\|^{1/l}$, and one defines a Hölder condition number of order $1/l$.

Finally we remark that the notion of singularity is *relative* to the computational process under study. For instance, let λ be a simple eigenvalue of the matrix A. Then λ is a regular point with respect to the problem $Ax = \lambda x$ but is a singular point for the computation of the resolvent $(A - zI)^{-1}$. Now if λ is double defective, it is also a singular point for the eigenvalue problem.

4.4.2 Condition number of an eigenvector

An eigenvector is a nonzero solution associated with the solution of the ill-posed, or singular, problem

$$(A - \lambda I)x = 0 \iff Ax = \lambda x \quad \text{with} \quad x \ne 0.$$

Because of the nonuniqueness of the definition of an eigenvector x (kx is also an eigenvector for all $k \ne 0$ in $\mathbb{C}$), there is no unique way to define a condition number. Wilkinson (1965) and Stewart (1971, 1973a) proposed two different definitions. These definitions have been unified in a general framework by Chatelin (1986, 1988c, 1993a).

First we present this framework and derive the general formulation of the condition number for an eigenvector associated with a simple eigenvalue. Then we detail several applications that can be found in the literature.

The main problem in defining the conditioning of an eigenvector lies in the freedom for the definition of the variation $\Delta x = x' - x$. One way to solve it is to prescribe the linear subspace to which Δx has to belong. We denote by M the eigendirection $\{x\}$ and by N the direction defined by $\{y\}$, where y is an arbitrary vector nonorthogonal to x. Therefore, the space X is the direct sum $X = M \oplus N^{\perp}$.

One defines the projection Π on M along $N^{\perp}$. If we normalize y such that $y^*x = 1$, then the projection can be written as $\Pi = xy^*$. Let $M' = \{x'\}$ be the perturbed eigendirection. If one chooses to normalize x' such that $y^*x' = 1$, then $\Delta x = (I - \Pi)x'$ belongs to the subspace $N^{\perp}$ (see Figure 4.1). Indeed, one can easily check that $\Pi\Delta x = 0$. Of course, if y is almost orthogonal to x, the projection Π is ill conditioned ($\|\Pi\| = \|y\|$ large) and $\|\Delta x\|$ is large. The quantity $\|\Delta x\|$ is minimal if Π is the orthogonal projection on M (see Figure 4.2). Note that this approach corresponds to a *linear* normalization of x', contrarily to what is usually done. In particular, the normalization induced by the classical choice of the Euclidean norm ($\|x'\|_2^2 = x'^*x' = 1$) is *quadratic*.

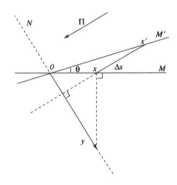

FIG. 4.1. *Choice of the projection Π on M.*

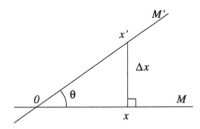

FIG. 4.2. *Orthogonal projection $\Pi^{\perp}$ on M.*

Let $[x \ \underline{X}]$ and $[y \ \underline{Y}]$ be two adjoint bases for $\mathbb{C}^n$. Writing A in these bases leads to

$$\begin{bmatrix} y^* \\ \underline{Y}^* \end{bmatrix} A[x \ \underline{X}] = \begin{bmatrix} \lambda & c \\ 0 & \underline{B} \end{bmatrix},$$

where $\underline{B} = \underline{Y}^* A \underline{X}$. One has $\Delta x = -\Sigma(\Delta A)x$ up to first order. The derivative of $A \longmapsto x$ eigenvector associated with a simple eigenvalue λ is the linear map $U \longmapsto -\Sigma U x$, where Σ is the partial inverse for $A - \lambda I$ in $N^{\perp}$: $\Sigma = \underline{X}(\underline{B} - \lambda I)^{-1}\underline{Y}^*$. This leads to the formulae for the relative condition number

Normwise $K_C(x)$	Mixed $K_G(x)$
$\alpha\|\Sigma\|$	$\dfrac{\||\Sigma||E||x|\|_\infty}{\|x\|_\infty}$

TABLE 4.1
Relative condition numbers for an eigenvector

of x given in Table 4.1. The subscript C refers to Chatelin (1988c, 1993a) for her general formulation, which allows a complete flexibility in the choice of normalization on the eigendirection. The subscript G refers to Geurts (1982), who proposed a *particular* partial inverse.

Proof: The upper bounds are respectively achieved by the perturbation:

1) $\Delta A = \alpha\delta wv^*$, where v and w are two vectors such that $v^*x = \|x\|$, $\|v\|_* = 1$, and $\|\Sigma w\| = \|\Sigma\|$, $\|w\| = 1$;

2) ΔA such that

$$\Delta a_{ij} = -\delta\frac{\overline{\sigma}_{ki}}{|\sigma_{ki}|}e_{ij}\frac{\overline{x}_j}{|x_j|},$$

where $\Sigma = (\sigma_{ij})$, $0/0$ is conventionally taken as 0, and k is the subscript of the maximum component of $|\Sigma||E||x|$. $\square$

Example 4.1 The Wilkinson condition number.

In 1965, Wilkinson proposed choosing $y = x_*$ corresponding to the choice of the projection Π equal to the *spectral* projection $P = xx_*^*$, which is the projection orthogonally to the left eigenvector x_*. In this case, $\Sigma = S$, where S is the *reduced resolvent* associated with $A - \lambda I$ (Kato (1976), Chatelin (1983)). In his proof, Wilkinson assumes A to be *diagonalisable* and computes, to first order,

$$x' - x = \Delta x = -S\Delta Ax = \sum_{\lambda_i \neq \lambda}\frac{x_{i*}^*\Delta Ax}{(\lambda - \lambda_i)x_*^*x_i}x_i.$$

Wilkinson thinks (*wrongly*) that he imposes the normalisation $\|x\|_2 = \|x'\|_2 = 1$, with $x' = x + \Delta x$ (see Golub and Van Loan (1989, pp. 345–346)). It is easy to check that in fact $x_*^*x = x_*^*x' = 1$ and that $\|x'\|_2$ may be much larger than 1 for nonnormal matrices. Note that $\|S\|_2$ is large as soon as $\|P\|_2$ is large and $\|P\|_2 = \|x_*\|_2$ is the absolute eigenvalue condition number.

With Wilkinson's choice, the eigenvalue and eigenvector condition numbers are *never independent for nonnormal matrices* ($\|P\|$ large implies $\|S\|$ large). $\triangle$

Example 4.2 The Stewart condition number.

The eigenvector and eigenvalue condition numbers need not be related. If one is interested in just the *eigendirection*, i.e., in the acute angle θ between the exact

eigendirection and the approximate one, then one may take the orthogonal projection
on the direction M, which leads, as indicated in Figure 4.2, to a measure of $\tan\theta$.

This projection, denoted $\Pi^\perp$, is xx^*; it amounts to the choice $N = M$. With the
Euclidean norm, the perturbation $\Delta x = -\Sigma^\perp \Delta A x$ is such that

$$\|\Delta x\|_2 = \|x' - x\|_2 = \tan\theta$$

because $x^* x = x^* x' = 1$.

This choice has been used by Stewart (1971), who proposes $\|\Sigma^\perp\|_2$ as a condition
number, where $\Sigma^\perp$ denotes the partial inverse corresponding to $y = x$, and the two
adjoint bases $[x, \underline{X}]$ and $[y, \underline{Y}]$ are identified into one *unitary* basis $Q = [x, \underline{Q}]$ (see
Chatelin (1988c)). Actually Stewart (1971, 1973a) deals with an invariant subspace
of dimension $m \geq 1$ and matrices under block triangular forms. If we restrict our
attention to the multiplicity $m = 1$, Stewart's results deal with

$$A = \begin{bmatrix} \lambda & c \\ 0 & \underline{B} \end{bmatrix};$$

$\Delta x = -\Sigma^\perp \Delta A x$ and the eigenvector condition number is $\|(\underline{B} - \lambda I)^{-1}\|_2 = \|\Sigma^\perp\|_2$.
Note that the choice of $\|\Sigma^\perp\|_2$ is optimal in the sense that for all possible partial
inverses Σ deriving from all possible choices of y, $\Sigma^\perp$ minimizes $\|\Sigma\|_2$:

$$\|\Sigma^\perp\|_2 = \min_{\substack{y \neq 0 \\ y \notin x^\perp}} \|\Sigma\|_2.$$

The eigenvalue and eigenvector condition numbers can now be *unrelated* ($\|P\|$ large
does not necessarily imply $\|\Sigma^\perp\|$ large).

If A is *normal* (Hermitian in particular), $x = x_*$, $P = \Pi^\perp$, and the two condition
numbers of Wilkinson and Stewart are identical: $\Sigma^\perp = S$. $\triangle$

The LAPACK library proposes the inverse of the Stewart condition
number, called *separation* (sep for short) after Varah (1979), in the two norms
$\text{sep}_2 = \|\Sigma^\perp\|_2^{-1}$ and $\text{sep}_F = \|\Sigma^\perp\|_F^{-1}$. However, such a choice may not be the
natural one in certain applications, as shown by the next example.

Example 4.3 Stationary state of a Markov chain.
We consider the eigenvector problem associated with an homogeneous irreducible
Markov chain. This problem can be stated as follows: find $x \neq 0$ such that

$$Px = x \iff Ax = 0$$

with $A = P - I$, where P is the matrix of transition probabilities, which is column
stochastic, and x is a vector of probabilities with real nonnegative components. The
constraint that the sum of the probabilities equals 1 applies to both the exact and the
approximate eigenvector and can be written

$$e^* x = e^* x' = 1, \tag{4.2}$$

where e is the vector of all ones.

Therefore, the natural choice is to take $y = e$ to define the projection $\Pi = xe^*$.
Moreover, the vector e happens to be the left eigenvector associated with P, because
P is column stochastic. Hence, the chosen projection Π is identical to the spectral
projection as used by Wilkinson, and the reduced resolvent S of P here is more

appropriate than any other partial inverse for $A = P - I$: with (4.2), $\Delta x = x' - x = -S\Delta Px$. The reduced resolvent S is often called the *group inverse* in the Markov chain literature and is denoted $(P - I)^\sharp$ (see Golub and Meyer (1986), Campbell and Meyer (1991)).

The second degree of freedom is the choice of the norm to express the condition number associated with the perturbations of the vector x of probabilities. Golub and Meyer (1986) give a general formulation of the condition number as $\|S\|$, where $\| \cdot \|$ can be any matrix norm. Rigorously, $\|S\|$ is only proportional to the condition number; one should take $\|S\|\|P\|$ as the relative condition number or $\|S\|\|x\|$ as the absolute condition number. Note that for the 1-norm, $\|S\|_1$ is the absolute condition number since $\|x\|_1 = e^*x = 1$. Funderlic and Meyer use the max norm of S as a vector, that is. $\max_{i,j} |S_{ij}|$.

Recently, Barlow (1993) has proposed the quantity $\|(P - I)^\sharp\|_1 \||P - I||x|\|_1$ as an "effective" condition number. This can be readily interpreted as an upper bound for the mixed condition number $\|(P - I)^\sharp |P - I||x|\|_1/\|x\|_1$ (see $K_G(x)$ with $\| \cdot \|_1$), where the matrix E is chosen to be equal to $|P - I|$ rather than to $|P| = P$. △

4.5 Distances to singularity

The numerical behaviour of a computation at a regular point depends on the distance to singularity, i.e., on the presence of a singular problem in the neighbourhood.

4.5.1 Linear problems

We define the following distances to singularity for inversion $A \longmapsto A^{-1}$:

$$\begin{aligned}
\delta_T &= \min\{\omega; \|\Delta A\| \leq \omega\alpha \text{ such that } A + \Delta A \text{ is singular}\}, \\
\delta_B &= \min\{\omega; |\Delta A| \leq \omega E \text{ such that } A + \Delta A \text{ is singular}\},
\end{aligned} \qquad (4.3)$$

which can be interpreted as the backward errors associated with the singularity of the matrix under relative normwise and componentwise perturbations, respectively.

Theorem 4.3 (Turing)

$$\delta_T = \frac{1}{\|A^{-1}\|\alpha} = \frac{1}{K_T(A)}.$$

This theorem, often attributed to Turing, seems to have already been proven by Banach in the 1920s. It was rediscovered by Eckart and Young in 1939 with the 2-norm and proved by Gastinel for an arbitrary norm. It shows that the normwise condition number of a matrix is the reciprocal of the distance to singularity.

Proof: Let $\theta = 1/(\|A^{-1}\|\alpha)$.

1) Let ΔA be such that $\|\Delta A\| < \theta\alpha$. Then $\|A^{-1}\Delta A\| < 1$ and $(I + A^{-1}\Delta A)$ is invertible. Since $(I + A^{-1}\Delta A)^{-1}A^{-1} = (A + \Delta A)^{-1}$, $A + \Delta A$ is nonsingular and $\delta_T \geq \theta$.

2) Let x and y be two vectors such that $\|x\| = \|y\|_* = 1$ and $\|A^{-1}x\| = y^*A^{-1}x = \|A^{-1}\|$. Let $\Delta A = -\|A^{-1}\|^{-1}xy^*$. Then $\|\Delta A\| = \theta\alpha$ and it is easy to check that $(A + \Delta A)A^{-1}x = 0$. Then $A + \Delta A$ is singular and $\delta_T \leq \theta$.   □

Example 4.4 (Mirsky (1960)).

A similar result holds for the Moore–Penrose inverse A^+ of a singular matrix A. Let A be a singular matrix of order n so that $\operatorname{rank}(A) < n$. One defines the distance to singularity by the distance from A to the set of matrices B so that $\operatorname{rank}(B) < \operatorname{rank}(A)$, i.e., $\delta_T = \min\{\|\Delta A\|_2/\|A\|_2,\ \operatorname{rank}(A + \Delta A) < \operatorname{rank}(A)\}$. Mirsky showed that $\delta_T = 1/(\|A^+\|_2\|A\|_2)$.   △

Example 4.5

Let λ be a simple eigenvalue of the matrix A. A singularity occurs when λ (which remains fixed) becomes at least double, i.e.,

$$\delta_T = \min\{\|\Delta A\|_2/\|A\|_2,\ \operatorname{rank}(A + \Delta A - \lambda I) < \operatorname{rank}(A - \lambda I) = n - 1\}.$$

Using the technique proposed by Demmel (1987, p. 260) to prove his Theorem 3, one can show that

$$\delta_T = 1/(\|(\underline{B} - \lambda I)^{-1}\|_2\|A\|_2) = 1/(\|\Sigma^\perp\|_2\|A\|_2)$$

in the notations of Chatelin (1993a, pp. 73–76). See also Shub and Smale (1993b). △

The componentwise distance to the nearest singular matrix is characterized in the following theorem.

Theorem 4.4 (Rohn (1990))

$$\delta_B = \frac{1}{\max_{D_1,D_2} \rho_0(D_1A^{-1}D_2E)},$$

where D_1, D_2 are diagonal matrices with diagonal entries equal to ± 1 and $\rho_0(B) = \max\{|\lambda|; \lambda \text{ is a real eigenvalue of } B\}$.

The componentwise distance δ_B is not easy to relate to K_B^{-1} (see Demmel (1988, 1992)). We shall see in Chapter 9, by means of PRECISE, that very often one can conjecture that δ_B is of the order of $1/K_B$, i.e., of the reciprocal of the componentwise condition number.

If one now considers the problem $(A, b) \longmapsto x = A^{-1}b$, it is clear that mathematically the singularity is determined by the matrix A only. But we shall see that numerically, for specific algorithms, the right-hand side may play a crucial role (see Chapter 9).

4.5.2   Nonlinear problems

How can Theorem 4.3 be extended to *nonlinear* problems? We begin our study by looking at two simple examples.

Example 4.6 Double root of a polynomial.

We consider the quadratic polynomial $p(x) = x^2 - 2bx + c$, which has two real simple roots $x = b \pm \sqrt{b^2 - c}$ if the discriminant $D = b^2 - c$ is positive. The linear condition number K is proportional to the reciprocal of the derivative, that is,

$$K \propto \frac{1}{|p'(x)|} = \frac{1}{2|\sqrt{D}|}.$$

As expected, K is infinite when $D = 0$, that is, when $x = b$ is a double root for p. For $D \neq 0$, the natural question is: can $|\sqrt{D}|$ be considered as proportional to some appropriately defined distance to singularity of $p(x) = 0$? The answer is yes, if one considers the *constrained* distance to singularity Δ, defined as

$$\Delta = \min \{ \Delta p | \text{ such that } p + \Delta p \text{ has a double root at } x \}.$$

Such a distance is called constrained because only the polynomial p is allowed to vary, whereas the solution x is kept fixed. Let us compute Δp. The simple root $x = b - \sqrt{D}$ of $p(z) = 0$ becomes a double root for $(p+\Delta p)(z) = z^2 - 2(b - \sqrt{D})z + 2b^2 - c - 2b\sqrt{D} = p(z) + 2D - 2b\sqrt{D} - 2z\sqrt{D}$. Therefore, $\Delta p(z) = -2z\sqrt{D} + 2D - 2b\sqrt{D}$. Hence, with the $\| \cdot \|_\infty$ norm for polynomials, $\Delta = |\Delta p| = \max\{|2\sqrt{D}|, |2D - 2b\sqrt{D}|\}$, which is of the order of $\sqrt{D}$ for D small enough. But, of course, the constrained distance to singularity may not realize the *minimal* distance to singularity δ, defined as

$$\delta = \min \{|\Delta p| \text{ such that } p + \Delta p \text{ has a double root near } x \}.$$

In such a definition, both the polynomial p and the solution x are allowed to vary, so clearly $\Delta \geq \delta$. For $p(x) = x^2 - 2bx + c$, $\delta \leq d$ with $d = |p(x) - (x - b)^2| = |c - b^2| = |D|$. This shows that $\Delta \sim |\sqrt{D}|$ is much larger than $d = |D|$ for $|D|$ smaller than 1. Note that d (resp., Δ) is proportional to $1/K^2$ (resp., $1/K$) when D approaches 0. $\triangle$

Example 4.7 Double defective eigenvalue of a matrix.
We consider the two simple eigenvalues a and b for

$$A = \begin{pmatrix} a & 1 \\ 0 & b \end{pmatrix}$$

for $a \neq b$. The linear condition number $K = \sqrt{1 + 1/(a - b)^2}$ is infinite when $a = b$ is a double defective eigenvalue. A simple calculation shows that
  i) the constrained distance to singularity $\Delta = |b - a|$ is achieved for

$$\Delta A = \begin{pmatrix} 0 & 0 \\ 0 & a - b \end{pmatrix} :$$

   the simple eigenvalue a becomes double;
  ii) the distance to singularity $d = (a - b)^2/4 \ll \Delta$ is achieved for

$$\Delta A = \begin{pmatrix} 0 & 0 \\ (a - b)^2/4 & 0 \end{pmatrix} :$$

   the nearby eigenvalue $(a + b)/2$ becomes double.
One sees again that Δ is proportional to $1/K$, but we have exhibited a distance d, which is proportional to $1/K^2$ when $|b - a|$ tends to 0. $\triangle$

These two simple examples have been proposed to illustrate that there is not a unique answer to the question of the extension of Theorem 4.3 to nonlinear equations. It is clear that the distinction between Δ and δ vanishes in the case of linear problems, since in that case one does not have the option to let x vary because no unique solution exists at the singularity.

We now review the two approaches for nonlinear problems found in the literature. Without loss of generality, we can write (P) in the form $F(x) = 0$.

The constrained and minimal distances of the problem (P) to singularity are therefore defined as

$$\begin{cases} \Delta = \min\left\{\|\Delta F\|,\ (F + \Delta F)(x) = 0 \text{ has a multiple root at } x\right\}, \\ \delta = \min\left\{\|\Delta F\,|,\ (F + \Delta F)(y) = 0 \text{ has a multiple root } y \text{ near } x\right\}. \end{cases}$$

1) Shub and Smale (1993a, 1993b) are interested in defining, in the general framework of systems of polynomial equations, a distance to singularity (or a distance to the discriminant variety) in such a way that a generalized form of Theorem 4.3 remains valid. This is achieved by considering essentially the constrained distance Δ, which yields $\Delta = 1/K$.

2) Demmel (1987, 1988) is primarily concerned with δ and establishes the asymptotic upper and lower bounds (valid as $K \to \infty$):

$$\frac{a}{K^2} \leq \delta \leq \frac{b}{K}, \tag{4.4}$$

where a and b are constants.

Is it computationally meaningful to distinguish between the constrained and minimal distances to singularity? We believe that the answer is yes for the following reasons:

- The price to pay to be able to extend Theorem 4.3 straightforwardly is to consider Δ, where only F is allowed to vary but x remains fixed. As a result such a constrained distance may be much larger than the minimal one δ. Therefore, we feel that Δ should not be called the "distance to singularity" without a warning about the possibility that, in the reality of the computation, $\Delta \gg \delta$. If this happens, $1/K$ does not estimate δ reliably: the singularity may be much closer than indicated by $1/K$ for computation purposes.

- In finite precision computations, an essential parameter is what we call the "distance to singularity viewed by the computer" (see Chapters 8 and 9); that is, the maximal size of perturbations to which a regular problem can be submitted while remaining regular for the computer. Such a distance is often in practice a good approximation to δ: this reflects the fact that the actual computation at a regular point x is influenced by the presence of the closest singularity y in the neighbourhood of x. This is why we find results such as (4.4) that relate δ to K to be of *much greater computational significance* than the equality $\Delta = 1/K$.

Our experiments on defective eigenvalues lead us to the following conjecture, which makes (4.4) more precise.

Conjecture 4.1 *If x is close to a Hölder singularity of order $\gamma > 1$, then*

$$\delta = c/K^{\gamma/(\gamma-1)}, \tag{4.5}$$

where c is a constant.

Sketch of a proof: Let us assume that the problem is well posed and corresponds to a multiple root of a polynomial $p(x) = 0$ of multiplicity $m \geq 2$

($\gamma = m$, $2 \le \gamma < \infty$). A perturbation of size t on the polynomial results in a variation Δx of x such that $|\Delta x| = O(t^{1/m})$. Therefore, $|\Delta x|/t = O(t^{1/m-1})$, that is, $K \propto t^{(1-m)/m}$. This indicates that $t \propto K^{m/(1-m)} = 1/K^{m/(m-1)}$.
□

The upper (resp., lower) bound in (4.4) is retrieved for $\gamma \to \infty$ (resp., $\gamma = 2$).

Computational experiments that confirm Conjecture 4.1 are amply described in Chapter 9 (§ 9.3), after a presentation in Chapter 8 of the "dangerous border," which is the *distance to singularity viewed by the computer*. These experiments rely upon the toolbox PRECISE presented in Chapter 8. It provides a software environment to explore "the reality of finite precision computation."

4.6   Unfolding of singularity

Theorem 4.3 and Conjecture 4.1 relate the condition number K to the distance to singularity in case of a linear or a nonlinear problem, respectively.

It may be interesting to look at the more general question of the behaviour of the condition number when the distance to singularity δ is increased: the problem, initially singular for $\delta = 0$, is subject to perturbations that take it *away* from the singularity. We call such process an *unfolding of singularity*. Conjecture 4.1 leads to the following conjecture.

Conjecture 4.2 *The condition number $K(\delta)$ of problems at distance δ from the singularity behaves as*

   i) *$1/\delta$ for linear problems,*

   ii) *$1/\delta^{1-1/\gamma} = \delta^{1/\gamma-1}$ for nonlinear problems (Hölderian singularity of order $\gamma > 1$).*

Proof: i) $K(\delta) = 1/\delta$ is a rewriting of Theorem 4.3.

   ii) $K(\delta) \propto \delta^{1/\gamma-1}$ for nonlinear problems is equivalent to Conjecture 4.1.
□

According to this proposition, the behaviour of $K(\delta)$ away from singularity depends on the characteristics (type and order) of this singularity. We shall give ample computational evidence in Chapter 9, which strengthens Conjecture 4.1. See also Conjecture 8.1 in Chapter 8.

4.7   Spectral portraits

One way to get a graphical insight about the "computational diffusion" of singularities in their neighbourhood consisting of regular points is to look at the condition map $z \longmapsto \|(A - zI)^{-1}\|$ for z in $\mathbb{C}$. The map $z \longmapsto \log_{10} \|(A - zI)^{-1}\|$ is known as the *spectral portrait* of A (Godunov (1992b)). The singularities of $A - zI$ are the eigenvalues of A, where $A - \lambda I$ is singular, and $\|(A - \lambda I)^{-1}\|$ is infinite. The way $\|(A - zI)^{-1}\|$ decreases from infinity for z around λ is related to the stability of the eigenvalue λ, according to the following proposition.

Proposition 4.1 *The absolute condition number of a simple eigenvalue λ satisfies*

$$C(\lambda) = \frac{\|x\|\|x_*\|_*}{|x_*^* x|} = \lim_{z \to \lambda} \|(A - zI)^{-1}\||z - \lambda|.$$

Proof: If λ is a *simple* eigenvalue of A, the resolvent $R(z) = (A - zI)^{-1}$ can be expanded in Laurent series (Chatelin (1988c, p. 59)) and one gets

$$R(z) = \frac{-P}{z - \lambda} + \sum_{k=0}^{\infty} (z - \lambda)^k S^{k+1}.$$

Then $(z - \lambda)R(z) = -P + \sum_{k=0}^{\infty}[(z - \lambda)S]^{k+1}$ and $\lim_{z \to \lambda} \|R(z)\||z - \lambda| = \|P\| = \|x\|\|x_*\|_*/|x_*^* x|$, with the notations of Chapter 3. □

$C(\lambda)$ can be interpreted as the limit of the ratio of the absolute condition number of $A - zI$ to $1/|z - \lambda|$, which would represent the same condition number if A were normal. The interested reader can look at Chapter 11 for several spectral portraits and more about this topic.

4.8 Bibliographical comments

The first condition number for a Hölder singularity was proposed by Wilkinson (1963) for multiple roots of polynomials (with a componentwise metric). Gratton (1995a) treats the normwise case. Chatelin (1986) deals with multiple defective eigenvalues. Although very natural (Kiełbasiński (1975)), this notion failed to catch the interest of numerical analysts beyond very special cases such as eigenvectors and least-squares solutions. Important references in the area deal with *constrained* perturbations, which may not be generic enough to represent the perturbations generated by finite precision computations (Kahan (1972), Demmel (1987), Shub and Smale (1993a, 1993b)).

Chapter 5

Arithmetic Quality of Reliable Algorithms

This chapter is concerned with the central question of the quantification of the arithmetic quality of an algorithm in order to assess the choice of this algorithm to solve the problem (P) on a given computer.

In this chapter we present the *backward error analysis* introduced by Givens in the late 1950s and developed by Wilkinson in the 1960s to analyse the reliability of algorithmic computations in finite precision.

N. B. All quantities overlined by a tilde represent computed versions of the exact ones.

5.1   Forward and backward analyses

As was indicated in Chapter 2, the notion of numerical stability with respect to round-off is specific to the exact perturbation $(\widetilde{G} - G, \tilde{y} - y)$ generated by round-off. A more generic notion of reliability is obtained if the data y and G are allowed to vary.

In Chapter 2 we presented a forward error analysis that involves the direct consistency error $\widetilde{G}(t) - G(t)$, t around y. It is often hard to get a reasonable bound on $\Delta x = x - \tilde{x}$ by a forward analysis. And it is often simpler to use a backward analysis based on the residual consistency error $\widetilde{F}(z) - F(z)$, z around x. Even though this rule has many counterexamples, the backward analysis has proved itself an extremely powerful tool.

5.2   Backward error

The essence of the backward error analysis is to set the exact and the finite precision computations in a common framework by means of the following trick, which we call the *Wilkinson principle*:

71

> Consider the computed solution $\tilde{x}$ the exact solution of a nearby problem.

This almost trivial idea turns out to be much more powerful than it looks:

i) It allows one to get rid of the details of the computer arithmetic: the errors made during the course of the computation are interpreted in terms of equivalent perturbations in the given problem, and the computed quantities are *exact* for the perturbed problem.

ii) One advantage is that rounding errors are put on the same footing as errors in the original data. And the effect of uncertainty in data has usually to be considered in any case.

iii) It enables to draw on powerful tools such as derivatives and perturbation theory.

iv) It allows one to factor out in the error bound, the contribution of the algorithm from the contribution of the problem.

v) Finally, it allows a great flexibility in the sensitivity analysis by providing a large choice of perturbations on the data of the problem.

Such an error analysis is referred to as backward error analysis because the errors are *reflected back* into the original problem. One essential ingredient is the *backward error*, which we proceed to define.

Let $\tilde{x} = \widetilde{G}(y) = \tilde{g}(z)$ be the computed solution for the problem (P) $F(x) = y$. The backward error measures the minimal distance of (P) to the set of perturbed problems that are solved exactly by $\tilde{x}$. Such a notion requires to specify the admissible perturbations, of (P), that is, the class (τ) of admissible perturbations Δz of the data z in Z and the norm $\| \cdot \|_Z$ on Z.

Definition 5.1 *The* backward error *at $\tilde{x}$ associated with (τ) is defined by*

$$B(\tilde{x}) = \inf \left(\|\Delta z\|_Z; \ \Delta z \in (\tau) \ and \ g(z + \Delta z) = \tilde{x} \right).]$$

This definition requires that the set $\mathcal{E} = \{\Delta z \in (\tau); \ g(z + \Delta z) = \tilde{x}\}$ be nonempty.[1] The backward error at $\tilde{x}$ gives the minimal size of the perturbation Δz of the data z when Δz varies in the set $\mathcal{E}$. If the class (τ) of the perturbations for Δz is a good model for the perturbations actually generated by the computer, then $B(\tilde{x})$ gives the minimal size of the perturbation of the data which is equivalent to the computation in finite precision.

5.3   Quality of reliable software

The arithmetic quality of a reliable algorithm/numerical method is related to the size of the backward error, which should be as small as possible compared

---

[1]When solving a problem such as (P), $\mathcal{E}$ is nonempty since at least one element $z + \Delta z$ can be deduced from $F(\tilde{x}) = \tilde{y}$. But this may not be always true. For Example 2.2, $G(y) = (1 + y - 1)/y$, we have $\widetilde{G}(y) = \tilde{x} = 0$ for y small enough, and for all $t = y + \Delta y$, we have $G(t) = 1 \neq \tilde{x} = 0$.

to machine precision Ψ. The best one can do by running an algorithm on a computer is to introduce no more uncertainty than the unavoidable one that results from introducing the data in the computer. Indeed, the reliability of the algorithm proves that the backward error is of order 1 in Ψ at regular points. However, the algorithm is of poor quality when the constant C such that $B(\tilde{x}) \leq C\Psi$ is too large.

Definition 5.2 *The* quality index *of a reliable algorithm at $\tilde{x}$ is defined by*

$$J(\tilde{x}) = \frac{B(\tilde{x})}{\Psi},$$

$J(\tilde{x}) \geq 1$. The best quality corresponds to $J = 1$, and a poor quality corresponds to J significantly larger than 1.

Definition 5.3 *A reliable algorithm is said to be* optimal *when $J \sim 1$.*

In the numerical software literature, the property of an algorithm that we have just defined as *optimal reliability* is referred to as *backward stability* since Wilkinson (1961). It entails computability in finite precision (Chapter 2). Such an algorithm enjoys two properties:

i) arithmetic stability in the mathematical sense; that is, $G_\varepsilon = F_\varepsilon^{-1}$ is equicontinuous with respect to ε in a neighbourhood of y,

ii) residual consistency of order 1: $B(x_\varepsilon) \leq C(y, F)\varepsilon$, with a constant $C(y, F)$ close to 1.

Hence, optimal reliability is more than arithmetic stability in the mathematical sense. However, the term *backward stable* is so widespread among software designers in the Wilkinson acception that we use it also to refer to a *reliable software of good quality* (J reasonably close to 1).

When the data are known with an accuracy of the order of η (i.e., $\|\Delta A\| \sim \eta \|A\|$ for instance), then the backward error should be compared to η; this is important when η is significantly larger than machine precision. Such a situation is frequent in most applications outside mathematics: for instance, uncertainty in physical measurements leads to inaccurate data. But of course, the accuracy on the computed solution may decrease accordingly.

The two principles of Lax and Wilkinson complement each other beautifully. On the one hand, the Lax principle is used to prove computability in finite precision. Once this first step is achieved, the Wilkinson principle is required to grade the quality of the algorithm, with machine precision or data accuracy as the gauge.

In numerical software, the essence of the backward analysis is to set the exact and computed problems into the common framework of perturbation theory, in order to derive, for *regular* problems, an estimation of the error on the computed solution via the first-order bound:

$$\textbf{forward error} \leq \textbf{condition number} \times \textbf{backward error}. \qquad (5.1)$$

The accuracy of this error estimation depends on the ability of the model for the perturbations (data, metrics, structure), chosen to derive the condition number and the backward error, to represent accurately the perturbations actually created by the implemented algorithm when run on a given computer.

We shall see that the formula for the backward error associated with the computed solution $\tilde{x}$ for a problem of the kind $F(x) = y$ can always be derived, in the field of linear algebra, from the computation of the residual $r = F(\tilde{x}) - y$ with an appropriate normalisation.

The backward error analysis allows us to factor the error bound (5.1) into the product of the following two quantities:

i) *condition number*, which depends on the equation $F(x) = y$ only;

ii) *backward error*, which depends on the algorithm and the arithmetic of the computer.

The condition number is imposed by the problem, and it is the aim of software developers to propose algorithms that provide a backward error of the order of machine precision. This is, of course, not always possible.

The bound (5.1) assumes that x is a regular point. In the neighbourhood of a *singular point* of Hölderian order $\gamma = 1/h$, $h < 1$, (5.1) should be replaced by the nonlinear bound

$$\textbf{forward error} \ \leq \ \left(\begin{array}{c} \textbf{Hölderian} \\ \textbf{condition number} \end{array} \right)_{(h)} \times \ (\textbf{backward error})^h.$$

$$(5.2)$$

5.4 Formulae for backward errors

We present the formulae for normwise and componentwise backward errors for a variety of problems in linear algebra. $\| \cdot \|$ is a vector or subordinate matrix norm.

5.4.1 Linear systems

Let $\tilde{x}$ be the computed solution and $r = A\tilde{x} - b$ be the associated residual vector.

1) The *normwise* backward error associated with the approximate solution $\tilde{x}$ of the linear system $Ax = b$ is defined by

$$\begin{aligned} \eta^{\mathcal{N}} &= \inf\{\omega; \|\Delta A\| \leq \omega\alpha, \ \|\Delta b\| \leq \omega\beta \ \text{and} \ (A + \Delta A)\tilde{x} = b + \Delta b\}, \\ &= \frac{\|r\|}{\alpha\|\tilde{x}\| + \beta} \end{aligned}$$

(Rigal and Gaches (1967)).

2) The *componentwise* backward error associated with the approximate solution $\tilde{x}$ of the system $Ax = b$ is defined by

$$\begin{aligned} \eta^{\mathcal{C}} &= \inf\{\omega; \ |\Delta A| \leq \omega E; \ |\Delta b| \leq \omega f \ \text{and} \ (A + \Delta A)\tilde{x} = b + \Delta b\} \\ &= \max_{1 \leq i \leq n} \frac{|b - A\tilde{x}|_i}{(E|\tilde{x}| + f)_i} \end{aligned}$$

(Oettli and Prager (1964)), where, as usual, $0/0$ is interpreted as 0 and $\xi/0$ is interpreted as ∞, and in this case, the backward error is not defined.

Proof: Let $\theta^\mathcal{N} = \|r\|/(\alpha\|\tilde{x}\| + \beta)$ and $\theta^\mathcal{C} = \frac{|b - A\tilde{x}|_i}{(E|\tilde{x}| + f)_i}$: they are *lower* bounds for the normwise and the componentwise backward errors, respectively, i.e., $\eta^\mathcal{N} \geq \theta^\mathcal{N}$ and $\eta^\mathcal{C} \geq \theta^\mathcal{C}$.

1) $\theta^\mathcal{N}$ is achieved for the perturbations $\Delta A = -\alpha\gamma r v^*$ and $\Delta b = \beta\gamma r$, where v satisfies $v^*\tilde{x} = \|\tilde{x}\|$ and $\|v\|_* = 1$ and with $\gamma = (\alpha\|\tilde{x}\| + \beta)^{-1}$.

2) $\theta^\mathcal{C}$ is achieved for the perturbations $\Delta A = DE\mathrm{diag}(\tilde{x}_i/|\tilde{x}|_i)$ and $\Delta b = -Df$, where D is a diagonal matrix such that $r = D(E|\tilde{x}| + f)$.   □

Here again, the values of the normwise (resp., componentwise) backward error according to the three different choices for the data of the linear system can be obtained by appropriately choosing the values of α and β (resp., E and f). These formulae are gathered in Table 5.1.

Normwise	Componentwise
$\dfrac{\|r\|}{\alpha\|\tilde{x}\| + \beta}$	$\displaystyle\max_{i=1,n} \dfrac{|r|_i}{(E|\tilde{x}| + f)_i}$

TABLE 5.1
Backward errors for linear systems, $r = A\tilde{x} - b$

Remark: From the identity $x - \tilde{x} = A^{-1}r$ it follows that $\|x - \tilde{x}\| \leq \|A^{-1}r\| \leq \|\,|A^{-1}|\,|r|\,\|$, where r is the residual $A\tilde{x} - b$ computed in exact arithmetic. We denote by $\tilde{r}$ the residual computed in working precision; then the maximal componentwise error satisfies $|r - \tilde{r}| \leq n\mathbf{u}(|A|\,|\tilde{x}| + |b|)$ (Higham (1991b)). Therefore, $\|x - \tilde{x}\| \leq \|\,|A^{-1}|\,[\,|\tilde{r}| + n\mathbf{u}(|A|\,|\tilde{x}| + |b|)]\,\|$.

5.4.2   Matrix inversion

Let $R = A\widetilde{X} - I$ be the matrix residual associated with the computed inverse $\widetilde{X}$.

1) The *normwise* backward error associated with the approximate inverse $\widetilde{X}$ of a matrix A is defined by

$$
\begin{aligned}
\eta^\mathcal{N} &= \inf\left\{\omega;\ \|\Delta A\| \leq \omega\alpha \text{ and } (A + \Delta A)\widetilde{X} = I\right\} \\
&\geq \frac{\|R\|}{\alpha\|\widetilde{X}\|}.
\end{aligned}
$$

If the normalised residual $\|R\|/(\alpha\|\widetilde{X}\|)$ is large, then one is sure that the algorithm that produced $\widetilde{X}$ is backward unstable. However, the equality

$A\widetilde{X} - I = R$ implies $\widetilde{X} - A^{-1} = A^{-1}R$ and $\frac{\|\widetilde{X}-A^{-1}\|}{\|A^{-1}\|} \le \|R\|$, assuming that A is nonsingular. If $\|R\| < 1$, then we know that A and $\widetilde{X}$ are nonsingular (write $I + R = A\widetilde{X}$).

2) The *componentwise* backward error associated with $\widetilde{X}$ when A is perturbed is defined by

$$
\begin{aligned}
\eta^{\mathcal{C}} &= \min\{\omega; |\Delta A| \le \omega E \text{ and } (A + \Delta A)\widetilde{X} = I\} \\
&\ge \max_{1\le i,j\le n} \frac{|R|_{ij}}{(E|\widetilde{X}|)_{ij}}.
\end{aligned}
$$

5.4.3   Eigenproblems

Let $\tilde{x}$ and $\tilde{\lambda}$ be respectively an approximate eigenvector and an approximate eigenvalue of the matrix A. We define $r = A\tilde{x} - \tilde{\lambda}\tilde{x}$ as the associated residual vector.

1) The *normwise* backward error associated with $(\tilde{\lambda}, \tilde{x})$ is defined by

$$
\begin{aligned}
\eta^{\mathcal{N}}(\tilde{\lambda}, \tilde{x}) &= \min\{\omega; \|\Delta A\| \le \omega\alpha \text{ such that } (A + \Delta A)\tilde{x} = \tilde{\lambda}\tilde{x}\} \\
&= \frac{\|r\|}{\alpha\|\tilde{x}\|}.
\end{aligned}
$$

We note that if $x' = k\tilde{x}$ and $r' = Ax' - \lambda'x'$, then we have $\frac{\|r'\|}{\alpha\|x'\|} = \frac{\|r\|}{\alpha\|\tilde{x}\|}$. Consequently, the backward error does not depend on the normalization chosen for the approximate eigenvector.

2) The *componentwise* backward error associated with the approximations $\tilde{\lambda}$ and $\tilde{x}$ is defined by

$$
\begin{aligned}
\eta^{\mathcal{C}}(\tilde{\lambda}, \tilde{x}) &= \min\{\omega; |\Delta A| \le \omega E \text{ such that } (A + \Delta A)\tilde{x} = \tilde{\lambda}\tilde{x}\} \\
&= \max_{1\le i\le n} \frac{|r|_i}{(E|\tilde{x}|)_i}.
\end{aligned}
$$

Proof: The two demonstrations are similar to the case $A \longmapsto x = A^{-1}b$, where b is replaced by $\tilde{\lambda}\tilde{x}$. $\quad\square$

Table 5.2 gives the formulae for the backward error for the eigenproblem where λ is not assumed to be simple.

5.4.4   Cluster of eigenvalues

Let $\widetilde{X}$ be an approximate invariant subspace for the matrix A for which we suppose to know an orthogonal basis $\widetilde{Q}$. We define $\widetilde{B} = \widetilde{Q}^*A\widetilde{Q}$. The residual associated with $\widetilde{Q}$ and $\widetilde{B}$ is $R = A\widetilde{Q} - \widetilde{Q}\widetilde{B}$. The *normwise* backward error associated with $\widetilde{Q}$ is defined by

$$
\eta^{\mathcal{N}}(\widetilde{Q}) = \min\left(\omega; \|\Delta A\| \le \omega\|A\| \text{ such that } (A + \Delta A)\widetilde{Q} = \widetilde{Q}\widetilde{B}\right).
$$

Normwise	Componentwise
$\dfrac{\|r\|}{\alpha\|\tilde{x}\|}$	$\max_{1 \leq i \leq n} \dfrac{|r_i|}{(E|\tilde{x}|)_i}$

TABLE 5.2

Backward errors form the eigenproblem, $r = A\tilde{x} - \tilde{\lambda}\tilde{x}$.

Proposition 5.1 *Set*

$$\theta^{\mathcal{N}} = \frac{\|R\|}{\|A\|\|\widetilde{Q}\|}.$$

Then $\eta^{\mathcal{N}}(\widetilde{Q}) \geq \theta^{\mathcal{N}}$, with equality when $\widetilde{Q}$ is exactly orthogonal, and $\| \cdot \|$ is any unitarily invariant norm.

Proof: The proof is straightforward since $R = -\Delta A\widetilde{Q}$ and $\|R\| \leq \|\Delta A\|\|\widetilde{Q}\|$. Then $\|\Delta A\|/\|A\| \geq \|R\|/(\|A\|\|\widetilde{Q}\|)$. Not all computed orthogonal bases are orthogonal within machine precision. We shall return to this question in §5.7. If $\widetilde{Q}$ is *exactly* orthogonal, $\|\widetilde{Q}\|_2 = 1$ and the lower bound $\theta^{\mathcal{N}} = \|R\|/\|A\|$ is achieved for $\Delta A = -R\widetilde{Q}^*$, which implies $\|\Delta A\| = \|R\|$ for $\| \cdot \|$ unitarily invariant.   □

5.4.5   Roots of polynomials

1) The *normwise* backward error associated with the approximate root $\tilde{x}$ of the monic polynomial $p(x) = \sum_{i=0}^{n} a_i x^i$ is defined by

$$\begin{aligned}
\eta^{\mathcal{N}} &= \inf \{\omega;\ \|\Delta a\| \leq \omega\beta \text{ and } (p + \Delta p)(\tilde{x}) = 0\} \\
&= \frac{|r|}{\|\tilde{\underline{x}}\|_* \beta},
\end{aligned}$$

where $a = (a_0, \ldots, a_n)^T$, $\tilde{\underline{x}} = (1\ \tilde{x}\ \tilde{x}^2 \ \ldots\ \tilde{x}^n)^T$, and $r = p(\tilde{x})$.

2) The *componentwise* backward error associated with the approximate root $\tilde{x}$ of the polynomial $p(x) = \sum_{i=0}^{n} a_i x^i$ is defined by

$$\begin{aligned}
\eta^{\mathcal{C}} &= \inf \{\omega;\ |\Delta a_i| \leq \omega f_i,\ i = 1, \ldots, n, \text{ and } (p + \delta p)(\tilde{x}) = 0\} \\
&= \frac{|r|}{\sum_{i=0}^{n} f_i |\tilde{x}|^i} = \frac{|r|}{f^T |\tilde{\underline{x}}|}
\end{aligned}$$

(Mosier (1986)). See Table 5.3.

Proof: 1) The lower bound $\eta^{\mathcal{N}}$ is achieved for the perturbation $\Delta a = -(1/\|\tilde{\underline{x}}\|_*)rv$ with v such that $v^T\tilde{\underline{x}} = \|\tilde{\underline{x}}\|_*$ and $\|v\| = 1$.

2) The lower bound $\eta^{\mathcal{C}}$ is achieved by $\Delta a_i = -r f_i \overline{\tilde{x}}^i/(|\tilde{x}^i| \sum_{k=0}^{n} f_k |\tilde{x}^k|)$.

□

Normwise	Componentwise
$\dfrac{|r|}{\|\tilde{x}\|_* \beta}$	$\dfrac{|r|}{f^T |\tilde{x}|}$

TABLE 5.3

Backward errors for $p(x) = 0$, $r = p(\tilde{x})$

Example 5.1 Newton's method.

We consider the Newton algorithm for solving the polynomial equation $p(x) = 0$. The iteration

$$x_0, \quad x_{k+1} = x_k - \frac{p(x_k)}{p'(x_k)}, \quad k = 1, 2, \ldots,$$

is stopped when $|x_{k+1} - x_k|/|x_k|$ is less than a prescribed threshold α.

1) We choose $p(x) = (x - 1)(x - 3)$, and set $x_0 = 4$, $\alpha = 10^{-3}$. The computed solution $\tilde{x}$ has a forward error $|\Delta x|/|x| \sim 1.5 \times 10^{-8}$. The normwise condition number is $K_W = 8.11$, and the backward error associated with $\tilde{x}$ is $\eta^{\mathcal{N}} = 1.9 \times 10^{-9}$. Applying (5.1) leads to the upper bound $K_W \times \eta^{\mathcal{C}} = 1.5 \times 10^{-8}$, in agreement with the forward error. The componentwise analysis produces the same result on this example.

2) The polynomial $p(x) = x^2 - 14x + 49 - \beta$ admits the two roots $x = 7 \pm \sqrt{\beta}$, becoming double as $\beta \to 0$. We choose $\beta = 10^{-12}$, $x_0 = 8$, and $\alpha = 10^{-5}$. The computed solution $\tilde{x}$ verifies $|\Delta x|/|x| \sim 8.6 \times 10^{-6}$. The normwise condition number is $K_W = 1.8 \times 10^8$, and the associated normwise backward error is $\eta^{\mathcal{N}} = 1.48 \times 10^{-12}$. The product $K_W \times \eta^{\mathcal{N}} = 2.66 \times 10^{-4}$ overestimates the forward error, and so would the componentwise analysis.

If we consider that we are solving a problem in the neighbourhood of a singularity of order 2, we can apply (5.2) with $K_{1/2}^{\mathcal{C}} = 2$ (see Theorem 4.2) and $\eta^{\mathcal{C}} = 1.9 \times 10^{-11}$. This leads to the upper bound $K_{1/2}^{\mathcal{C}}(\eta^{\mathcal{C}})^{1/2} = 8.7 \times 10^{-6}$, which is now an accurate prediction for the forward error. Alternatively, $K_{1/2}^{\mathcal{N}} = 7.18$ leads to the same upper bound. $\triangle$

The above example shows that the linear bound (5.1) is valid only far enough from a singularity. It also illustrates that the formulae for the backward error at $\tilde{x}$ do not depend whether x is a singular or a regular point.

5.5   Influence of the class of perturbations

5.5.1   Pertinence of the model for perturbations

How relevant are the various condition numbers introduced above to assess the computation error $x - \tilde{x}$? Clearly, the condition number relative to a given class of perturbation (τ) is an *upper bound* for the *potential* instability resulting from the actual perturbation of the data chosen in this class.

Two most useful classes of perturbations for the analysis of computational stability are defined by means of the scaled norms on Z and X defined with $\alpha = \|A\|$, $\beta = \|b\|$ and $E = |A|$, $f = |b|$, respectively. We illustrate this on the example of solving $Ax = b$, that is, $(A, b) \longmapsto x = A^{-1}b$.

The largest possible class of perturbations of size ω corresponds to

$$(\tau)_\omega^{\mathcal{N}} = \{(\Delta A, \Delta b); \|\Delta A\| \leq \omega\|A\|, \|\Delta b\| \leq \omega\|b\|\}.$$

The associated Turing condition number $K_T(A, b)$ corresponds to a *worst-case* analysis: there are no constraint other than in size on the way A and b may vary; that is, ΔA and Δb are as general as possible in "balls" of radius ω, $\omega \to 0$.

On the other hand, the smallest possible class of perturbations compatible with the floating-point representation of data corresponds to

$$(\tau)_\Psi^{\mathcal{C}} = \{(\Delta A, \Delta b); |\Delta A| \leq \Psi|A|, |\Delta b| \leq \Psi|b|\},$$

where Ψ is the machine precision. The associated Skeel condition number, $K_S(A, b)$, corresponds in some sense to a *best-case* (or optimal) analysis. The error is no greater than the unavoidable one of the order of Ψ, generated by introducing the data in the computer. The constraint is borne by each entry of A and b. Zero elements cannot be perturbed; the sparsity pattern of the matrix is respected.

We note that $K_S \leq K_T$ (because of the use of monotonic norms on X), which means that a linear system may be much better conditioned in the mixed sense than in the normwise sense. This explains why the normwise bounds for the computation error may be pessimistic if the perturbations generated by the finite precision computation belong to $(\tau)^{\mathcal{C}}$.

On the contrary, we have $\eta_\infty^{\mathcal{C}} \geq \eta_\infty^{\mathcal{C}}$ in infinity norm: this implies that a small componentwise backward error is more difficult to achieve than a small normwise backward error.

In conclusion, there exist at least two measures of stability that are useful in numerical linear algebra: they correspond to the Turing and Skeel condition numbers. In the literature, the concept of ill-conditioning refers implicitly to Turing. However, it proves useful to distinguish between Turing and Skeel ill-conditioning in certain cases. We illustrate now the two cases where the effective instability is much less than the potential instability.

5.5.2   When the results are better than predicted

It is important to remember that the potential instability is only an upper bound of the *effective* instability of the computation resulting from the perturbation actually generated by the computer arithmetic.

Indeed the potential instability is related to the nearness to singularity of A: K_T and K_S in general depend on A^{-1}. Here are two cases where the effective instability is much smaller than the potential instability, indicated by K_T or K_S.

- Case 1: the effective instability is much less than indicated by K_T. This may happen when K_S can be bounded independently of A^{-1} for certain triangular matrices (Higham (1989)). In this case, a componentwise analysis is more appropriate than a normwise analysis to describe the computation.
- Case 2: the effective instability is much less than indicated by K_S. This may happen when the effective perturbation generated by the computation has not only a *size* constraint as above (i.e., $|\Delta A| \leq \omega|A|$, $|\Delta b| \leq \omega|b|$) but also a *directional* constraint. For example, only certain entries of the data are allowed to be be perturbed, or the particular structure of the matrix has to be preserved. It is the case for the Björck–Pereyra (BP) algorithm to solve certain Vandermonde systems (Higham (1987a)) and for the fast Poisson solver (Chan and Foulser (1988)).

We illustrate below these two cases.

Example 5.2 Solutions of triangular systems (case 1).

Wilkinson (1961, 1963) and Stewart (1973b) have emphasized the fact that the solution of triangular systems $Tx = b$ is generally computed with high accuracy. As far as backward stability is concerned, Wilkinson (1963, p. 100) proved that the approximation $\tilde{x}$ (resulting from the application of any standard algorithm for solving a triangular system by substitution) satisfies exactly $(T + E)\tilde{x} = b$ with $|E| \leq (n+1)c\mathbf{u}|T|$: this therefore implies that solving a triangular system is backward stable in a componentwise sense. The same analysis could be done in a normwise metric, but Wilkinson notes that it gives very pessimistic bounds.

We consider the particular case of triangular M-matrices. Let $T \longmapsto M(T)$ be the transformation such that

$$M(T) = (m_{ij}) \text{ with } m_{ij} = \begin{cases} -|m_{ij}| \ i \neq j, \\ +|m_{ij}| \ i = j. \end{cases}$$

Matrices such that $T = M(T)$ are called M-matrices. Higham (1989) states that if T is an M-matrix and if all entries of b are nonnegative, then

$$K_S(T) = \frac{\||T^{-1}||T||x|\|_\infty}{\|x\|_\infty} \leq 2n - 1,$$

independently of T^{-1}. Since the algorithm has been proven componentwise backward stable, the immediate consequence is that the computed solution is accurate even if T is almost singular. It is clear that, in such a situation, a normwise analysis would give pessimistic results: the potential instability contained in a large normwise condition number $K_T(T)$ is not excited by the actual computation. The componentwise model for perturbations is appropriate to describe the computation in the case of M-matrices.
$\triangle$

Example 5.3 An accurate Vandermonde solver (case 2).

An efficient solver for Vandermonde systems is extremely useful because such systems are encountered many different domains, such as polynomial interpolation, polynomial root finding, and moments problems. A Vandermonde matrix V of order $n+1$ can be written as

$$V = \begin{pmatrix} 1 & 1 & \dots & 1 \\ \alpha_0 & \alpha_1 & \dots & \alpha_n \\ \vdots & \vdots & & \vdots \\ \alpha_0^n & \alpha_1^n & \dots & \alpha_n^n \end{pmatrix}.$$

The generic parameters α_j of the matrix represent the nodes, and the right-hand side represents the moments, whose weights are given by the solution x. For such a problem, one can allow perturbations in the nodes and in the moments, but arbitrary perturbations in the matrix coefficients are not allowed in order to retain the characteristics of a moment problem. This is an example of *structured* perturbations.

We consider the solution of a Vandermonde system by the BP algorithm (1970): BP is very competitive not only because of its CPU time performance but also because it produces very accurate solutions and generates perturbations that respect the moment structure of the problem (Higham (1987a)).

1) The forward analysis of this algorithm leads to the bound $|x - \tilde{x}| \leq 5n\mathbf{u}|V^{-1}||b| + O(\mathbf{u}^2)$; therefore,

$$\frac{\|x - \tilde{x}\|_\infty}{\|x\|_\infty} \leq 5n\mathbf{u}\frac{\| \ |V^{-1}||b| \ \|_\infty}{\|x\|_\infty} + O(\mathbf{u}^2). \tag{5.3}$$

An interesting case is obtained when the right-hand side b has a sign oscillation property, e.g., $(-1)^i b_i \geq 0$, $i = 0, \dots, n$. Then $|V^{-1}||b| = |V^{-1}b| = |x|$, and thus the computed solution satisfies

$$|x - \tilde{x}| \leq 5n\mathbf{u}|x| + O(\mathbf{u}^2).$$

Therefore, the computed solution is very accurate because the error bound is independent of V^{-1} (Higham (1987a)).

2) The componentwise backward analysis (with perturbations of b only) yields

$$\frac{\|x - \tilde{x}\|_\infty}{\|x\|_\infty} \leq K_S(b)\eta^C(b)$$

$$\leq \frac{\| |V^{-1}||b| \|_\infty}{\|x\|_\infty} \times \max_i \frac{|r_i|}{|b_i|}. \tag{5.4}$$

When comparing this inequality with (5.3), can we deduce that the backward error is of order $\mathbf{u}$? No (see Chapter 9): it is possible that the solution $\tilde{x}$ is accurate but the backward error is large. In such cases, (5.4) is an overestimation of the forward error, whereas (5.3) is realistic. One partial explanation is that BP can create only perturbations of the right-hand side and of the $\alpha_i, i = 0, \dots, n$, since the matrix V itself is not built.

Therefore, the bounds given by the general theory of Skeel may lead to a large overestimation of the error because they take into account a class of perturbations which is too large. We look at the next question: is it sufficient to consider componentwise perturbations of the $n+1$ parameters α_i, $i = 0, \dots, n$? Let C_α be the structured mixed condition number of V with respect to componentwise perturbations of the parameters $\alpha_i, i = 0, \dots, n$. Higham (1987a) proves that

$$C_\alpha = \frac{\| \ |V^{-1}H_nV||x| \ \|_\infty}{\|x\|_\infty}$$

with H_n = diag$(0, 1, \ldots, n)$. C_α is to be compared with $K_S(V)$ = $\|V^{-1}\|\|V\|\|x\|\|_\infty / \|x\|_\infty$. One has $C_\alpha \leq nK_S(V)$, but there are matrices for which $C_\alpha \ll K_S(V)$. Is $C_\alpha \Psi$ therefore a reliable prediction for the forward error? Again, no (see Chapter 9).

In conclusion, BP tends to respect the Vandermonde structure better than GEPP. However, perturbations of the α_i only are not sufficient to describe faithfully the computational behaviour. The right-hand side b also has to be taken into account. $\triangle$

5.6   Iterative refinement for backward stability

Algorithms are said to be backward stable or reliable whenever, for given data and approximate solution, the associated backward error at regular points is of the order of machine precision. Otherwise they are declared backward unstable. This defines a *local* backward stability since it is restricted to specific data. Assessing the *global* (or generic) backward stability of an algorithm (i.e., for all possible choice of data) can be very difficult: one has to perform a thorough study of both the mathematical problem and the algorithm in order to determine the critical data that would produce a singularity or a degeneracy. However, it is sometimes possible to prove the global backward stability. Proving that an algorithm can be backward unstable for certain data is easier in a way, since it is sufficient to exhibit counterexamples. We show examples of both cases and then explain how backward instability can be sometimes corrected via iterative refinement techniques.

Normwise backward stability

Gaussian elimination with partial pivoting is known to be possibly *normwise backward unstable*. For example, if A is the Wilkinson matrix WIL of order 50 (which is the well-conditioned matrix W_{50} of §2.5), $\eta^N(A) = 1.2 \times 10^{-4}$, which is 10^{12} times larger than machine precision. This backward instability results from the bad sequence of pivots generated by the algorithm on this example. This may happen more frequently without pivoting.

QR, implemented with Householder transformations or Givens rotations, is *backward stable* with respect to the Euclidean norm. Indeed Wilkinson (1965) proved that $(A + \Delta A)\tilde{x} = b + \Delta b$, with $\|\Delta A\| \leq p(n)\Psi\|A\|$ and $\|\Delta b\| \leq p(n)\Psi\|b\|$, where $p(n)$ is a linear polynomial. Formulations for the polynomial $p(n)$ can be found in Golub and Van Loan (1989). It results that $\eta^N \leq p(n)\Psi$, which assesses the backward stability, provided that $p(n)$ is not too large.

Componentwise backward stability

An algorithm is said to be backward stable in a componentwise sense if the componentwise backward error can be bounded by a reasonable factor of the machine precision. Neither GEPP nor QR is componentwise backward stable. This is illustrated for GEPP with the matrix VAND5 of order 10 $(a_{ij} = j^{i-1})$

with the right-hand side $b_i = i$, $i = 1, \ldots, n$, and for QR with the matrix IPJ of order 10 ($a_{ij} = (i + j)!$) with the right-hand side $b = e$. Table 5.4 gives the componentwise backward errors corresponding to the three choices of data: (A, b), A, or b. However, GEPP and QR, when used in conjunction with iterative refinement, can be backward stable.

	GEPP	QR
Data	VAND5	IPJ
A, b	$2.6 \times 10-13$	4.6×10^{-8}
A	$2.6 \times 10-13$	4.6×10^{-8}
b	$3.0 \times 10-9$	1.0×10^{-3}

TABLE 5.4
Examples of large componentwise backward errors

Iterative refinement

Iterative refinement is a technique used to improve a computed solution $\tilde{x}$. Three steps are necessary and take the following form for a linear system $Ax = b$:

1. compute the residual $r = b - A\tilde{x}$;
2. solve the system $Ad = r$, which gives the computed solution $\tilde{d}$;
3. update $\tilde{y} = \tilde{x} + \tilde{d}$.

Wilkinson (1961) made an analysis of iterative refinement in single precision requiring that the residual r is computed in double precision to increase accuracy. Later, Jankowski and Woźniakowski (1977) proved that iterative refinement, using a residual computed to working precision, can make a solver that is not too unstable normwise backward stable, as long as the matrix A is not too ill conditioned. This result was important because it showed that iterative refinement could be used without extra precision in the purpose of backward stability. Then Skeel (1980) studied in detail iterative refinement on GE with partial pivoting and proved that one step is enough to guarantee componentwise backward stability. Higham (1991b) showed that, provided that some conditions are satisfied (A^{-1} not too ill conditioned and $|A||\tilde{y}|$ not too badly scaled), one step of iterative refinement is enough to make QR componentwise backward stable.

Remark: We caution that iterative refinement without extra precision does not guarantee a better accuracy in the corrected solution $\tilde{y}$ than in the previous solution $\tilde{x}$. It can only guarantee a smaller backward error. If iterative refinement is used to improve the accuracy of an approximate solution, then the residual should be computed with extra precision (double the working precision, for example).

It is not always possible to improve the backward stability of an algorithm through iterative refinement. This happens for instance with BP on Vandermonde systems, which are classically ill conditioned. Often the computed solution leads to a large componentwise backward error, whereas the computed solution is accurate to working precision. The backward error is not decreased by iterative refinement, and after the first step, the forward error increases. BP produces very specific perturbations that permit us to obtain good accuracy in the solution; iterative refinement introduces additional perturbations that can be significantly amplified by the mathematical instability.

5.7 Robust reliability and arithmetic quality

The bound

$$B(\tilde{x}) \leq C(F, y)\Psi \tag{5.5}$$

plays an essential role in the assessment of the reliability and quality of the algorithm, as we have seen. However, the constant $C(F, y)$ may depend on the data F and y in a way that might decrease dramatically the arithmetic quality if the reliability is not robust enough to accommodate certain difficult problems.

A very important case is provided by the *loss of orthogonality* in the computation of an orthogonal matrix by the Gram–Schmidt or modified Gram–Schmidt (MGS) algorithm (Björck (1994)). We consider the computation of the factorization $A = QR$ for the matrix A of size $n \times m$. We define $K(A) = \sigma_{\max}/\sigma_{\min}$. Let $\tilde{Q}$ be the computed factor by MGS or Householder/Givens (H/G). The loss of orthogonality is now defined.

Definition 5.4 *The* loss of orthogonality *of the computed matrix $\tilde{Q}$ is*

$$\omega(\tilde{Q}) = \min\left(\|\tilde{Q} - Q\|_2, \ Q \ exactly \ orthonormal\right).$$

It can be measured by $\|I - \tilde{Q}^*\tilde{Q}\|_2$ because of the equivalence stated by the following proposition.

Proposition 5.2

$$\omega(\tilde{Q}) \leq \|I - \tilde{Q}^*\tilde{Q}\|_2 \leq 2\omega(\tilde{Q}) + \omega(\tilde{Q})^2.$$

Proof: The proof is based on the polar decomposition $\tilde{Q} = WP$, where W is orthogonal and P is Hermitian and semidefinite. Fan and Hoffman (1955) showed that $\omega(\tilde{Q}) = \|\tilde{Q} - W\|_2$.

1) Left inequality: see Higham (1994).

2) Right inequality: straightforward by taking the 2-norm of $\tilde{Q}^*\tilde{Q} - I = (\tilde{Q} - W)^*(\tilde{Q} - W) + (W^*\tilde{Q} - I) + (\tilde{Q}^*W - I)$. □

It has been shown that

- for MGS (Björck (1967)): $\|I - \tilde{Q}^*\tilde{Q}\|_2 \leq C(n, m)K(A)\Psi$,
- for H/G (Wilkinson (1963)): $\|I - \tilde{Q}^*\tilde{Q}\|_2 \leq C(n, m)\Psi$.

If A has column vectors that are poorly independent, then $\widetilde{Q}$ computed by MGS will not be orthogonal to machine precision. This shows that the computation of Q by MGS is *weakly stable* in the sense of Bunch (1987): he defines a weakly stable algorithm as forward stable for well-conditioned problems.

The possible *forward instability* of the computation by MGS of the orthogonal factor Q may occur when A is square and highly nonnormal, because $K_2(A)$ is large. We recall that the computed factorization QR has, however, a small residual error with all three implementations.

As a consequence, all methods that require the computation of orthonormal bases for powers of A, such as many methods to compute eigenvalues, should be very carefully implemented when intended for use on highly nonnormal matrices (Bennani and Braconnier (1994b), Chaitin-Chatelin (1994a)).

The reader will find more developments on the robustness to nonnormality in Chapter 10, which is devoted to that topic.

5.8   Bibliographical comments

The main aspects of backward error analysis are presented in Wilkinson (1961, 1963, 1965). Backward error analysis for Sylvester equations (Higham (1993)), least-squares problems (Waldén, Karlson, and Sun (1995)), and the Riccati equations (Ghavimi and Laub (1995)) are examples for which the backward error cannot be formulated in terms of a normalized residual.

Better-than-predicted results are discussed in Wilkinson (1961) and Higham (1987a, 1989). Forward analysis is studied in Stummel (1985a, 1985b), Bauer (1974), Voïévodine (1980), Higham (1987a), and Yalamov (1991, 1994). Bunch (1987) introduces more refined notions of numerical stability (see also Bunch, Demmel, and Van Loan (1989)).

Loss of orthogonality in MGS has a long history (Björck (1994)). Practical implications of this possible loss of orthogonality in eigenvalue computations are discussed in Bennani and Braconnier (1994b) and Braconnier (1994b, 1994c).

Chapter 6

Numerical Stability in Finite Precision

In this chapter we study the behaviour on a computer of numerical methods that require an infinite number of steps to converge in exact arithmetic toward an exact or approximate solution. How is their convergence affected by finite precision? We present a backward error analysis that extends to numerical analysis in finite precision the ideas of Givens and Wilkinson, which were developed for numerical software (finite algorithms).

6.1 Iterative and approximate methods

The question of the computability in finite precision for iterative and approximate methods has already been addressed in § 2.9. We have seen that the numerical stability or convergence proved in exact arithmetic may become *conditional to the arithmetic* in finite precision, because of the possible coupling between the convergence parameters and the computer precision ε. If this is the case, numerical stability is guaranteed only when the variation of the convergence parameters satisfies the constraints imposed by the arithmetic (see Example 2.10).

A typical situation in numerical analysis corresponds to the approximation of $F(x) = y$ by $F_h(x_h) = y_h$ such that $x_h \to x$ as $h \to 0$. Often, only a good enough approximation x_h of x is sought. This is achieved by solving, for a fixed h, $F_h(x_h) = y_h$ to working precision by means of some iterative solver.

We therefore turn to the convergence of iterative methods in finite precision.

6.2 Numerical convergence of iterative solvers

Let G be an iterative method such that $x = G(y)$ is obtained in the limit $k \to \infty$ of the sequence $x_k = G_k(y)$, where each G_k, for k finite, is an algorithm. Let $\tilde{x}_k$

be the computed value of x_k in finite precision. The best we can expect from a convergent iteration is a backward error of the order of machine precision Ψ. Therefore, the following definition is natural.

Definition 6.1 *The* convergence index *of a convergent iterative solver at the kth iteration is given by*

$$J(\tilde{x}_k) = \frac{B(\tilde{x}_k)}{\Psi}, \quad k = 1, 2, \ldots .$$

The optimal value for the convergence index is 1. When the value is reached, the iteration should be stopped. The history of the convergence on the computer is told by the map $k \longmapsto J(\tilde{x}_k)$ or equivalently by the map $k \longmapsto B(\tilde{x}_k)$. The numerical quality of the convergence depends on two elements:

   i) the order of magnitude η_{conv} of the backward error $B(\tilde{x}_k)$ when it stabilizes as k increases,
   ii) the speed at which η_{conv} is reached.

From the error analysis given in Chapter 2, it is clear that the best we can expect in finite precision is that $\eta_{\text{conv}} \sim \Psi$ or equivalently $J_{\text{conv}} \sim 1$. If this is at all realized, it takes place necessarily after a finite number of steps.

> The clear-cut difference in behaviour in exact arithmetic between algorithms and iterative solvers is blurred by finite precision.

This allows us to *extend to iterative methods* the definition of backward stability proposed by Wilkinson for algorithms. See Definition 5.3. However, if the convergence is conditional to the arithmetic, the optimal floor value Ψ may be impossible to reach for $B(\tilde{x}_k)$. This will be discussed later (§ 6.3).

Example 6.1

The algorithm QR converges mathematically after an infinite number of steps at best. However, *in practice*, with appropriate shifts, it can be used as a finite algorithm, since the backward error is always reduced to machine precision. $\triangle$

We saw above that iterative methods can be treated as algorithms by means of the backward error. Conversely, it is often the case for very large problems that finite algorithms, such as conjugate-gradient–like methods, are treated as iterative solvers and are stopped much before the exact mathematical termination.

In the above study of the convergence of iterative methods, we have let the iterations continue until stabilization of the backward error at a floor value η_{conv}. Such a strategy for termination can be called *natural termination* because one can safely stop the iterations once the minimal value for the backward error is reached. Doing more iterations cannot decrease the backward error anymore. There are circumstances where an a priori stopping criterion is imposed on the iterations, of the type $\|x_{k-1} - x_k\|/\|x_k\| \leq tol$. Such a strategy is called *forced termination*, because the process may be stopped before η_{conv} is reached, that is, before the natural termination.

6.3 Stopping criteria in finite precision

We have illustrated why it is important in practice to use the *backward error* to assess the quality of an algorithm or of an iterative method. The price to pay for matrix problems is the necessity to estimate $\|A\|$, and this may be considered expensive for very large matrices. This is the price for greater security. The role of $\|A\|$ may be crucial, for example, in those cases where A is highly nonnormal and therefore $\|A\|$ is large. Luckily, a rough estimate of $\|A\|$ can often be inferred cheaply from the mathematical partial differential equation.

Let us look at an other illuminating example of the essential role of the backward error as a stopping criterion provided by a Krylov-based eigensolver.
Example 6.2 Arnoldi–Tchebycheff on the Schur matrix (Bennani and Braconnier (1994b)).
The Schur matrix has been defined in Chatelin (1993a, p. 162). Let S_ν be the real Schur form of order $n = 2p$ defined by

$$
S_\nu = \begin{bmatrix}
x_1 & y_1 & & & & & \\
-y_1 & x_1 & \nu & & & & \\
& & x_2 & y_2 & & & \\
& & -y_2 & x_2 & \nu & & \\
& & & & \ddots & \nu & \\
& & & & & x_p & y_p \\
& & & & & -y_p & x_p
\end{bmatrix},
$$

where x_i, y_i, and ν are real numbers. The exact eigenvalues of S_ν are $x_j \pm i y_j$, $j = 1, \ldots, p$. With the choice $x_j = -(2j-1)^2/1000$ and $y_j = +(2j-1)/100$, $j = 1, \ldots, p$, the eigenvalues lie on the parabola $x = -10y^2$. Now let $A_\nu = QS_\nu Q$, where Q is the symmetric unitary matrix consisting of the eigenvectors of the second difference matrix,

$$
q_{ij} = \sqrt{\frac{2}{n+1}} \sin \frac{ij\pi}{n+1}, \qquad i, j = 1, \ldots, n.
$$

We set $n = 300$, $p = 150$, and $\nu = 10^4$ and proceed to compute the eigenvalues of largest imaginary part. We use the incomplete Arnoldi algorithm (Krylov subspace of dimension $m = 20$ based on a starting vector $u^{(0)}$, $u^{(k)} \neq 0$) with Tchebycheff acceleration (polynomial of degree $l = 20$) iteratively for $k = 0, 1, 2, \ldots$ (see Chatelin (1988c, 1993a)). It computes at each step k an orthonormal basis $V_m = [v_1, \ldots, v_m]$ for the Krylov subspace of order m such that

$$
AV_m = V_m H_m + h_{m+1,m} v_{m+1} e_m^T. \tag{6.1}
$$

Let (λ, x) (resp., (λ, y)) be an approximate (resp., exact) eigenpair for A (resp., H_m). From (6.1) follows the identity in *exact arithmetic*,

$$\|Ax - \lambda x\|_2 = h_{m+1,m}|y_m| \text{ with } y_m = e_m^T y, \qquad (6.2)$$

which gives a cheap way to compute the direct residual $r_D = \|Ax - \lambda x\|_2$ by means of the Arnoldi residual $r_A = h_{m+1,m}|y_m|$. However, the mathematical identity (6.2) is not always satisfied in *finite precision*, as is illustrated by Figure 6.1 for the computation of the eigenvalues $\lambda_j = x_j \pm iy_j$, $j = 1, \ldots, 4$.

The phenomenon is clear if one interprets Figure 6.1 in terms of backward errors with $\|A\| \sim 10^5$. The identity $r_D = r_A$ is valid in finite precision until convergence has been reached $(r_D/\|A\| \sim \Psi)$ at the 25th iteration. If k increases beyond 25, r_D remains constant at its minimum value 10^{-11}, whereas r_A continues to decrease.

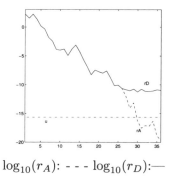

$$\log_{10}(r_A): \text{- - -} \quad \log_{10}(r_D): \text{—}$$

FIG. 6.1. *Computed residuals r_D and r_A versus the iteration number k.*

Therefore, if the convergence is monitored by the Arnoldi residual, one gets the misleading message, based on wrong values for r_A, that convergence can be improved with more iterations beyond $k = 25$.

This phenomenon of possible divergence between r_D and r_A in finite precision was first noticed by Bennani (1991). The mechanism that creates such a difference in behaviour is not yet well understood. The phenomenon always occurs for any Krylov-based method used to solve $Ax = \lambda x$ or $Ax = b$ in the symmetric (Lanczos and conjugate gradient) and the nonsymmetric (iterative Arnoldi) cases.   △

This example shows clearly how the backward error allows us to circumvent the possible difficulty created by the unreliability in finite precision of the identity (6.2). The backward error is also useful to resolve the ambiguity created by a nonmonotonic decrease of the residual or of the backward error.
Example 6.3 Jacobi on $B_\nu = S_\nu^T S_\nu$ (Bennani and Braconnier (1994b)).
We set $n = 150$, $p = 75$, $\nu = 10^4$ and compute all the eigenvalues λ_i of the symmetric matrix $B_\nu = S_\nu^T S_\nu$, $\|B_\nu\| \sim 10^5$. The convergence history is plotted in Figure 6.2: it gives $k \longmapsto \eta_k = \log_{10} \max_i \eta_{ik}$, where η_{ik} is the backward error associated with the ith computed approximate eigenpair at step k of the Jacobi iteration, $i = 1, \ldots, 150$.

The backward error stalls at 10^{-11} between iterations $k = 150$ and $k = 300$. However, it makes sense to continue to iterate since we expect this backward stable method to produce the optimal floor value of machine precision. It is indeed reached in this case after 800 iterations (shown as .-.- in Figure 6.2).   △

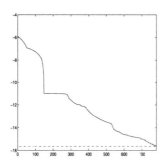

FIG. 6.2. $\log_{10} \max_i \eta_{ik}$ *versus the iteration number k.*

6.4 Robust convergence

In exact arithmetic, the general situation is that numerical stability for an approximation method can be proved under restrictive conditions. Therefore, numerical convergence (in exact arithmetic) is guaranteed to take place if these conditions are fulfilled. How is this theoretical framework modified by finite precision?

Clearly it can be affected in two ways:

i) the sufficient condition for convergence may not hold anymore,

ii) the quality of convergence may not be optimal.

Such phenomena can take place when any of these properties is highly sensitive to perturbations in the data created by the computer arithmetic. It is important to realize that case i) is not restricted to finite precision computation. It may happen in exact arithmetic as well, as will be developed in § 10.3. However, case ii) is specific to finite precision computation in a way that we now describe.

The optimal reliability or backward stability of finite and iterative methods can be analysed by means of the backward error at the converged computed solution $\tilde{x}$. Usually one can prove a bound of the type

$$B(\tilde{x}) \leq C(F,y)\Psi, \tag{6.3}$$

where C is a constant that depends on the details of the arithmetic and the data F, y (see §§ 2.11 and 5.7). If the dependence of C in y and F is highly unstable, then C can vary widely in a neighbourhood of the data y and F. This indicates how the backward stability can be deteriorated.

This twofold phenomenon is illustrated now on the method of successive iterations that converges in exact arithmetic under a condition on the iteration matrix.

Example 6.4 Successive iterations for $x = Ax + b$ (Chatelin (1993b), Chaitin-Chatelin and Gratton (1995)).

Consider the family of linear systems

$$x = A_\nu x + b, \tag{6.4}$$

which depend on the parameter ν. The matrix A_ν is the Schur matrix defined in Example 6.2. It is nonnormal and its nonnormality is controlled by ν: $\|A_\nu A_\nu^T - A_\nu^T A_\nu\|_F > \nu^2\sqrt{n-2}$. We study the solution by successive iterations:

$$x_0, \quad x_{k+1} = A_\nu x_k + b, \quad k \geq 0, \tag{6.5}$$

which is *convergent in exact arithmetic* because the necessary and sufficient condition for convergence is satisfied: $\rho(A_\nu) < 0.41$ for all ν. The right-hand side b is chosen such that the exact solution is $x = (\sqrt{i})$, $i = 1, \ldots, n$. We choose $n = 20$. Let $\tilde{x}_k$ be the kth computed iterate. Convergence histories are plotted in Figure 6.3 for the four values of ν: $\nu = 1, 10, 100,$ and 300, where

$$E(\tilde{x}_k) = \frac{\|x - \tilde{x}_k\|_\infty}{\|x\|_\infty}, \qquad J(\tilde{x}_k) = \frac{1}{\Psi}\frac{\|\tilde{x}_k - A_\nu \tilde{x}_k - b\|_\infty}{\|I - A_\nu\|_\infty\|\tilde{x}\|_\infty + \|b\|_\infty}.$$

The vertical axis shows either $\log_{10}(E(\tilde{x}_k))$ or $\log_{10}(J(\tilde{x}_k))$; the respective captions are E and J. For $\nu = 1$, convergence occurs as predicted: the forward error E and the

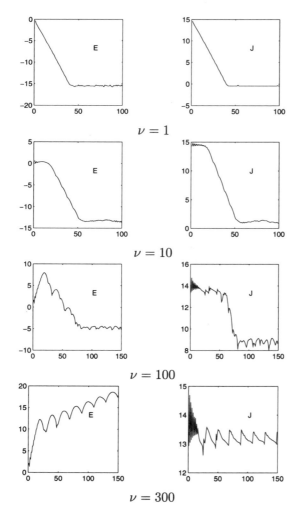

FIG. 6.3. *Successive iterations versus k.*

quality index J decrease monotonically until J almost reaches the optimal value 1. This is not true anymore for $\nu = 10$, where E and J slightly increase and oscillate before convergence is recovered.

Below, E does not behave like J anymore. For $\nu = 100$, the forward error increases drastically and reaches 10^8 at the 20th iteration, whereas the quality index oscillates around 5×10^{13}. However, both quantities resume decrease until J is almost stabilized around $8 \times 10^8 \gg 1$. Finally, for $\nu = 300$, divergence occurs, as shown clearly by the forward error E but not by the quality index, which oscillates around 10^{13}.

The source of the computational difficulty lies, in this example, in the nonnormality of A_ν. We shall study more the resulting spectral instability in Chapter 10. Due to finite precision arithmetic, the iteration matrix becomes $A_\nu + \Delta A_\nu$ with $\rho(A_\nu + \Delta A_\nu) \geq 1$. The mathematical necessary and sufficient condition for convergence $\rho(A_\nu) < 1$ is not robust enough to hold in finite precision (case i)). In addition, the backward stability of successive iterations has significantly deteriorated *much earlier than* the computed spectral radius reaches 1 (case ii)).   △

ν	1	10	100	300
computed spectral radius	0.407947	0.407948	0.634915	1.189894

It is interesting to compare with such a difficult example the results of the backward error applied to two different solvers:

a) a direct method, such as GEPP;

b) an iterative solver, such as successive iterations.

Example 6.5 GE versus successive iterations on (6.5).
Because $I - A_\nu$ is increasingly nonnormal, we expect that it is, in particular, increasingly ill conditioned. This is confirmed by the sequence of values for $K_T(I - A_\nu)$. The results are summarized in Table 6.1, where BE (resp., FE) stands for the backward (resp., forward) error. One remarks that GEPP is not affected by the increasing nonnormality of A_ν.

ν	K_T	BE	FE	BE	FE
1	10	10^{-16}	10^{-15}	10^{-16}	10^{-15}
10	10^3	10^{-14}	10^{-14}	4×10^{-17}	2×10^{-14}
100	10^{11}	10^{-7}	10^{-5}	3×10^{-17}	2×10^{-7}
300	7×10^{15}	$[10^{-2}, 10^{-3}]$	$\nearrow$	5×10^{-17}	2×10^{-1}
Solver		Successive Iterations		GEPP	

TABLE 6.1
Comparative normwise backward error analysis

The values of the actual forward errors should be compared with the predicted values obtained by means of (5.1), that is, $K_T \times BE$.

The difference in prediction accuracy between the direct and iterative solver is striking. For GEPP, the backward error analysis provides an accurate prediction of the actual error. In contradistinction, the backward error analysis is accurate for successive iterations only as long as the method is reasonably backward stable. For

ν	1	10	100	300
GEPP	10^{-15}	4×10^{-14}	3×10^{-6}	3.5×10^{-1}
Succ. Iter.	10^{-15}	10^{-11}	10^4	7×10^{13}

TABLE 6.2
Predicted forward errors

$\nu = 100$, the actual error 10^{-5} is already 10^9 times smaller than the predicted value 10^4.   △

The above example examplifies the fact that the basic bound (5.1) for backward error analysis is based on a *first-order expansion* in the neighbourhood of the exact solution. It may not be valid when the size of the perturbation (measured here by the backward error) is too large with respect to machine precision. This shows again the importance of using, for finite precision computations, methods that are *backward stable*.

However, this is not always possible. Chapter 10 will be devoted to the important aspect of *robustness with respect to nonnormality*, as nonnormality appears to be one of the major sources of deterioration of the backward stability.

6.5   The computed logistic revisited

The computed logistic was presented in § 2.12 as an example of the variation, with the parameter r, of the stability of the successive iterations for solving the fixed-point equation (2.25)

$$x = f_r(x) = rx(1 - x).$$

The computer plots shown in Figures 2.12–2.15 are meaningful if the computational process (2.27) can be shown to be *backward stable* in some sense. Each iteration step is very simple (one subtraction and two multiplications). However, for values of r corresponding to the chaotic regime, a computed iterate $\tilde{x}_k$ may have lost all significant figures before $k = 100$. It is therefore important to show that this inaccuracy is not created by finite precision only but reflects the high sensitivity of the computational scheme (2.27) to arbitrary perturbations, including finite precision as a special case.

This has been done by Hammel, Yorke, and Grebogi (1987) in the language of dynamical systems. First they introduce the ε-pseudotrajectories by inserting a perturbation bounded by ε at each iteration k for N steps at most:

$$|f(z_{k-1}) - z_k| < \varepsilon, \quad 1 \leq k \leq N.$$

Then they show that, given an ε-pseudotrajectory $\{z_k\}$, for a small enough ε, there exist δ and an *exact* trajectory $\{y_k\}_{k=0,...,N}$ that approximates or *shadows* the pseudotrajectory within the precision δ, i.e., with $y_k = f(y_{k-1})$, $|y_k - z_k| < \delta$, $0 \le k \le N$. Finally they show that a computed trajectory $\{\tilde{x}_k\}$ can be considered an ε-pseudotrajectory, with ε of the order of machine precision.

δ can be interpreted as a backward error for the computation process (2.27) in the more general sense of Kahan (1966) and Stewart (1973b): the computed trajectory is *close* (but not equal) to the exact trajectory corresponding to a slightly perturbed initial condition: $|x_0 - y_0| < \delta$.

Example 6.6

It is shown in Hammel, Yorke, and Grebogi (1987) that on a CRAY X-MP with 14 decimal digits, the computed trajectory for $N = 10^7$ is an ε-pseudotrajectory for $\varepsilon < 3 \times 10^{-14}$. Then for $x_0 = 0.4$ and $r = 3.8$, the backward error is $\delta = 10^{-8}$ for the computation of $N = 10^7$ steps. Similar results are given for other values of x_0 and r. They conjecture that for any map producing the same behaviour as f_r, the computed trajectory would correspond to a backward error $\delta \sim \Psi^{1/2}$ for the computation of $N \sim \Psi^{-1/2}$ steps. $\triangle$

6.6 Care of use

The backward error analysis of Wilkinson is essential to scientific computing. It allows the user to choose the algorithms which are guaranteed to make the *best use* of the arithmetic of the computer. However, it should be used with care and common sense.

Suppose that we are required to compute $x = G(y)$, where we are not provided with an equation of the type $F(x) = y$, with $F = G^{-1}$. How can we assess the quality of the computed $\tilde{x}$ without the help of a residual? Let us look at a slowly converging series.

Example 6.7 (Forsythe, Malcom, and Moler (1977)).

$$e^x = \lim_{j \to \infty} s_j, \quad s_j = \sum_{k=0}^{j} \frac{x^k}{k!}, \quad j = 0, 1, 2 \ldots . \tag{6.6}$$

For $x = -20$, the exact value $a = e^{-20}$ is equal to $2.061153622438558 \ldots \times 10^{-9}$. If we attempt to compute e^{-20} by the formula (6.6), we get an apparent convergence at the value $\tilde{a} = \tilde{s}_{94} = 6.138 \ldots \times 10^{-9}$, which remains constant for $j > 94$. However, the exact value (Mathematica) of the 94th iterate is $s_{94} = 2.0611536224385575 \times 10^{-9}$. The computed value $\tilde{a}$ has no correct digit.

Without a residual, it is not possible to realize that the apparent limit $\tilde{a}$ is actually wrong.

One possible way around the difficulty is to find a mathematical identity that should be statisfied by a. For example, $e^{-20} \times e^{20} = 1$. If we compute e^{-20} as $b = (e^{20})^{-1}$, we deal with the same series (6.6) for $x = 20$, which now converges much more rapidly, and we get the satisfactory answer $\tilde{b} = 2.061153622438559 \times 10^{-9}$. $\triangle$

Not all instability phenomena can be captured by perturbations. Example 2.13 provides an illustration of some inherent limitations to perturbation methods. The example shows an instability with respect to initial conditions.

A backward error analysis on $p(x) = 0$ would give a backward error of the order of machine precision. The condition numbers of the three simple roots of $p(x) = x^3 - 111x^2 + 1130x - 3000 = 0$ are moderate. For 5, 6, and 100, respectively, the normwise condition numbers are 8.6×10^2, 1.25×10^3, and 3.59×10^3. Because the three possible limits of $\{x_k\}$ are roots of $p(x) = 0$, the backward error is necessarily small. However, despite the small backward error, the *algorithm* can be unstable: it cannot be proved convergent for *all* initial conditions.

6.7   Bibliographical comments

The possibly bad convergence for successive iterations has been known for a long time. See, for example, Hammarling and Wilkinson (1976), where it is recommended that there should exist a "natural" norm $\| \, . \, \|$ for the iteration matrix such that $\|A\| < 1$, instead of the mere condition $\rho(A) < 1$. The role of nonnormality in the convergence of such iterations is hinted at in Arioli and Romani (1992) and more fully described in Chatelin (1993a, 1993b) and Chaitin-Chatelin and Gratton (1995).

The importance of an optimal stopping criterion for iterative solvers is discussed in Arioli, Duff, and Ruiz (1992). Templates (Barrett, et al. (1994)) recommends stopping iterative linear solvers with the backward error. See also Kasenally (1995). Bennani and Braconnier (1994b) illustrate the importance of choosing the backward error as a stopping criterion for eigensolvers. This is the choice made in the Arnoldi–Tchebycheff codes proposed by Braconnier (1993, 1994a) and Scott (1993).

Chapter 7

Software Tools for Round-off Error Analysis in Algorithms

7.1 A historical perspective

The concern about the overall effect of the addition of a large number of experimental elementary errors goes back at least to the Marquis Pierre-Simon de Laplace (1778). It is to model such a random variable that he introduced the so-called normal law (Laplace (1812)). This law of experimental errors has been the source of very active research in probability and statistics. To mention only a few landmarks along this path we recall the various forms of the law of large numbers and the central limit theorems, which, among other things, aimed at weakening the assumption of independency between the individual errors. Until the second half of the twentieth century, the main focus of this theoretical work has been on consequences of inaccurate data in *experimental sciences*, especially physics, with the only noticeable exception of the works of a few *astronomers*, such as Newcomb (1881), Schlesinger (1917), and Brouwer (1937). Because computation was done by hand, the cumulative behaviour of errors could be controlled at each step. It is no wonder that the concern about the effect of round-off errors in large computations was the strongest in the astronomical community. Astronomy is a science that has always put a great emphasis on the accuracy of predictions, and these predictions often require a huge amount of calculations. Since antiquity, human affairs have been scheduled by astronomical events. Gauss became famous for accurately predicting the return of the asteroid Ceres in 1801, for which he invented the method known today as Gaussian elimination (Stewart (1993a)). The depth and brilliance of his *Disquisitiones Arithmeticae* remained known only to the happy few.

It was only in 1945, with the potential availability of electronic computers, that some scientists began to worry about the cumulative effect in large-scale scientific computing. However, it was soon discovered that this effect was not as negative as had been feared (Hotelling (1943)). The famous papers by von Neumann and Goldstine (1947), Goldstine and von Neumann (1951), and Turing (1948) follow the trend of works on experimental errors. They open an era for scientific computing on computers where the propagation of rounding errors is *simulated by probabilistic models* to analyse either the result of a long sequence of computations (von Neumann and Goldstine (1947), Turing (1948), Henrici (1966), Hull and Swenson (1966)) or the result of one elementary arithmetic operation (Feldstein and Goodman (1976)).

This elegant approach will be presented in § 7.5. Since it does not allow estimation of the resulting error on the solution, it became gradually obsolete in the 1970s among software developers.

Probabilistic models are remembered for their theoretical meaning. In software practice, they were progressively superseded by the equally elegant but deterministic approach known as *backward error analysis*, which now enjoys the widest popularity in the numerical software community. The seminal idea in Givens (1954) came into fruition at Turing's National Physical Laboratory in Teddington, England, under the skillful care of Wilkinson (1961, 1963) over more than three decades.

Although of dominating importance in software practice today, the backward error analysis is not the only approach that is in practical use to control round-off errors. We survey below the uses of sensitivity analysis and automatic differentiation, interval computations as well as computer algebra. They are all very important tools and they have proved efficient in their own rights. They often provide automatic error bounds on the computer itself. It is not generally realized that A. M. Turing himself thought a good deal about these modes of calculations as early as 1946 and considered the possibility of including appropriate hardware in the computer.

7.2   Assessment of the quality of numerical software

Aspects of quality control that are unique to numerical software are well described in the quotation to follow (Ford and Rice (1994)). It is taken from the rationale for the IFIP Working Conference on the same topic, to be held in Oxford, England, July 8–12, 1996 (Chairmen Ford and Rice), and organized by the IFIP Working Group WG2.5 on Numerical Software:

Numerical software is central to our computerized society, it is used to design the airplanes and bridges, to operate manufacturing lines, to control power plants and refineries, to analyse future options for financial markets and the economy. It is essential that it be of high quality; fast, accurate, reliable, easily moved to new machines, and easy to use. Quality control of numerical software faces all the challenges of software in general; it is large and complex, expensive to produce, difficult to maintain and hard to use. Numerical software has two characteristics that distinguish it from general software. First, much of it is built upon a long established and elaborately developed foundation of mathematical and computational knowledge. Second, it routinely solves problems of types where it is known that no algorithm can provide an accurate solution. ...

Five somewhat independent components or criteria for software quality can be listed:

Speed. This component measures the consumption of computer resources: processor time, memory used, network bandwidth utilization, and similar resources. This is traditionally the most heavily weighted criterion of quality (and performance).

Accuracy. This measures the difference between the solution actually provided and the true solution of the problem. The speed criterion is usually used with an implicit assumption that a prescribed accuracy criterion is met. ...However, since achieving a prescribed accuracy is rarely easy—or even assured—in numerical computations, the importance of this component of quality is often underweighted.

Reliability. Since prescribed accuracy are not alway achieved, one measures how "often" the software fails. ... Ideally, software that fails to solve a problem should recognize this fact and return the information (along with control) to the user.

Modifiability. This criterion measures the ease of modifying the software for such purposes as fixing bugs, making enhancement, moving it to new computing environments, and combining it with other software.

Ease of use. In addition to the usual human engineering aspects of software, this criterion measures the number of user inputs required and the difficulty of providing good values. For example, software modules whose inputs require the number of discretization points needed in order to achieve the prescribed accuracy are not easy to use.

There are two other important aspects of software that are closely related to quality:

Cost. The expense of developing, buying, maintaining and using software.

Ratings. It is not easy to objectively measure some of the components of software quality. It is difficult to evaluate the trade-offs between the components. Nevertheless, it is important that meaningful rating information be available which is appropriate for users, for software developers, and for researchers.

7.3   Backward error analysis in libraries

LAPACK (Linear Algebra Package) is a high-quality software for linear algebra that builds upon the expertise developed from extensive use of previous libraries such as LINPACK and EISPACK. It incorporates the most up-to-date developments for backward error analysis for linear systems, eigenvalues, and least squares. LAPACK guarantees achievement of componentwise backward stability almost always for the following problems: linear equations, bidiagonal singular value decompositions, and symmetric tridiagonal eigenproblems. Many routines provide the user with an estimation of the condition number (componentwise for linear systems, normwise for eigenproblems) of the backward and the forward errors.

Templates (Barrett, et al. (1994)) is a recent numerical library that proposes state-of-the-art iterative solvers for linear systems. The recommended stopping criterion is the normwise backward error.

7.4   Sensitivity analysis

The stability analysis of an algorithm $x = G(y)$ with the implementation $G_{alg} = \Pi G^{(i)}$ depends on the partial derivatives $\frac{\partial G^{(i)}}{\partial y_j}$ computed at the various nodes of the computational graph (see § 2.6). The partial derivatives show how inaccuracies in data and rounding errors at each step are propagated through the computation. The analysis can be conducted in a forward (or bottom-up) mode or a backward (or top-down) mode. There have been several efforts to automate this derivation. One can cite the following:

1. Miller and Spooner (1978);
2. the B-analysis: Larson, Pasternak, and Wisniewski (1983), Larson and Sameh (1980);
3. the functional stability analysis: Rowan (1990);
4. the automatic differentiation (AD) techniques: Rall (1981), Griewank (1989), Iri (1991).

The impact of AD tools on industrial problems is such that the first Theory Institute on Combinatorial Challenges in Computational Differentiation was held at Argonne National Laboratory, May 24–26, 1993 (*SIAM News*, March 1994).

7.5   Interval analysis

Interval analysis (Moore (1966), Kulisch and Miranker (1981)) is a very efficient tool for computer-aided proofs in analysis by providing, in some cases, computed solutions that are provably of maximum quality, that is, for real numbers, there is no floating-point number between the computed solution ξ and the exact solution x. This is done by computing, whenever possible, maximum-quality inclusions for the solution (Rall (1991), Moore (1991)) by iterative refinement. This supposes that the problem is amenable in the form of a fixed-point equation with a contraction. The method makes heavy use of the maximum-quality scalar product. It is implemented in the ACRITH software and in the high-level language extension PASCAL-SC (Bleher, et al. (1987), Kulisch (1987)). One can also cite the Novosibirsk school of Godunov and its software PALINA (Godunov, et al. (1993), Kirilyuk and Kostin (1991)).

Another approach to computer-aided proof uses a combination of interval analysis, a safe subset of the IEEE computer arithmetic, and Prolog as a high-level programming language (Meyer and Schmidt (1991)).

7.6   Probabilistic models

7.6.1   Model for the rounding error $x - \text{fl}(x)$

The rounding error $\alpha = x - \text{fl}(x)$ is deterministic. However, it may be useful to model α by a random variable u uniformly distributed around the pth digit in a representation with a mantissa of length p. This is a very old idea used by astronomers that has been theoretically justified in Goodman and Feldstein (1975). It seems very natural, but the same paper proves the much less intuitive property that the distribution of the first digit is not uniform but *logarithmic* (see also Turner (1982)).

This fact was well known to astronomers (Newcomb (1881)) but has been frequently rediscovered by engineers and scientists (Benford (1938), Knuth (1969), Stewart (1993c)). There is a more than 30% chance that the first digit is 1 and a less than 4.5% chance than it is 9, in base 10. From this counterintuitive result follows what we call the *Newcomb–Borel paradox* on randomness in numbers (Chaitin-Chatelin (1994b)).

In 1909, Borel proved that almost all real numbers are normal; i.e., in any base, the first digit is *uniformly* distributed. Consequently, there seems to be an important difference in nature between a number chosen at random from the set $I\!R$ of real numbers in mathematics and one from the set of all results of nonlinear algorithmic calculations.

7.6.2   Model for round-off propagation

From the model u for the elementary rounding error α and from the hypothesis that the errors at each step are independant, one can derive, by means of a *forward error analysis*, a probabilistic model that predicts the random variable U representing the solution x (Brouwer (1937), Rademacher (1948), Henrici (1962b, 1963), Stewart (1990)). Let m be the mean of the law of U. In general, $m \neq x$ for iterative and approximate methods. When $m \neq x$, knowing the law of U is not enough to control the error $U - x$. This puts a limit to the practical use of probabilistic models to perform a forward error analysis (Chatelin (1988b, 1989b)). This difficulty is resolved in Bennani, Brunet, and Chatelin (1988) for matrix computations by means of a backward as well as a forward error analysis. Moreover, that paper shows that the normal law for U obtained by Henrici (1962b) and verified experimentally by Hull and Swenson (1966) is valid only at regular points.

A normal law does not hold any longer for the error in the neighbourhood of singular points.

The case of a multiple defective eigenvalue is treated in Chatelin (1988a, 1989b) and Chatelin and Brunet (1990).

7.6.3   The school of Vignes

The group of Professor Vignes at the University of Paris VI has worked on the quality of numerical software for more than 20 years. The CESTAC method (Vignes (1986)) originates in the permutation-perturbation method (La Porte and Vignes (1974)), which follows the trend of probabilistic models and randomisation of data and arithmetic proposed by Forsythe (1950). CESTAC provides the user with a *forward* error analysis based on a random perturbation of the last bit of the result in each elementary arithmetic operation (Pichat and Vignes (1993)). It is proven valid under the hypothesis of a normal law for the error, plus several technical assumptions (Chatelin (1988b), Chesneaux (1988)) that amount to a guarantee that the problem being solved is far enough from a singularity. The newest software tool is CADNA, for programs written in

Fortran or ADA (Chesneaux (1992a, 1992b)). SCALP is a similar tool (using perturbations of varying size for data and possibly for arithmetic operations) developed at IMAG, Grenoble (Francois (1989)) and INRIA/IRISA, Rennes (Erhel (1991)). Both SCALP and CESTAC will be available in the toolbox for numerical quality called AQUARELS, which is currently under development as a collaborative effort of CNES, INRIA, and SIMULOG (its first release is scheduled for June 1995; Erhel and Philippe (1991a, 1991b)).

7.7 Computer algebra

In its principle, computer algebra uses exact arithmetic and therefore avoids the problems caused by round-off. It is therefore a very powerful tool for computing exactly at singular points of ordinary differential equations, for example (Duval (1992)). There is a growing interest in developing interfaces between numeric and symbolic computations.

7.8 Bibliographical comments

The previous bird's-eye view of software tools for round-off error analysis in numerical software does not do justice to this extremely rich and active domain of software development. The interested reader should definitely consult some of the many books on the topic. As good state-of-the-art presentations, one can cite the three most recent proceedings of the working conferences organized every three years by the IFIP Working Group WG2.5 on Numerical Software, which are Ford and Chatelin (1987), Wright (1989), and Gaffney and Houstis (1992).

Chapter 8

The Toolbox PRECISE for Computer Experimentation

Toutes les sciences sont vaines et pleines d'er-
reurs si elles ne sont pas nées de l'expérience,
mère de toute certitude, et si elles ne sont pas
soumises à l'expérience.

Leonardo da Vinci

We have seen the role of the notions of backward errors and condition numbers in assessment of the reliability of a resolution process and the quality of its computed solution. In linear algebra, the condition numbers and the backward errors are easy to characterize and can be estimated (see LAPACK), but for more complex nonlinear problems, one does not always enjoy such convenient formulations. The following questions are pressing:

1. Is it possible to perform a backward error analysis in a general framework when no formulae for backward errors are known?
2. How can the quality of numerical methods and software be assessed?

In this chapter we describe the toolbox PRECISE (PRecision Estimation and Control In Scientific and Engineering computing), which offers a variety of software tools developed under MATLAB (see Annex) to conduct experiments about stability with a computer.

PRECISE is not intended to be yet another software for automatic control of round-off error propagation. The review conducted in the previous chapter has shown that the user is already facing a large collection of efficient tools to choose from. It is as much a matter of personal taste as of performance that should guide his choice amongst the available methods and software for automatic control of accuracy. We view PRECISE as a help to investigate difficult cases, such as computations in the neighbourhood of a singularity and computations in the presence of high nonnormality, to get better insight on the underlying mathematical instability. The better understanding of the problem provided by PRECISE allows in turn a better use of current software for error control.

8.1   What is PRECISE?

PRECISE is a set of tools provided to help the user set up computer experiments to explore the impact on the quality of convergence of numerical methods of finite precision as well as other types of prescribed perturbations of the data. Because *stability* is at the heart of the phenomena under study—mathematical as well as numerical stabilities—PRECISE allows experimentation about stability by a straightforward *randomisation* of selected data, then lets the computer produce a sample of perturbed solutions and associated residuals or a sample of perturbed spectra.

The idea of using random perturbations on a selection of data or parameters to obtain information on the stability of dynamical processes is natural and old. It has been used extensively in physics and technology, but it has not gained popularity in numerical analysis or numerical software. However, the idea has often been recommended by the best specialists, as illustrated by the following quotation from Dahlquist and Björck (1980):

> In larger calculational problems, the relations between input data and output data are so complicated that it is difficult to directly apply the general formulas for the propagation of error. One should then investigate the sensitivity of the output data for errors in the input data by means of an *experimental perturbational calculation:* one performs the calculations many times with perturbed input data and studies the relation between the changes (perturbations) in the input data and the changes in the output data. . . .
>
> Such a perturbational calculation often gives not only an error estimate, but also a greater insight into the problem. Occasionally, it can be difficult to interpret the perturbational data correctly, since the disturbances in the output data depend not only on the mathematical problem but also on the choice of the numerical method and the details in the design of the algorithm. The round-off errors during the computation are not the same for the perturbed and the unperturbed problem. Thus if the output data reacts more sensitively than one had anticipated, it can be difficult to immediately point out the source of the error. It can be then profitable to plan a series of perturbation experiments with the help of which one can separate the effects of the various sources of error. If the dominant source is the method or the algorithm, then one should try another method or another algorithm.
>
> It is beyond the scope of this book to give further comments on the planning of such experiments; imagination and the general insights regarding error analysis which this chapter is meant to give play a large role. Even in the special literature, the discussion of the planning of such numerical experiments is surprisingly meager.

This long quotation serves as an excellent introduction to PRECISE, which provides an experimental environment for the engineer or the software developer to test the robustness of a numerical method or of an algorithm with respect to finite precision and data uncertainty.

It allows performance of a complete statistical backward error analysis on a numerical method or an algorithm to solve a general nonlinear problem of the form $F(x) = y$ (matrix or polynomial equation) at regular points and in the neighbourhood of algebraic singularities. It provides an estimate of the distance to the nearest singularity viewed by the computer, as well as of the order of this singularity. It can also help to perform a sensitivity analysis by means of graphical displays of samples of perturbed solutions.

PRECISE offers the following facilities:

1. a module for statistical backward error analysis: it provides a statistical estimation for
   - condition numbers at regular and singular points for the algorithm/method and the problem,
   - backward errors,
   - reliability and quality indexes,
   - distances to singularity, or dangerous borders,
   - order of Hölder-singularities.
2. a module for sensitivity analysis: it provides graphical displays of
   - perturbed spectra,
   - spectral portraits and pseudospectra for matrices,
   - sensitivity portraits and sets of pseudozeroes for polynomials,
   - divergence portraits for iterations depending on a parameter.

PRECISE has been used intensively since 1988 in several industrial environments (IBM-France, Thomson-CSF, and CERFACS) to test various *laws of computation* that emerge from invariant patterns of behaviour for computations in finite precision. We present them in these lectures as conjectures (see Conjecture 3.1, for example). It has also been used, more classically, to assess the numerical quality of computations in industrial problems such as

- the flutter phenomenon for Aerospatiale (Braconnier, Chatelin, and Dunyach (1995)),
- an aeroelasticity problem for ONERA (Division Hélicoptères) (Braconnier (1994c)),
- electromagnetic guided waves for Thomson-CSF (Braconnier (1994c)),
- the reliability of an orbitography software for CNES (Gratton (1994)).

8.2 Module for backward error analysis

8.2.1 A framework for parametric study

The main difficulty in analysing computer results is that the finite precision of the computer introduces itself as a parameter ε in a very complicated way. We have seen that even for an algorithm that seems as "simple" as GE the detailed analysis is a formidable task that has not been fully completed. However complex, the dependence on ε of the computation plays a crucial role in the behaviour of numerical methods on a computer and therefore needs to be understood as thoroughly as possible. A way to gain insight on this dependence is to simulate the unknown dependence on ε by a model giving the influence of perturbations of variable size δ chosen at random in a given class (τ) of admissible perturbations on data. The unknown dependence on ε is modelled by the dependence on δ, which can be either statistically analysed from samples produced by the computer or theoretically investigated.

The construction of the model relies on the class (τ) of perturbations. One has to specify which data to perturb and how they are perturbed. The central question is then: when does the dependence on δ give information about the dependence on ε? Wilkinson's principle of backward error analysis shows that the modelling is meaningful under the following hypothesis on (τ):

Hypothesis (H_ε): *Computation with variable precision ε, $\varepsilon \to 0$, produces solutions x_ε that are equivalent to data perturbations in the class (τ) on the exact problem $(\varepsilon = 0)$.*

Of course, such an approach is valid for any type of parameter dependence. It is not bound to the interpretation of ε as machine precision, so it can serve the purpose of a general sensitivity analysis with respect to an arbitrary parameter θ. In this case, (H_ε) is modified into the following hypothesis.

Hypothesis (H_θ): *Varying θ produces solutions x_θ that are equivalent to data perturbations in the class (τ) on the exact problem $(\theta = 0)$.*

To answer the central question asked above, one has to judge whether the hypothesis (H_θ) is appropriately fulfilled by the chosen model (τ) of perturbations. This step is delicate and cannot always receive a clear yes or no answer.

8.2.2   The indicators of stability and reliability

Let the class (τ) be given as our model for perturbations. We consider the problem (P) : $F(x) = y$, which is solved by means of an algorithm/method G_θ. For a fixed θ, let x_θ be the solution computed by G_θ, that is, $x_\theta = G_\theta(y) = g_\theta(z)$, where we have specified the data z chosen to be perturbed among all the data that define the equation $F(x) = y$. Let $\| \cdot \|$ be the chosen norm on the perturbation specified by (τ) in the parameter space Z. The computational scheme that is performed is

$$z \;\overset{g_\theta}{\longmapsto}\; x_\theta \;\overset{F}{\longmapsto}\; \zeta_\theta = F(x_\theta).$$

To quantify the sensitivity to perturbations of the various components of this scheme $(F^{-1}, g_\theta, F \circ g_\theta)$, we introduce random perturbations on the data z, which belong to (τ). For a given perturbation Δz of the data z, we define

$$z + \Delta z \;\overset{g_\theta}{\longmapsto}\; x_\theta + \Delta x_\theta \;\overset{F}{\longmapsto}\; \zeta_\theta + \Delta\zeta_\theta = y + \Delta w_\theta. \tag{8.1}$$

Note that $\Delta\zeta_\theta$ (resp., Δw_θ) measures the variation with respect to ζ_θ (resp., y). Let δ be a positive parameter that measures the variable size of the data perturbations: $\|\Delta z\| = \delta$. For brevity we call the sensitivity of a map to perturbations of size δ on the data δ-*sensitivity*.

- The δ-sensitivity of g_θ at z is measured by

$$\mathcal{L}_{\theta\delta} = \sup_{\|\Delta z\|=\delta} \frac{1}{\delta}\|\Delta x_\theta\|. \tag{8.2}$$

- The δ-sensitivity of F^{-1} at ζ_θ, with $x_\theta = F^{-1}(\zeta_\theta)$, is measured by

$$\mathcal{K}_\delta = \sup_{\|\Delta z\|=\delta} \frac{\|\Delta x_\theta\|}{\|\Delta\zeta_\theta\|}. \tag{8.3}$$

The δ-sensitivity of F^{-1} is estimated at ζ_θ and not at y because $x = F^{-1}(y)$ is unknown. This is meaningful only if F has a similar behaviour around x_θ and x. This is related to the possibility of considering g_θ as an approximate inverse for F.

- The reliability of considering g_θ as an approximation to F^{-1} is measured by

$$\mathcal{I}_{\theta\delta} = \sup_{\|\Delta z\|=\delta} \frac{1}{\delta}\|\Delta w_\theta\|. \tag{8.4}$$

Several remarks are in order:

1. If the maps $\delta \longmapsto \mathcal{I}_{\theta\delta}$, $\mathcal{L}_{\theta\delta}$, $\mathcal{K}_\delta$ are continuous and not decreasing, then $\sup_{\|\Delta z\|=\delta}$ also represents $\sup_{\|\Delta z\|\leq\varepsilon}$.

2. In (8.3), the perturbation $\Delta\zeta_\theta$ on ζ_θ is deduced from the perturbation Δx_θ on x_θ, which itself results from Δz on z, whereas according to Definition 3.2, the perturbation on ζ_θ should be arbitrary. We shall see later when such an estimation is allowed.

3. The asymptotic indicators $\mathcal{I}_\theta$, $\mathcal{L}_\theta$, and $\mathcal{K}$ are defined in the limit $\delta \to 0$.

4. The Hölder sensitivities $\mathcal{L}_{\theta\delta(h)}$ and $\mathcal{K}_{\delta(h)}$, for $h < 1$, are measured by similar formulae. We use the notation $\mathcal{K}_\delta^h = \mathcal{K}_{\delta(1/l)}$ for $h = 1/l$, $l > 1$ (see Chapter 4).

5. In (8.4), Δw_θ represents the residual $F(x_\theta + \Delta x_\theta) - y$ for the exact equation $F(x) - y = 0$ at the solution $x_\theta + \Delta x_\theta$ computed by g_θ from $z + \Delta z$. It will be related later to the quality/convergence index $J(\tilde{x}_\theta)$ defined in Chapters 5 and 6 in relation to backward stability.

In Table 8.1 we sum up the definitions of the indicators of stability and reliability (θ is fixed and δ varies).

8.2.3   Simulation by randomisation of the data

The indicators $\mathcal{I}$, $\mathcal{L}$, and $\mathcal{K}$ defined previously are mathematical quantities that cannot be computed directly. In order to perform a *statistical estimation* of these quantities later, we *randomise* the data z by choosing Δz at random in $(\tau)_\delta = \{\Delta z; \|\Delta z\| = \delta\}$ in the following way. Let u be chosen at random in a finite set representing some (often crude) approximation of $(\tau)_1$. The set $(\tau)_\delta$ is approximated by a sample $(\check{\tau})_t$ of N elements of the form tu, where t is the parameter (analogous to δ) specifying the size of the perturbation. To be

Backward stability or reliability	$\mathcal{I}_{\theta\delta} = \max\limits_{\|\Delta z\|=\delta} \dfrac{\|\Delta w_\theta\|}{\delta}$	$\mathcal{I}_\theta = \lim\limits_{\delta\to 0}\mathcal{I}_{\theta\delta}$
Sensitivity of the method/algorithm	$\mathcal{L}_{\theta\delta} = \max\limits_{\|\Delta z\|=\delta} \dfrac{\|\Delta x_\theta\|}{\delta}$	$\mathcal{L}_\theta = \lim\limits_{\delta\to 0}\mathcal{L}_{\theta\delta}$
Sensitivity of the problem	$\mathcal{K}_\delta = \max\limits_{\|\Delta z\|=\delta} \dfrac{\|\Delta x_\theta\|}{\|\Delta\zeta_\theta\|}$	$\mathcal{K} = \lim\limits_{\delta\to 0}\mathcal{K}_\delta$
Hölder sensitivity of the problem	$\mathcal{K}_{\delta(1/l)} = \max\limits_{\|\Delta z\|=\delta} \dfrac{\|\Delta x_\theta\|}{\|\Delta\zeta_\theta\|^{1/l}}$	$\mathcal{K}_{1/l} = \lim\limits_{\delta\to 0}\mathcal{K}_{\delta(1/l)}$

TABLE 8.1

Indicators of sensitivity and reliability for variable δ

more specific, we describe the model of random perturbations for matrices A and vectors b that we adopted in the experiments reported in these lectures. We introduce

- a random variable μ taking the values ± 1 with equal probability,[1]
- a parameter t, which controls the size of the perturbation. In double precision (with a mantissa of 53 bits), t is chosen as 2^{-p}, where p is an integer ranging from 52 to 0, which makes t vary from Ψ to 1. This amount roughly to a perturbation of the pth bit.

The randomisation of A and b is defined by adding to A and b a family of perturbations ΔA and Δb such that

i) for a normwise analysis, $\Delta A = \alpha t F$, $\Delta b = \beta t g$, where F and g are random matrix and vector respectively, with entries equal to μ. By default, $\alpha = \|A\|$, $\beta = \|b\|$;

ii) for a componentwise analysis, $\delta a_{ij} = \mu t e_{ij}$, $\Delta b_i = \mu t f_i$, where $E = (e_{ij})$ and $f = (f_i)$ are a given matrix and vector with nonnegative entries. By default, $E = |A|$ and $f = |b|$.

8.2.4 Statistical estimation

For a given value of t, we create a sample of perturbed data denoted Z_t. To each element in Z_t, we apply the algorithm g_θ. This creates the sample of computed solutions X_t. Then we compute the image sample $Y_t = F(X_t)$. The operation is repeated for each value of t taken in the interval $[\Psi, 1]$. From

---

[1] In practice, μ is computed by a linear congruence and is pseudorandom.

these samples we derive a *statistical estimation* of the indicators of stability and reliability $\mathcal{I}_{\theta\delta}$, $\mathcal{L}_{\theta\delta}$, and $\mathcal{K}_\theta$ as explained now.

We denote by m_t (resp., ρ_t) and by σ_t (resp., v_t) the mean and the standard deviation of the sample X_t (resp., $Y_t = F(X_t)$). The size of the perturbations on the initial data is controlled by the parameter t and $\| \, . \, \|$ denotes any subordinate norm.

i) Solving a linear system $Ax = b$

The data to be perturbed can be A or b or both. We keep the notations used in §2.6 for condition numbers and in §4.4 for backward errors. The scheme (8.1) (with $\zeta_\theta = Ax_\theta$) takes the form

$$
\left. \begin{array}{c} A + \Delta A \\ b + \Delta b \end{array} \right\} \quad \overset{g_\theta}{\longmapsto} \quad x_\theta + \Delta x_\theta \quad \overset{A}{\longmapsto} \quad \zeta_\theta + \Delta\zeta_\theta = b + \Delta w_\theta.
$$

$$
\quad\;\; \downarrow \qquad\qquad\qquad \downarrow \qquad\qquad\qquad \downarrow
$$

$$
\quad\;\; Z_t \qquad\qquad\qquad X_t \qquad\qquad\qquad Y_t
$$

$$(8.5)$$

The principles of the statistical estimation are the following:

a) The perturbations Δx_θ and $\Delta\zeta_\theta$ are estimated by the standard deviations σ_t and v_t, respectively. The perturbation Δw_θ is estimated by $\hat{v}_t$ defined by $(\hat{v}_t)_i = \left(v_{ti}^2 + |(\rho_t - b)_i|^2\right)^{1/2}$, $i = 1, \ldots, n$, to take into account the bias $\rho_t - b = \nu_t$.

b) Scaled norms are used. For Δx_θ, the choice is easy: Δx_θ is measured by an *average distance* of the sample X_t to the computed solution x_θ defined by

$$
\|X_t - x_\theta\|_{\mathrm{av}} = \frac{\|\sigma_t\|}{\|x_\theta\|}.
$$

For $\Delta\zeta_\theta$ and Δw_θ, the choice of the normalization is less obvious. For $\Delta\zeta_\theta$, one could consider the choice $\|Y_t - \zeta_\theta\|_{\mathrm{av}} = \|v_t\|/\|\zeta_\theta\|$, which is similar to the choice made for $X_t - x_\theta$.

However, another choice seems more appropriate to take better advantage here of the context of backward error analysis. Indeed the backward error at x_θ is

$$
B(x_\theta) = \frac{\|Ax_\theta - b\|}{\alpha\|x_\theta\| + \beta} = \frac{\|\Delta w_\theta\|}{\alpha\|x_\theta\| + \beta}.
$$

It represents the perturbation Δw_θ scaled by taking into account the weight $\alpha\|x_\theta\| + \beta$ on the data A and b. This is the properly scaled perturbation on A and b equivalent to the computation of x_θ. The dispersion of the image sample $Y_t = AX_t$ around ζ_θ or b can be normalised by means of $\alpha\|x_\theta\| + \beta$.

$\Delta\zeta_\theta$ and Δw_θ are therefore measured by the *average distance* of the sample Y_t to ζ_θ and b, respectively, defined by

$$\|Y_t - \zeta_\theta\|_{\text{av}} = \frac{\|v_t\|}{\alpha\|x_\theta\| + \beta},$$

$$\|Y_t - y\|_{\text{av}} = \frac{\|\hat{v}_t\|}{\alpha\|x_\theta\| + \beta}.$$

The normwise statistical estimators of $\mathcal{I}_{\theta\delta}$, $\mathcal{L}_{\theta\delta}$, and $\mathcal{K}_{\theta\delta}$ are taken as

$$\begin{cases} \mathrm{I}_{\theta t}^{\mathcal{N}} = \dfrac{\|Y_t - y\|_{\text{av}}}{t} = \dfrac{\|\hat{v}_t\|}{t(\alpha\|x_\theta\| + \beta)}, \\[2ex] \mathrm{L}_{\theta t}^{\mathcal{N}} = \dfrac{\|X_t - x_\theta\|_{\text{av}}}{t} = \dfrac{\|\sigma_t\|}{t\|x_\theta\|}, \\[2ex] \mathrm{K}_t^{\mathcal{N}} = \dfrac{\|X_t - x_\theta\|_{\text{av}}}{\|Y_t - y_\theta\|_{\text{av}}} = \dfrac{\|\sigma_t\|(\alpha\|x_\theta\| + \beta)}{\|v_t\|\|x_\theta\|}, \end{cases}$$

where the upper $\mathcal{N}$ refers to the *normwise* analysis. Note that the maximal values of the ratios have been replaced by ratios of "average" values in the above given meaning.

The indicator $\mathrm{I}_{\theta t}^{\mathcal{N}}$ is a statistical estimation of the quality index $J(X_t)$ of the sample X_t: $J(X_t) = \frac{1}{t}B(X_t)$ is estimated by $\mathrm{I}_{\theta t}^{\mathcal{N}} = \frac{1}{t}\|Y_t - y\|_{\text{av}}$. The indicator $\mathrm{I}_{\theta t}^{\mathcal{N}}$ will play an essential role to assess the internal coherence of considering g_θ as an approximation of F^{-1}.

Table 8.2 gives the formulations for $Ax = b$, for normwise and componentwise analyses. Table 8.3 does the same for matrix inversion (where X_θ is the computed inverse). The error estimation is given by $\mathrm{E}_{\theta t} = \mathrm{K}_t \times B(x_\theta)$.

ii) Eigencomputations $Ax = \lambda x$

We have seen in Chapter 5 that a backward error analysis of $Ax = \lambda x$ is similar to that of $Ax = b$, where only A is perturbed.

If $(\lambda_\theta, x_\theta)$ is a computed eigenpair, then the associated residual is $Ax_\theta - \lambda_\theta x_\theta$. The normwise backward error is $B(x_\theta) = \|Ax_\theta - \lambda_\theta x_\theta\|/(\alpha\|x_\theta\|)$. For each size t of perturbations, we compute a sample of eigenvalues Λ_t (mean m_t, standard deviation σ_t), eigenvectors X_t, and a sample of residuals $R_t = AX_t - \Lambda_t X_t$ (mean ρ_t, standard derivation v_t). The means m_t and ρ_t can be real or complex.

If λ is a defective eigenvalue of ascent l, K_t is not the appropriate indicator. It should be replaced with

$$\mathrm{K}_{t(1/l)} = \frac{\sigma_t}{|\lambda_\theta|}\left(\frac{\|A\|\|x_\theta\|}{\|v_t\|}\right)^{1/l}.$$

	Normwise	Componentwise
$\mathbf{I}_{\theta t}$	$\dfrac{\left\|\left(\sqrt{v_{ti}^2 + \lvert \rho_t - b\rvert_i^2}\right)_i\right\|}{t(\alpha\|x_\theta\| + \beta)}$	$\dfrac{1}{t}\max_{1\le i\le n}\dfrac{\sqrt{v_{ti}^2 + \lvert \rho_t - b\rvert_i^2}}{(E\lvert x_\theta\rvert + f)_i}$
$\mathbf{L}_{\theta t}$	$\dfrac{\|\sigma_t\|}{t\,\lvert x_\theta\rvert}$	$\dfrac{\|\sigma_t\|_\infty}{t\|x_\theta\|_\infty}$
$\mathbf{K}_t$	$\dfrac{\|\sigma_t\|(\alpha\|x_\theta\| + \beta)}{\|x_\theta\|\|v_t\|}$	$\dfrac{\|\sigma_t\|_\infty}{\|x_\theta\|_\infty}\dfrac{1}{\max_{1\le i\le n}\dfrac{v_{ti}}{(E\lvert x_\theta\rvert + f)_i}}$
$\mathbf{E}_{\theta t}$	$\dfrac{\|\sigma_t\|}{\|x_\theta\|}\dfrac{\|Ax_\theta - b\|}{\|v_t\|}$	$\dfrac{\|\sigma_t\|_\infty}{\|x_\theta\|_\infty}\dfrac{\max_{1\le i\le n}\dfrac{\lvert Ax_\theta - b\rvert_i}{(E\lvert x_\theta\rvert + f)_i}}{\max_{1\le i\le n}\dfrac{v_{ti}}{(E\lvert x_\theta\rvert + f)_i}}$

TABLE 8.2
Statistical estimates for $Ax = b$. Default: $\alpha = \|A\|$, $\beta = \|b\|$, $E = \lvert A\rvert$, and $f = \lvert b\rvert$

The corresponding error estimation is given by $\mathbf{E}_{\theta t(1/l)} = \mathbf{K}_{t(1/l)}(B(x_\theta))^{1/l}$. All the corresponding formulae are gathered in Table 8.4.

iii) Roots of a polynomial $p(x) = 0$

Let $p(x) = \sum_{i=0}^n a_i x^i$ be a polynomial. The componentwise backward error for the root x_θ has been given in Chapter 5 as

$$B(x_\theta) = \frac{\lvert p(x_\theta)\rvert}{\sum_{i=0}^n f_i \lvert x_\theta\rvert^i}.$$

We set $\zeta_\theta = p(x_\theta)$. For each t, we compute a sample of roots X_t (mean m_t, standard deviation σ_t) and a sample of residuals $Y_t = p(X_t)$ (mean ρ_t, standard deviation v_t). We measure Δx_θ by

$$\lvert X_t - x_\theta\rvert_{\mathrm{av}} = \frac{\sigma_t}{\lvert x_\theta\rvert},$$

	Normwise	Componentwise
$\mathbf{I}_{\theta t}$	$\dfrac{\left\\|\left(\sqrt{v_{tij}^2 + \|\rho_{tij} - \delta_{ij}\|^2}\right)_{ij}\right\\|}{t\alpha\\|X_\theta\\|}$	$\dfrac{1}{t}\max_{1\le i\le n}\dfrac{\sqrt{v_{tij}^2 + \|\rho_{tij} - \delta_{ij}\|^2}}{(E\|X_\theta\|)_{ij}}$
$\mathbf{L}_{\theta t}$	$\dfrac{\\|\sigma_t\\|}{t\\|X_\theta\\|}$	$\dfrac{\\|\sigma_t\\|_\infty}{t\\|X_\theta\\|_\infty}$
$\mathbf{K}_t$	$\dfrac{\\|\sigma_t\\|\alpha}{\\|v_t\\|}$	$\dfrac{\\|\sigma_t\\|_\infty}{\\|X_\theta\\|_\infty}\dfrac{1}{\max_{1\le i,j\le n}\dfrac{v_{tij}}{(E\|X_\theta\|)_{ij}}}$
$\mathbf{E}_{\theta t}$	$\dfrac{\\|\sigma_t\\|}{\\|X_\theta\\|}\dfrac{\\|AX_\theta - I\\|}{\\|v_t\\|}$	$\dfrac{\\|\sigma_t\\|_\infty}{\\|X_\theta\\|_\infty}\dfrac{\max_{1\le i,j\le n}\dfrac{\|AX_\theta - I\|_{ij}}{(E\|X_\theta\|_{ij}}}{\max_{1\le i,j\le n}\dfrac{v_{tij}}{(E\|X_\theta\|_{ij}}}$

TABLE 8.3

Statistical estimates for $A \longmapsto A^{-1}$. Default: $\alpha = \\|A\\|$, $E = \|A\|$

$\Delta\zeta_\theta$ by

$$|Y_t - \zeta_\theta|_{\mathrm{av}} = \frac{v_t}{\sum_{i=0}^n f_i|x_\theta|^i},$$

and Δw_θ by

$$|Y_t - 0|_{\mathrm{av}} = |Y_t|_{\mathrm{av}} = \frac{\sqrt{v_t^2 + |\rho_t^2|}}{\sum_{i=0}^n f_i|x_\theta|^i} = \frac{\hat{v}_t}{\sum_{i=0}^n f_i|x_\theta|^i}.$$

The resulting formulae for the indicators are given in Table 8.5. m represents the multiplicity of the root.

iv) Solving $F(x) = y$

The three situations that we have treated so far correspond to the existence of a well-established theory for backward error analysis. This has been an essential ingredient to choose the normalisations of the image sample $Y_t = F(X_t)$. What can be done when such a theory is lacking? The difficulty lies in finding an appropriate scaling for the standard deviations v_t and $\hat{v}_t$.

	Normwise	Componentwise
$\mathrm{I}_{\theta t}$	$\dfrac{1}{t}\dfrac{\left\|\left(\sqrt{v_{ti}^2+|\rho_{ti}|^2}\right)_i\right\|}{\alpha\|x_\theta\|}$	$\dfrac{1}{t}\max_i \dfrac{\sqrt{v_{ti}^2+|\rho_{ti}|^2}}{(E|x_\theta|)_i}$
$\mathrm{L}_{\theta t}$	$\dfrac{\sigma_t}{t|\lambda_\theta|}$	$\dfrac{\sigma_t}{t|\lambda_\theta|}$
K_t	$\dfrac{\sigma_t}{|\lambda_\theta|}\dfrac{\alpha\|x_\theta\|}{\|v_t\|}$	$\dfrac{\sigma_t}{|\lambda_\theta|}\dfrac{1}{\max_i \dfrac{v_{ti}}{(E|x_\theta|)_i}}$
$\mathrm{E}_{\theta t}$	$\dfrac{\sigma_t}{|\lambda_\theta|}\dfrac{\|Ax_\theta-\lambda_\theta x_\theta\|}{\|v_t\|}$	$\dfrac{\sigma_t}{|\lambda_\theta|}\dfrac{\max_i \dfrac{|Ax_\theta-\lambda_\theta x_\theta|_i}{(E|x_\theta|)_i}}{\max_i \dfrac{v_{ti}}{(E|x_\theta|)_i}}$
$\mathrm{K}_{t(1/l)}$	$\dfrac{\sigma_t}{|\lambda_\theta|}\left(\dfrac{\alpha\|x_\theta\|}{\|v_t\|}\right)^{1/l}$	$\dfrac{\sigma_t}{|\lambda_\theta|}\dfrac{1}{\max_i\left(\dfrac{v_{ti}}{(E|x_\theta|)_i}\right)^{1/l}}$
$\mathrm{E}_{\theta t(1/l)}$	$\dfrac{\sigma_t}{|\lambda_\theta|}\left(\dfrac{\|Ax_\theta-\lambda_\theta x_\theta\|}{\|v_t\|}\right)^{1/l}$	$\dfrac{\sigma_t}{|\lambda_\theta|}\left(\dfrac{\max_i \dfrac{|Ax_\theta-\lambda_\theta x_\theta|_i}{(E|x_\theta|)_i}}{\max_i \dfrac{v_{ti}}{(E|x_\theta|)_i}}\right)^{1/l}$

TABLE 8.4
Statistical estimates for $Ax=\lambda x$. Default: $\alpha=\|A\|$, $E=|A|$

A simple approach, which is often taken when $y\neq 0$, consists of choosing $\beta=\|y\|$ and $f=|y|$ for the scalings. This leads, for a normwise analysis, to the formulae given in Table 8.6.

Such a scaling is based only on the right-hand side y and does not take into account the weight of the data in F. In the particular case $Ax=b$, this would amount to replacing $\mathrm{I}_{\theta t}=\frac{\|\hat{v}_t\|}{t(\alpha\|x_\theta\|+\beta)}$ with $\mathrm{I}'_{\theta t}=\frac{\|\hat{v}_t\|}{t\beta}$, which corresponds

Componentwise	
$\mathrm{I}_{\theta t} = \dfrac{\sqrt{v_t^2 + \|\rho_t\|^2}}{t \sum_{i=0}^{n} f_i \|x_\theta\|^i}$	$\mathrm{L}_{\theta t} = \dfrac{\sigma_t}{t \|x_\theta\|}$
$\mathrm{K}_t = \dfrac{\sigma_t \sum_{i=0}^{n} f_i \|x_\theta\|^i}{v_t \|x_\theta\|}$ $\mathrm{K}_{t(1/m)} = \dfrac{\sigma_t}{\|x_\theta\|} \left(\dfrac{\sum_{i=0}^{n} f_i \|x_\theta\|^i}{v_t} \right)^{1/m}$	
$\mathrm{E}_{\theta t} = \dfrac{\sigma_t \|\zeta_\theta\|}{v_t \|x_\theta\|}$ $+\mathrm{E}_{\theta t(1/m)} = \dfrac{\sigma_t}{\|x_\theta\|} \left(\dfrac{\|\zeta_\theta\|}{v_t} \right)^{1/m}$	

TABLE 8.5
Statistical estimates for $p(x) = 0$. Default: $f = |a|$

$\mathrm{I}_{\theta t}$	$\mathrm{L}_{\theta t}$	K_t	$\mathrm{E}_{\theta t}$
$\dfrac{\|\hat{v}_t\|}{t\beta}$	$\dfrac{\|\sigma_t\|}{t\|x_\theta\|}$	$\dfrac{\|\sigma_t\|}{\|v_t\|} \dfrac{\beta}{\|x_\theta\|}$	$\dfrac{\|\sigma_t\|}{\|x_\theta\|} \dfrac{\|F(x_\theta) - y\|}{\|v_t\|}$

TABLE 8.6
Normwise statistical estimates for $F(x) = y$. Default: $\beta = \|y\|$

to the backward error formula for a perturbation of y only, and one has the inequality $\mathrm{I}_{\theta t} \leq \mathrm{I}'_{\theta t}$.

8.3   Sample size

As a rule, the size of the samples can be kept *very small*. In practice, samples of size between 5 to 20 give very satisfactory results. The indicators $\mathrm{I}_{\theta t}$, $\mathrm{L}_{\theta t}$, and K_t correspond, at least for t small enough, to estimations of the sensitivity of the maps $F \circ g_\theta$, g_θ, and F^{-1}. Thus, the definition of the size of the samples to compute the three indicators amounts to the definition of the size of the sample required for statistical condition estimate.

This question has been addressed by Kenney and Laub (1994), who show by rigorous probability arguments that for a real-valued map $f : \mathbb{R}^n \longmapsto \mathbb{R}$, the evaluation of $\|f'(x)\|$ requires only a few function evaluations. For example, they show that with *two* function evaluations, the chance of being off by more than a factor of 100 is less than 1 in 100. These results can be readily extended to vector-valued functions, which can be considered as functions which map matrices into matrices, by means of the vec transform.

8.4   Backward analysis with PRECISE

In §8.2 we proposed the statistical estimates $\mathsf{L}_{\theta t}$, K_t, and $\mathsf{I}_{\theta t}$ for the mathematical quantities $\mathcal{L}_{\theta \delta}$, $\mathcal{K}_{\delta}$, and $\mathcal{I}_{\theta \delta}$. When are these estimates *reliable*? Not surprisingly, when g_θ is itself reliable to solve $F(x) = y$. Of the three indicators $\mathsf{L}_{\theta t}$, K_t, and $\mathsf{I}_{\theta t}$, the two most important are K_t and $\mathsf{I}_{\theta t}$: K_t will give information on the problem once the reliability has been assessed by $\mathsf{I}_{\theta t}$.

By giving access to the behaviour of these indicators as functions of the perturbation size t, PRECISE is able to assess the orders of convergence achieved in effect by the finite precision computation, provided that the chosen model of perturbations is realistic, that is, provided that (H_ε) is satisfied.

8.4.1   Reliability interval and backward error

The generic behaviour of $t \longmapsto \mathsf{I}_{\theta t}$ and $t \longmapsto \mathsf{L}_{\theta t}$ is given in Figure 8.1.
Definition 8.1 *The interval* $\mathbf{R} = [s, r]$ *of* $[\Psi, 1]$ *on which the map* $\mathsf{I}_{\theta t}$ *is constant and such that* $\mathsf{I}_{\theta \sharp} \sim 1$ *is called the* reliability interval *for* g_θ *to solve* $F(x) = y$.

The map $t \longmapsto \mathsf{I}_{\theta t} \sim J(X_t) = B(X_t)/t$ is constant whenever the backward error at X_t is of order of 1 in t, which is the definition of reliability for G_θ given in Chapter 2 (modulo the obvious change of ε into t).

> The condition $\mathsf{I}_{\theta t}$ constant in t is *essential*: it guarantees the internal coherence of the model and, in particular, of the statistical estimation.

To be satisfied, it requires that g_θ can be considered as an approximate inverse for F with respect to perturbations in $(\check{r})$. It should be clear that what

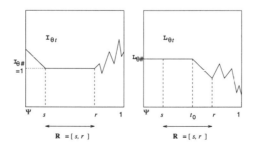

FIG. 8.1. *General behaviour of the statistical estimates* $\mathsf{I}_{\theta t}$ *and* $\mathsf{L}_{\theta t}$.

is really important for the reliability assessment of g_θ is the fact that there exists a nonempty interval where $\mathcal{I}_{\theta t}$ is *constant* in t. The value $\mathcal{I}_{\theta\sharp}$ of the constant value is secondary, since it is a consequence of the scaling chosen for $\|\hat{v}_t\|$.

The value s is the lower threshold of reliability for the estimations given by PRECISE for the three indicators $\mathcal{L}_{\theta\delta}$, $\mathcal{K}_\delta$, and $\mathcal{I}_{\theta\delta}$. It also measures the backward error associated with the computer solution x_θ, according to the following fact.

Fact 8.1 *Let x_θ be the solution to $F(x) = y$ computed by g_θ. The value s is of the order of the backward error at x_θ, associated with the model $(\breve{\tau})$ of perturbations.*

Proof: The value s is the lowest value of the size t of perturbations such that the approximate method g_θ, considered as a perturbation of F^{-1}, behaves in a way which is indistinguishable from that of F^{-1} at the level of uncertainty on the data defined by t. □

The upper threshold r will be discussed later in relation with $\mathcal{K}_t$.

In practice **R** may be empty if $r \le \Psi$ or $s \ge 1$. In this case, PRECISE provides no statistical estimation, either because the problem is too unstable ($r \le \Psi$) or because g_θ is backward unstable for all t ($s \ge 1$).

The condition for backward stability within machine precision is of course $s \le \Psi$. However, one can work with *mildly* backward unstable algorithms: many numerical methods (in particular, iterative methods that are forced to stop) have in general a threshold of reliability larger than Ψ.

8.4.2   Dangerous border

The generic behaviour of $t \longmapsto \mathcal{K}_t$ is shown in Figure 8.2. In general the indicators $\mathcal{K}_t$ and $\mathcal{L}_{\theta t}$ are constant on an interval $\mathbf{S} = [s, t_0[$, with $t_0 \le r$, included in the reliability interval **R**.

Definition 8.2 *The value t_0 for which $\mathcal{K}_t$ ceases to be constant is called the* dangerous border.

It is possible that $t_0 < \Psi$ so that **S** is empty (see Figure 8.2, at right).

Fact 8.2 *The dangerous border t_0 is of order of the distance to singularity relative to the model $(\breve{\tau})$ of perturbations.*

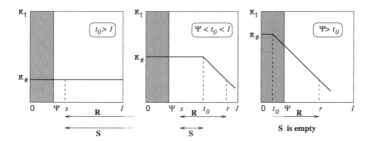

FIG. 8.2.   *Machine precision Ψ and dangerous border t_0.*

THE TOOLBOX PRECISE 117

Computational evidence will be given in Chapter 9.

8.4.3 Error estimation

Fact 8.3 *If the interval* **S** *is not empty, the constant values* $K_\sharp$ *and* $L_{\theta\sharp}$ *for* K_t *and* $L_{\theta t}$, *respectively, are of the order of the condition numbers for* F^{-1} *and* g_θ *associated with the model* $(\tilde{r})$ *of perturbations.*

Sketch of a proof: From Fact 8.2, we see that t_0 is of the order of the distance to the nearest singularity. Thus, for small perturbations such that $t \leq t_0$, K_t and $L_{\theta t}$ estimate, respectively, $\mathcal{K}_\delta$ and $\mathcal{L}_{\theta\delta}$, which are continuous and nondecreasing functions of $\delta < \delta_s$ so that the condition numbers are obtained in the limit $\delta \to 0$. $\quad\square$

Using Facts 8.1 and 8.2, we can estimate the computing error $x - x_\theta$ by

$$\frac{\|x - x_\theta\|}{\|x\|} \sim K_\sharp \times s. \tag{8.6}$$

Such a *linear law of errors* is valid for perturbations t in $\mathbf{S} = [s, t_0[$. It expresses the fact that the computation is done at a regular point.

Definition 8.3 *The interval* $\mathbf{S} = [s, t_0[$ *is the* regularity interval *for the problem.*

8.4.4 Global versus arithmetic reliability

For a direct algorithm that involves only one level of approximation, that is only the arithmetic level, the parameter θ has dimension 1: $\theta = \varepsilon$ and $x_\theta = x_\varepsilon$ represents the exact solution as computed by the algorithm run on a computer. Then the indicator $I_{\varepsilon t}$ allows one to assess the choice of the algorithm G, when $I_{\varepsilon t} \sim 1$. However, iterative solvers and numerical methods involve *more than one level* of approximation: θ is a vector of parameters of dimension ≥ 2. And the indicator $I_{\theta t}$ allows one to assess a *global* reliability with respect to all parameters.

Example 8.1

We consider Newton's method to compute a root of $p(x) = 0$ described in Example 5.1. The convergence is described by the vector parameter $\theta = (\alpha, \varepsilon)$ of *dimension* 2. The computed solution is $\tilde{x}_\alpha = x_{\alpha\varepsilon}$, and the exact approximate solution is x_α (unknown because computed in exact arithmetic). Suppose that $I_{\theta t} = I_{\alpha\varepsilon t}$ allows detection of a backward instability: is it attributable to the method G_α ($\|x - x_\alpha\|$ too large) or to the arithmetic ($\|x_\alpha - x_{\alpha\varepsilon}\|$ too large)? In order to answer that question, one has to introduce an indicator of arithmetic reliability $I_{\varepsilon t}$, where $\zeta_{\alpha\varepsilon} = p(x_{\alpha\varepsilon})$ is compared with $\zeta_\alpha = p(x_\alpha)$ and not with $0 = p(x)$. The difficulty is that x_α and ζ_α are unknown. Example 9.11, treated by PRECISE in Chapter 9, shows that one *cannot* replace ζ_α with $\zeta_{\alpha\varepsilon}$ for that purpose. $\quad\triangle$

In conclusion, the discrimination between numerical and arithmetic reliabilities can be done only *if the arithmetic reliability has been assessed first*. This can be done by using extra information such as the exact x_α, for example.

8.4.5   Side effects

Section 8.4.1 has presented the generic pattern for the indicators $I_{\theta t}$, $L_{\theta t}$, and K_t taking into account some backward instability seen on $I_{\theta t}$ (see Figure 8.1). We observe in this case the following behaviour for the standard deviations v_t and σ_t:

- $t \in [\Psi, s]$: $\|v_t\| \ll \|\nu_t\|$ with $\nu_t = \rho_t - y$ and $\|v_t\|$ increases with t until the two terms are of the same order;
- $t \in [s, t_0]$: $\|v_t\|$ increases with the perturbation size, and we observe $\|v_t\| \sim \|\nu_t\| \sim t$;
- $t \in [\Psi, t_0]$: $\|\sigma_t\|$ increases with t.

Note: Usually, on the interval $[\Psi, s]$, the standard deviation of the sample of solution $\|v_t\|$ is smaller than the bias $\|\nu_t\|$ (that is the case for linear systems, for instance), which remains almost constant. Then this standard deviation $\|v_t\|$ increases proportionally to t until it reaches the order of magnitude of the bias, which occurs for a perturbation size $t \sim s$. Above this perturbation size s, the two quantities $\|v_t\|$ and $\|\nu_t\|$ remain of the same order of magnitude and increase proportionally to t.

However, this is not the only way for v_t or σ_t to vary. We present a typology of the different cases that can be obtained. All these side effects will be illustrated in Chapter 9.

Forward stable algorithms

We consider the case where σ_t varies proportionally to t (as in the generic behaviour described earlier) but where v_t behaves in the following way:

- $t \in [\Psi, s]$: $\|v_t\|$ is constant, and we have $\|v_t\| \sim \|\nu_t\|$;
- $t \in [s, t_0]$: $\|v_t\|$ increases with the perturbation size, and we observe $\|v_t\| \sim \|\nu_t\| \sim t$.

This does not modify the behaviour of $I_{\theta t}$ and of $L_{\theta t}$ (which remain as in Figure 8.1) but does affect the behaviour of K_t, since $K_t \propto \|\sigma_t\|/\|v_t\|$, as represented in Figure 8.3. On the interval $[\Psi, s]$, $K_{\theta t}$ is not constant anymore: it increases. This is what we call a *side effect*. The value chosen for estimating

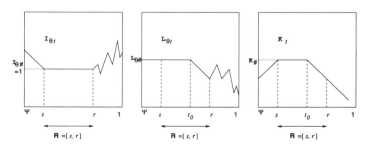

FIG. 8.3. *Side effects with a forward stable algorithm.*

the asymptotic condition number is now the constant value K_t on $[s, t_0]$. Note that the algorithm transmits proportionally to the solution the perturbations imposed on the data, $L_{\theta\sharp}$ being the constant of proportionality; the algorithm G_θ is forward stable.

Forward unstable algorithms

The second type of side effects is more complex and not yet fully understood. It can be itself divided into two subcases. The common feature is the behaviour of σ_t: there exists a value s' such that

- $\forall t \in [\Psi, s']$, $\|\sigma_t\|$ remains constant and is of the same order as the bias $\|m_t - x\| = \|\mu_t\|$, with $\mu_t = m_t - x$;
- $\forall t \in [s', t_0]$, $\|\sigma_t\| \sim \|\mu_t\|$ and they both increase proportionally to t.

Therefore, unlike in the previous case, $L_{\theta t}$ is not constant in the interval $[\Psi, s]$ but decreases until $t = s'$. Statistically, it is due to the fact that for $t \in [\Psi, s']$, the standard deviation $\|\sigma_t\|$ is constant and its value is close to the exact bias $\|\mu_t\|$. σ_t increases only when $t \geq s'$. For $t = \Psi$, the sample of perturbed solution is already as "large" as for $t = s'$ (in terms of average distances): that is why we say that the algorithm G_θ is *forward unstable*. However, this instability shows for t small enough, since as soon as $t > s'$, the indicator $L_{\theta t}$ is constant: this indicates that the algorithm recovers its stability.

The division into two cases comes from the two possible behaviours of v_t that were already encountered: in Figure 8.4, v_t varies proportionally with t right from the beginning (Case 1), and in Figure 8.5, v_t starts to increase only when $t > s$ (Case 2).

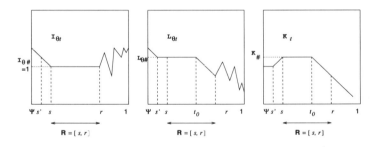

FIG. 8.4. *Backward and forward unstable algorithm: Case 1.*

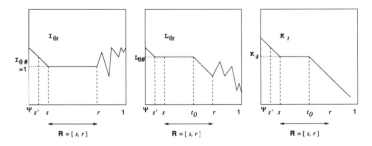

FIG. 8.5. *Backward and forward unstable algorithm: Case 2.*

In Case 1, the value of K_t remains constant on the interval $[\Psi, s']$ and leads to an extremely good estimation of the error, as can be seen in Figure 8.4, whereas generally the error estimate provided by the constant value $K_\sharp$ on $[s, t_0]$ is a slight overestimation. We have no satisfactory explanation of such a particularly good error estimation; the only clue is that on the interval $[\Psi, s']$, $\|\sigma_t\| \sim \|\mu_t\|$, and if m_t is close to x_θ, then $\|\sigma_t\|$ is a good estimation of the exact error. This situation has been obtained on many different examples. The interval $[s', s]$ is a transient zone.

When t is larger than s, all the estimates recover the usual behaviour, K_t reaching the value $K_\sharp$ given by the theory. On the reliability interval $\mathbf{R} = [s, t_0]$, the estimation of the error is feasible and its quality depends on (H_ε). Note that one may also obtain the case $s < s'$, but we do not present it here in order to keep the description simple.

It is important to note that the existence of a dangerous border t_0 is a genuine property of the mathematical problem related to the distance to singularity. The thresholds s and s' are related with the backward stability of the chosen algorithm. For a given mathematical problem, one may observe certain values for s and s' for a chosen algorithm and different values for another algorithm, but in all cases, the dangerous border t_0 is independent of the algorithm.

The quality of the statistical backward analysis provided by PRECISE will be illustrated in the following chapter. We wish to describe next another aspect of PRECISE, i.e., its use to obtain information about nearby singularities.

8.5   Dangerous border and unfolding of a singularity

This section is devoted to the behaviour of $t \longmapsto K_t$ for large values of t—in particular, values of t larger than t_0.

8.5.1   The dangerous border

For a perturbation of amplitude $t > t_0$, the *resolution process* is seen by the computer as *singular*. In other words, if one uses a computer with a precision $\Psi > t_0$, then the law of errors changes: $\mathbf{S}$ is empty and the linear law of error is no longer reliable. We distinguish two cases:

i) $Ax = b$: the system is almost singular, and no reliable solution can be computed with the current machine precision;

ii) a nonlinear equation: the root is almost multiple, corresponding to a singularity of order $1/h > 1$. Then a *nonlinear* law of error expressed by (5.2) holds:

$$\text{error} \ \leq \ K_{(h)} \times (\text{backward error})^h \quad \text{for some } h < 1.$$

This leads to the estimate

$$\frac{\|x - x_\theta\|}{\|x\|} \sim K_{\sharp(h)} \times s^h. \tag{8.7}$$

The value t_0 measures the maximum perturbation that a problem can bear while remaining at a given level of regularity. It can be interpreted as the *distance to singularity viewed by the computer* (see Chapter 4).

For a given machine precision Ψ, we have three possibilities for t_0 (see Figure 8.2):

- $s \leq \Psi$ and $t_0 \geq 1$ indicate that the problem can stand high relative perturbations and still gives a reliable answer.
- $s \leq \Psi$ and $t_0 \in [\Psi, 1]$ are the classical case described previously.
- $s \leq \Psi$ and $t_0 \leq \Psi$ correspond to the case where the problem is too ill conditioned and must be solved with a higher machine precision, for example. It corresponds to an almost singular matrix or an almost multiple root.

In Figure 8.2, the three cases correspond to a decreasing distance to singularity. The grey area of each picture corresponds to the interval $[0, \Psi]$, which is not accessible through finite precision computation. The unshaded area corresponds to perturbations greater than machine precision and represents what can be obtained on a computer. On the interval $[t_0, 1]$, the problem is seen as singular by the computer. The possible oscillations of $I_{\theta t}$ and $L_{\theta t}$ in this area (see Figure 8.1) are the reflection of the instability of the algorithm on a singular problem. K_t behaves more regularly because the computation of the image $F(X_t)$ smoothes the behaviour of X_t (as indicated in Figure 8.2).

More illustrations of the dangerous border t_0 will be given in Chapter 9.

8.5.2   Unfolding of singularity

The δ-sensitivity $\mathcal{K}_\delta$ of F^{-1} has been defined as the sensitivity of F^{-1} to perturbations of size δ. Let δ_s be the distance to singularity for the problem (P) : $F(x) = y$. As long as $\delta < \delta_s$, $C_\delta = \sup_{\|\Delta y\| \leq \delta} \|\Delta x\| / \|\Delta y\|$ is a continuous function of δ that is not decreasing in δ. Therefore

$$\mathcal{K}_\delta \sim C_\delta = \sup_{\|\Delta y\| = \delta} \frac{\|\Delta x\|}{\|\Delta y\|} \quad \text{for } \delta < \delta_s.$$

The generic behaviour of $\delta \longmapsto C_\delta$ is given in Figure 8.6. The δ-condition number is not defined for $\delta \geq \delta_s$, but the $\mathcal{E}$-sensitivity $\mathcal{K}_\delta$ is defined for

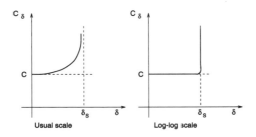

FIG. 8.6.   *Behaviour of the condition number C_δ.*

perturbations of size δ, $\delta > \delta_s$, if there exists no singularity for the problems (P_δ) that are at distance δ of (P).

Conjecture 8.1 *For $\delta \neq \delta_s$ and $\delta < \hat{\delta}$, the δ-sensitivity $\mathcal{K}_\delta$ is equal to $C(P_\delta)$, the asymptotic condition number of (P_δ), where (P_δ) is a problem of type (P) at distance δ of (P).*

Comments: The statement of this conjecture is loose to keep it general. A particular matrix version of this conjecture is stated in Chatelin and Fraysse (1993c, Proposition 6.1) and proven by simple calculations in Fraysse (1992, p. 88). See also Example 9.1.   □

Conjecture 8.1 deals with the behaviour of the condition number as a function of the distance to a given regular problem. It can be related to Conjecture 4.2, which considers the distance to a singular problem. Both conjectures will be checked on the computer by means of PRECISE in the next chapter.

If Conjecture 8.1 is valid, then $\mathcal{K}_t$ can be interpreted as the condition number of a problem of type (P) at distance t of (P) for $t \neq t_0$. It appears clearly that the value t_0 where $\mathcal{K}_t$ changes its behaviour corresponds to δ_s, the distance to singularity (see Figure 8.7 in a log-log scale). However, the peak at infinity for $\delta = \delta_s$, which appears in Figure 8.7 (left) is *not realized on the computer* for $t = t_0$ (right). The family of random perturbations of (P) of size t_0 does not contain the specific perturbation that realizes the mathematical singularity that exists at distance δ_s. Indeed such a perturbation contains exact information about the singularity that cannot be obtained from problems chosen at random.

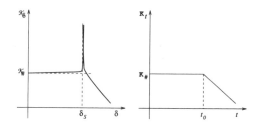

FIG. 8.7.   *Maps $\delta \longmapsto \mathcal{K}_\delta$ and $t \longmapsto \mathsf{K}_t$ around a singularity.*

Figure 8.7 (left) shows an unfolding around the singularity at distance δ_s. If Conjecture 4.2 is valid, then for $\delta > \delta_s$, $\log \mathcal{K}_\delta$ decreases linearly and the slope (-1 or $-1 + h = -1 + \frac{1}{\gamma}$) is characterized by the type and the order of the singularity. Examples are given in Chapter 9.

8.5.3   In the neighbourhood of a Hölderian singularity

When t_0 signals the presence of a singularity that is of Hölderian type and order $m > 1$, it is possible that there exists another value t_1 for which K_t changes its behaviour again in t. This can be interpreted as follows. The singularity is viewed as a regular point for perturbations $t < t_0$. It is then seen as a Hölder singularity of order m for $t_0 < t < t_1$ and afterwards, for $t > t_1$, as a Hölder singularity of larger order $m' > m$. The map $t \longmapsto \mathsf{K}_{t(1/m)}$ displays similar changes at t_0 and t_1 in Figure 8.8. The error estimation (8.6) is valid on $\mathbf{S} = [s, t_0[$, and (8.7) is valid on $\mathbf{S}_{(1/m)} = [t_0, t_1[$. Examples will be given in Chapter 9.

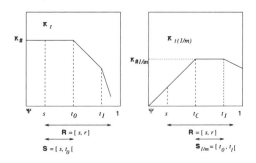

FIG. 8.8. *Linear and Hölder indicators of problem sensitivity.*

8.6 Summary of module 1

The first module of PRECISE, the module for statistical backward error analysis, can be summarized as follows:
1) Construction of the model:
   - Choose the class of perturbations (τ) depending on δ.
   - Define its discrete approximation ($\breve{\tau}$) depending on t.
2) Computation:
   - Plot the maps $t \longmapsto \mathsf{I}_{\theta t}$, K_t, and $\mathsf{L}_{\theta t}$.
   - Determine the reliability interval $\mathbf{R} = [s, r]$ and the regularity interval $\mathbf{S} = [s, t_0[$.
3) Error estimation and distance to singularity:
   - For linear equations, $t_0 = r$ and $\mathbf{R} = \mathbf{S}$:
     — If $t_0 > \Psi$, the error estimation is $\mathsf{E} = \mathsf{K}_\sharp \times s$. The distance to singularity viewed by the computer is given by t_0.
     — If $t_0 < \Psi$, the problem is too ill conditioned for the working precision.
   - For nonlinear equations, $t_0 < r$ and there may exist several dangerous borders. If $t_0 < \Psi < t_1$, the estimation with K_t is impossible. The order γ of the singularity is determined by the slope $-1 + \frac{1}{\gamma}$ of K_t. The error estimate is $\mathsf{E}_{(1/\gamma)} = \mathsf{K}_{\sharp(1/\gamma)} \times s^{1/\gamma}$.

This module allows analyses of the influence of perturbations that are *asymptotic* ($t \to 0$) but also *local* (t large, $t > t_0$) in order to explore the neighbourhood of singularities.

The possibility for PRECISE to capture the essence of finite precision computation (resp., the sensitivity to specific data perturbations) relies entirely on the choice of the class (τ) and its ability to fulfill (H_ε) (resp., (H_θ)). As we said in Chapter 1, this is the main difficulty. As an illustration, the validity of normwise and componentwise perturbations to represent algorithmic behaviour in finite precision will be discussed in Chapter 9 with the help of PRECISE.

In conclusion, the module offers a set of software tools designed to provide a *framework for computer experiments about stability and regularity*, such as

- performance of a statistical backward error analysis for general nonlinear equations $F(x) = y$ when no formula is known for the backward error or the condition number,
- experimentation with various types of perturbations on a chosen set of selected data,
- estimation of the distance to the nearest singularity and provision of the type and order of the singularity,
- study of the robustness to finite precision of numerical methods and iterative solvers.

This module applies to the computer solution of nonlinear well-posed problems and ill-posed problems that are linear. For certain ill-posed problems that are nonlinear, PRECISE allows a more qualitative approach which will be described in Chapter 11.

The second module of PRECISE, the module for sensitivity analysis, provides graphical displays of perturbed spectra, spectral portraits, and pseudospectra that give information about the sensitivity of the eigenvalues of a matrix to perturbations. The complete description is deferred until Chapter 11.

8.7   Bibliographical comments

The principles of PRECISE were presented first in Chatelin (1988b, 1989a, 1989b). The experimentation has been developed in several Ph.D. theses (Brunet (1989), Bennani (1991), Frayssé (1992), Braconnier (1994c)). Advanced training in PRECISE has been provided to scientists and engineers working in industry (Chatelin (1991), Chatelin and Frayssé (1993c), Chatelin and Toumazou (1995)). Papers that discuss the use of statistical estimates for condition numbers include Dixon (1983), Fletcher (1985), Stewart (1990), and Kenney and Laub (1989, 1994).

Chapter 9

Experiments with PRECISE

The advantage of small size examples is that it puts into sharp relief the cause of the trouble, whereas in examples of higher order, the trouble is more insidious.

J. H. Wilkinson, von Neumann Lecture,
Society for Industrial and Applied Mathematics
Meeting, Boston, Fall 1970

This chapter is devoted to the use of the first module of PRECISE, *the module for statistical backward error analysis*, in linear and nonlinear problems. We illustrate its efficiency through two issues:

i) We discuss the pertinence of normwise and componentwise perturbations to model algorithmic and numeric behaviour in finite precision.

ii) We check on the computer the two laws of computation that were expressed in Conjectures 4.2 and 8.1.

9.1 Format of the examples

We give, for each example, up to four plots consisting of each of the three indicators $I_{\theta t}$, $L_{\theta t}$, and K_t plus one plot that gives, in superimposition, the exact relative error $Ex = \frac{\|x - \tilde{x}\|}{\|x\|}$ (constant with t) and the estimation $E_{\theta t} = K_t \times B(x_\theta)$, where $B(x_\theta)$ is the backward error at x_θ. $E_{\theta t}$ is to be compared with Ex. The corresponding captions of the plots are I, L, K, Ex, and E. The map $t \longmapsto 1/t$ is superimposed on each plot. In case of a Hölderian singularity of order $l > 1$, K_t and $E_{\theta t}$ are replaced respectively with $K_{t(1/l)}$ and $E_{t(1/l)}$. The captions are K(1/1) and E(1/1), and the map $t \longmapsto 1/t$ is replaced by $t \longmapsto t^{(1-l)/l} = t^{-1+1/l}$. Computed graphs are displayed with o, whereas theoretical graphs are indicated by a solid line.

All graphs have a logarithmic scale on both axes. The horizontal axis represents the parameter t, the size of the perturbations, which varies from Ψ

to $6 \times 10-2$ under the form $t = 2^{-p}$, $p = 52$ to 4. The size of the samples for each t is fixed at 20 unless otherwise stated.

The maps $t \longmapsto t^{-1}$ and $t \longmapsto t^{-1+1/l}$ appear in the log-log scale as straight lines with slopes -1 and $-1 + 1/l$, respectively.

Only the values of the exponents are shown on both axes: the displayed value $\pm n$ should be read as $10^{\pm n}$.

9.2   Backward error analysis for linear systems

We compare, for several systems, the error analysis taken from the theory (see Chapters 3 and 5) to the statistical estimations provided by PRECISE.

9.2.1   The systems

The matrices are taken from Higham (1991a) and Frayssé (1992):
- **Dingdong**: $a_{ij} = (2(n - i - j) + 3)^{-1}$, $n = 10$;
- **Lotkin**: $a_{ij} = (i + j - 1)^{-1}$ for $i \neq 1$, $a_{1j} = 1$, and $n = 8$;
- **IPJ**: $a_{ij} = (i + j)!$, $n = 10$;
- **VAND**: $\alpha_i = n + i - 1/(n + 1)$, $a_{ij} = \alpha_i^j$, and $n = 18$;
- **DD**: $a_{ij} = d_i(i - j)/(i + j - 1)$ with $d_i = 10^6$ if i is even, $d_i = 10^{-6}$ if i is odd, and $n = 10$;
- **Kahan**: $a_{ij} = -(\sin \theta)^i \cos \theta$ for $i < j$, $a_{ii} = (\sin \theta)^i$, $a_{ij} = 0$ for $i > j$, $\theta = 0.25$, and $n = 20$;
- **WIL**: $\alpha = 0.9$, $n = 50$, and

$$A = \begin{bmatrix} 1 & 0 & \cdots & 0 & 1 \\ -1 & \ddots & \ddots & 0 & \vdots \\ -1 & \ddots & \ddots & 0 & \vdots \\ \vdots & \ddots & \ddots & 1 & 1 \\ -1 & \cdots & \cdots & -1 & \alpha \end{bmatrix}.$$

We denote by ξ the vector of size n such that $\xi_i = \sqrt{i}$, by e the vector of all ones, and by e_1 the first canonical vector $(1, 0, \ldots, 0)^T$. In most cases, we choose one of these three vectors as the exact solution of the linear system and deduce the right-hand side by a matrix-vector multiplication. In the present experiments, the matrices Dingdong, Lotkin, VAND, and DD are associated with the exact solution ξ. The IPJ matrix is associated with the exact solution e_1. The Wilkinson matrix is used with the right-hand side $b = e$. For the Kahan matrix, we first use ξ as the exact solution, and in a second case, we choose e as the right-hand side, the exact solution being determined by Mathematica.

9.2.2   The results

We gather in this paragraph the results obtained on the six first linear systems that we have defined. Table 9.1 shows the condition numbers K_T and K_S

matrix	data	K_T	$\mathrm{K}_{\#}^{\mathcal{N}}$	K_S	$\mathrm{K}_{\#}^{\mathcal{C}}$
Dingdong	A	1.3×10^{01}	4	7.8	2
	b	6.7	2	2.9	1
Lotkin	A	8.2×10^{10}	4×10^{10}	6.1×10^{09}	2×10^{09}
	b	5.9×10^{10}	3×10^{10}	6.1×10^{09}	3×10^{09}
IPJ	A	4.2×10^{21}		1.3×10^{05}	5×10^{04}
	b	6.5×10^{10}	3×10^{10}	1.3×10^{05}	6×10^{04}
VAND	A	2.8×10^{19}		2.1×10^{14}	
	b	2.4×10^{14}	2×10^{15}	1.8×10^{14}	3×10^{14}
DD	A	1.5×10^{12}	2×10^{12}	1.2	1
	b	1.3×10^{12}	1×10^{12}	1.3	1
WIL	A	5.0×10^{01}	3×10^{01}	1.1	7×10^{-1}
	b	1.0	4×10^{-1}	1.1	4×10^{-1}

TABLE 9.1

Normwise and componentwise condition numbers

given by the theory and compares them to the estimations $\mathrm{K}_{\#}^{\mathcal{N}}$ and $\mathrm{K}_{\#}^{\mathcal{C}}$ given by PRECISE. Table 9.2 compares the predicted forward errors E_T and E_S (resp., $\mathrm{E}_{\#}^{\mathcal{N}}$ and $\mathrm{E}_{\#}^{\mathcal{C}}$) given by (5.1); Ex denotes the exact relative error obtained with GEPP. A blank entry for a PRECISE estimation means that the reliability interval is empty so that no estimation is allowed.

Following the two tables are the figures corresponding to the experiments with PRECISE (perturbations of A or b) on the seven systems. We do not show the results for perturbations of A and b together, because they do not provide any supplementary information.

The experiments have been realized on a Sun SPARC 10 workstation using MATLAB 4.0 and Mathematica whenever necessary. The routines for the

matrix	data	E_T	$\mathrm{E}_{\#}^{\mathcal{N}}$	Ex	E_B	$\mathrm{E}_{\#}^{\mathcal{C}}$
Dingdong	A	1.5×10^{-15}	4×10^{-16}	2.1×10^{-16}	1.4×10^{-15}	3×10^{-16}
	b	1.5×10^{-15}	4×10^{-16}	2.1×10^{-16}	1.9×10^{-14}	5×10^{-15}
Lotkin	A	1.6×10^{-06}	8×10^{-07}	3.6×10^{-07}	8.3×10^{-07}	4×10^{-07}
	b	1.6×10^{-06}	8×10^{-07}	3.6×10^{-07}	8.3×10^{-07}	5×10^{-07}
IPJ	A	2.4×10^{-05}		2.7×10^{-12}	3.7×10^{-11}	2×10^{-11}
	b	2.4×10^{-05}	5×10^{-06}	2.7×10^{-12}	3.7×10^{-11}	3×10^{-11}
VAND	A	8.1×10^{-02}		3.5×10^{-03}	2.3×10^{-02}	
	b	8.1×10^{-02}	5×10^{-03}	3.5×10^{-03}	1.2×10^{-01}	8×10^{-01}
DD	A	2.3×10^{-04}	2×10^{-04}	3.8×10^{-13}	2.7×10^{-14}	5×10^{-13}
	b	2.3×10^{-04}	2×10^{-04}	3.8×10^{-13}	8.3×10^{-14}	2×10^{-12}
WIL	A	2.5×10^{-02}	2×10^{-02}	1.3×10^{-02}	2.7×10^{-02}	2×10^{-02}
	b	2.5×10^{-02}	1×10^{-02}	1.3×10^{-02}	2.5×10^{-02}	1×10^{-02}

TABLE 9.2

Normwise and componentwise forward errors: GEPP

algorithms GEPP and QR are provided by MATLAB. The infinity norm of
the inverse of A, i.e., $\|A^{-1}\|_\infty$, is estimated by the Harwell routine MC41.

9.2.3 Comments

Dingdong/GEPP

Both analyses give a good image of the computation: the forward error is well
estimated. The two models are equally good (Figures 9.1 and 9.2).

Lotkin/GEPP

Lotkin is ill conditioned: K_T and K_S are around 10^{10}. Both analyses give
a good estimation of the computation error. The reliability intervals are

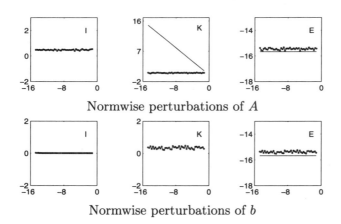

FIG. 9.1. *Dingdong/GEPP: normwise.*

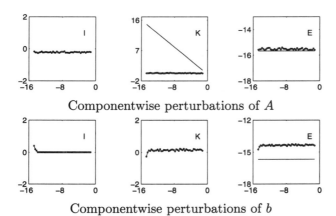

FIG. 9.2. *Dingdong/GEPP: componentwise.*

$\mathbf{R}^{\mathcal{C}} = [10^{-15}, 10^{-8}]$ and $\mathbf{R}^{\mathcal{N}} = [10^{-15}, 10^{-11}]$. As expected $\mathbf{R}^{\mathcal{C}}$ is larger than $\mathbf{R}^{\mathcal{N}}$. For $t \geq r = t_0$, $K_t^{\mathcal{N}}(A)$ and $K_t^{\mathcal{C}}(A)$ fit the map $t \longmapsto 1/t$ almost exactly. The dangerous border t_0 is of the order of the reciprocal of the condition number in both of the cases (Figure 9.3).

IPJ/GEPP and QR

Normwise and componentwise perturbations are not equivalent in this example (Figure 9.4). The componentwise perturbations are better suited to describe GEPP since they lead to a good approximation of the forward error. The normwise perturbations yield an empty reliability interval: $t_0 < \Psi$. However, normwise perturbations can be well suited for a different algorithm. We observe this when solving the same system using the QR algorithm: normwise perturbations of b now allow a good estimation of the forward error (see Figure 9.7).

Figure 9.5 is an illustration of side effects analysed in Chapter 8, which reveal the componentwise backward instability of QR on this example. Note

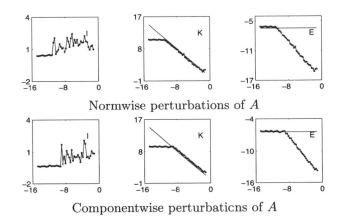

FIG. 9.3. *Lotkin/GEPP.*

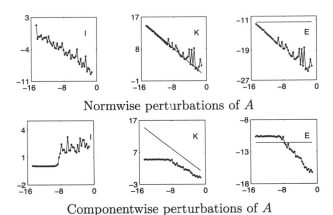

FIG. 9.4. *IPJ/GEPP.*

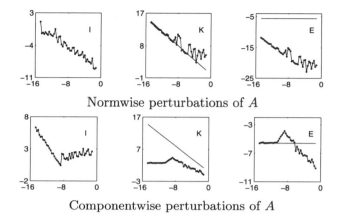

Normwise perturbations of A

Componentwise perturbations of A

FIG. 9.5. *IPJ/QR*.

that in this figure the quality of the error estimation is in the interval $[10^{-15}, s']$. These side effects do not appear under normwise perturbations, in this case because the QR is normwise backward stable.

VAND/GEPP

Whenever the Vandermonde matrix A is perturbed (with normwise or componentwise perturbations), PRECISE gives an empty interval of reliability and therefore no estimation is provided (see Figure 9.6). Figure 9.8 gives the Harwell, LINPACK, and PRECISE estimates of the normwise condition number $\|A^{-1}\|_\infty \|A\|_\infty$ and compares them with the exact value determined by Mathematica for $8 \leq n \leq 18$. PRECISE is reliable for $n \leq 11$, and this information is given by the computation. The Harwell and LINPACK estimations are reliable for $n \leq 14$. No warning is included in Harwell about a possible failure.

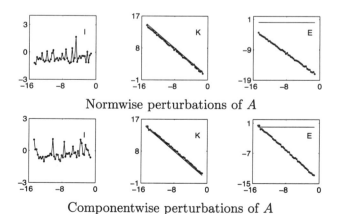

Normwise perturbations of A

Componentwise perturbations of A

FIG. 9.6. *VAND/GEPP*.

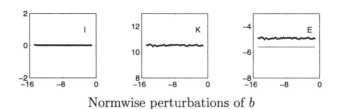

Normwise perturbations of b

FIG. 9.7. *IPJ/QR.*

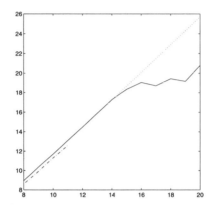

...: Mathematica, —: HARWELL and LINPACK,
— · — · — : PRECISE

FIG. 9.8. *VAND: estimations of the condition number $\|A\|_\infty\|A^{-1}\|_\infty$ for $8 \le n \le 20$.*

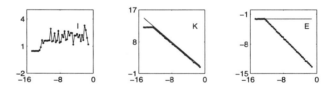

FIG. 9.9. *DD/GEPP: analysis of a given normwise perturbation of A.*

DD/GEPP

DD is a very badly scaled matrix. The componentwise backward error s is well estimated by PRECISE. The algorithm is normwise backward stable (see Figure 9.10). The computation error, which is quite low ($\sim 10^{-14}$), is well estimated by componentwise perturbations but overestimated by a factor of 10^{10} when normwise perturbations are used. Normwise perturbations are not relevant to model the behaviour of GEPP. In a normwise measure, the bad scaling of the matrix affects the condition number. In a componentwise measure, the condition number is row scaling independent; indeed, for GEPP, the bad scaling affects the computation through the backward error (the algorithm becomes backward unstable) but does not affect the mathematical problem (the condition number remains low).

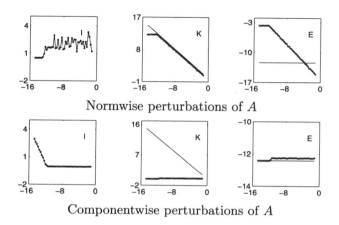

Normwise perturbations of A

Componentwise perturbations of A

FIG. 9.10. *DD/GEPP.*

With a normwise analysis, we are actually trying to measure the forward error issued from a problem which should be a normwise perturbation of the initial problem. Figure 9.9 is an illustration of this point. Let (A, b) be the initial system and (A', b') be a given normwise perturbation of the initial system. Let x be the exact solution of the initial problem and x' be the exact solution of the perturbed system. If $K_T(A)$ is the normwise condition number, we can write

$$\frac{\|x' - x\|}{\|x\|} \sim K_T(A) \frac{\|Ax' - b\|}{\|A\|\|x'\|}.$$

In Figure 9.9, we use the backward error $\|Ax' - b\|_\infty / (\|A\|_\infty \|x'\|_\infty)$ for the error estimation, and we compare the estimated error with $\|x' - x\|_\infty / \|x\|_\infty$. We observe now that the error is well estimated.

WIL/GEPP

This example has been designed by Wilkinson to show the potential instability of GEPP. Indeed, in this example, the normwise backward errors $\eta^N(A)$ and $\eta^N(b)$ are large (0.5×10^{-3} and 0.25×10^{-1}). The forward error is large too.

In Figure 9.11, one can analyse the effect of normwise perturbations of the right-hand side. The large backward error is well detected. On the interval $[10^{-15}, s]$ where $I_t^N(b)$ decreases, $K_t^N(b)$ is still constant and leads to a very good estimation of the error; this is a remarkable side effect similar to the second one described in Chapter 8.

However, the analysis with normwise perturbations of A does not show the large backward error. Indeed, this large backward error is accidental: it is due to the fact that GEPP on WIL produces a bad sequence of pivots and achieves a very high growth factor. But as soon as the matrix A is perturbed, the sequence of pivots is different and GEPP recovers its backward stability. This explains why PRECISE, which is based on a sample of perturbed data, cannot detect this backward instability, which is not generic. This example

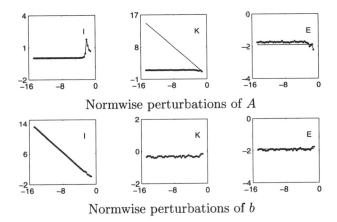

Normwise perturbations of A

Normwise perturbations of b

FIG. 9.11. *WIL/GEPP.*

indicates that perturbations of both A *and* b may be necessary to get a complete understanding of the numerical phenomenon.

Kahan/back substitution

Kahan is an upper triangular M-matrix chosen to illustrate the results of Higham (1989). We perform two experiments, one with a right-hand side b with mixed signed entries and one with a right-hand side with positive entries (see Figure 9.12). The system is solved by a backward substitution. We observe that the computation is always backward stable. The choice of the right-hand side with positive entries lowers the condition number and the forward error; PRECISE estimation of the condition number satisfies the bound given by Higham. Note the slight underestimation of the error by PRECISE, but the order of magnitude is still correct. More on this example will be said later in this chapter.

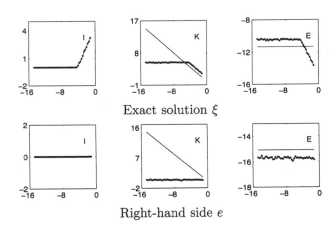

Exact solution ξ

Right-hand side e

FIG. 9.12. *Kahan/GEPP: componentwise perturbations of A.*

9.2.4   Structured perturbations on Vandermonde/BP

As explained in Example 5.3, the BP algorithm for solving Vandermonde systems is known to provide accurate solutions. In some cases, the componentwise analysis gives a large overestimation for the error, because the potential singularity of the matrix is not excited in finite precision by such an algorithm. We report here the results concerning two linear systems consisting of the same matrix V and two different right-hand sides. V is the Vandermonde matrix of order 10 defined by $\alpha_i = 1/(14 - i)$, $i = 1, \ldots, 10$, which satisfy $0 \leq \alpha_0 < \alpha_1 < \cdots < \alpha_n$. We will denote by

- VDM1 the system $Vx = b$, where $b_i = (-1/2)^{(i-1)}, i = 1, \ldots, 10$, presents the sign-oscillation property and the exact solution is determined by Mathematica;
- VDM2 the system $Vx = b$, where $x = e$.

All notations refer to Example 5.3.

Perturbation of the right-hand side b

The right-hand side of each system is submitted to componentwise perturbations (Figure 9.13). Table 9.3 gathers the main results. The agreement is good. These two examples show that, although very accurate, BP is not always backward stable with respect to componentwise perturbations of the right-hand side.

	Theoretical bounds		PRECISE	
	$K_S(b)$	$\eta^{\mathcal{C}}(b)$	$K_\sharp$	s
VDM1	1	2×10^{-6}	1	10^{-5}
VDM2	7×10^9	4×10^{-16}	5×10^9	10^{-15}
	$E_S(b)$	$H(b)$	Ex	$E_\sharp$
VDM1	2×10^{-6}	10^{-15}	9×10^{-16}	10^{-5}
VDM2	2×10^{-6}	7×10^{-6}	10^{-7}	8×10^{-6}

TABLE 9.3
BP: componentwise perturbations of the right-hand side

Perturbations of the matrix V

The structure of BP imposes that we consider componentwise perturbations only on each coefficient α_i. Therefore, the componentwise analysis is not appropriate because it allows componentwise perturbations of *all the entries* of the matrix. To model Higham's analysis, the perturbations on the entries are correlated in the following way: $a_{ij\text{per}} = [\alpha_i(1 + \varepsilon_i)]^j$: the perturbed matrix is still Vandermonde. $K_S(V)$ is the mixed condition number for perturbations of the whole matrix V, and $\eta^{\mathcal{C}}(V)$ is the componentwise backward error. C_α is the condition number derived by Higham when the α_i are perturbed and $H(\alpha) = \Psi C_\alpha$ is the corresponding error bound.

	Theoretical values			PRECISE
	$K_S(V)$	$\eta^C(V)$	C_α	$K_\sharp$
VDM1	2×10^8	10^{-16}	4×10^1	3×10^1
VDM2	7×10^9	2×10^{-16}	2×10^5	3×10^4
	$E_S(V)$	Ex	$H'(\alpha)$	$E_\sharp$
VDM1	2×10^{-8}	9×10^{-16}	4×10^{-15}	2×10^{-16}
VDM2	10^{-6}	6×10^{-8}	2×10^{-11}	5×10^{-12}

TABLE 9.4
BP: componentwise perturbations of V or α

Results for the two systems are given in Table 9.4. The estimation of C_α and $H(\alpha)$ by PRECISE is satisfactory.

Figure 9.15 shows the componentwise analysis for VDM1 (when V is perturbed) when the GEPP algorithm is used. We observe the presence of a dangerous border $t_0 \sim 10^{-8}$, which does not appear when BP is used (see Figure 9.14 (top)). The dangerous border is connected with the distance to singularity of the matrix and signals the potential instability of the system. The absence of a t_0 for the BP means that this algorithm does not excite the potential singularity of the matrix. This is an example of the difference between potential and effective instabilities.

For VDM2, we notice that the estimate of the condition number of the algorithm is not constant before the perturbations reaches $\sim 10^{-12}$ (see Figure 9.14 (bottom)). In the region of perturbations for which all the indicators are constant, the value of $K_\sharp$ is about 10^4 and the exact error is dramatically underestimated. However, the bad quality of the estimation is not due to an incorrect estimation of the condition number: the value for C_α given by PRECISE matches Higham's analysis within a factor of 10 (Table 9.4). The estimation is not satisfactory in both cases displayed in Figure 9.14, because perturbing α does not entirely reflect the behaviour of BP. The influence is less striking on VDM1 than on VDM2.

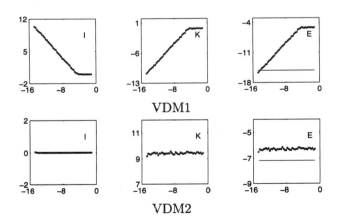

FIG. 9.13. *VDM1 and VDM2/BP: componentwise perturbations of b.*

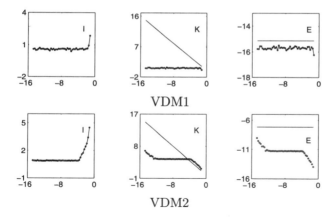

FIG. 9.14. *VDM1 and VDM2/BP: componentwise perturbations s of V.*

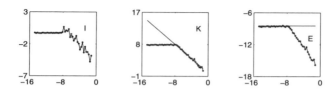

FIG. 9.15. *VDM1/GEPP: componentwise perturbations of V.*

9.2.5 Conclusion

These examples demonstrate that the quality of the statistical backward error analysis obtained with PRECISE allows to judge the relevance of the models of perturbations. The flexibility offered by PRECISE in the choice of perturbations and data is an asset, as was illustrated with the two Vandermonde systems with GEPP and BP.

9.3 Computer unfolding of singularity

We have proposed two conjectures in relation with computations in the neighbourhood of a singularity.

Conjecture 4.2 *The condition number $K(\delta)$ of problems at distance δ from the singularity behaves as*

    i) *$1/\delta$ for linear problems,*

    ii) *$1/\delta^{(1-1/\gamma)} = \delta^{1/\gamma-1}$ for nonlinear problems (Hölderian singularity of order $\gamma > 1$).*

Conjecture 8.1 *For $\delta \neq \delta_s$ and $\delta < \hat{\delta}$, the δ-sensitivity $\mathcal{K}_\delta$ is equal to $C(\mathrm{P}_\delta)$, the asymptotic condition number of (P_δ), where (P_δ) is a problem of type (P) at distance δ of (P).*

    We investigate how these conjectures are realized in finite precision and use PRECISE to decide whether there is computer evidence in their favor.

9.3.1   The linear case

We present here the unfolding of a singularity associated with a matrix for matrix inversion $A \longmapsto A^{-1}$.

Example 9.1

Let A be the 3×3 matrix $A = QDQ$ with $D = \text{diag}(10^{-5}, 1, 10^{6})$, and Q is the symmetric orthogonal matrix defined by $q_{ij} = \frac{1}{\sqrt{2}} \sin \frac{ij\pi}{4}$. We use the Euclidean norm and recall that $\delta_T = 1/(\|A\|_2 \|A^{-1}\|_2) = 10^{-5}/10^{6} = 10^{-11}$ is the relative distance to singularity.

Let E be the eigenprojection such that $S = A(I - E)$ achieves the closest singularity: $S = Q\text{diag}(0, 1, 10^{6})Q$. We then introduce the family $A(\delta) = A - \frac{\delta}{\delta_T} AE$. Clearly, $A(\delta_T) = S$. This defines the particular class of perturbations of dimension 1 by $\Delta A = -\frac{\delta}{\delta_T} AE$. We define, for $\delta \neq \delta_T$,

$$D_\delta(A) = \sup_{\frac{\|\Delta A\|_2}{\|A\|_2} = \delta} \frac{1}{\delta} \frac{\|A^{-1}(\delta) - A^{-1}\|_2}{\|A^{-1}\|_2}.$$

A simple calculation leads to $D_\delta = K_T(A)/|1 - \frac{\delta}{\delta_T}|$. The map $\delta \longmapsto D_\delta$ is plotted in a log-log scale in Figure 9.16.

When $\delta \to 0$, $D_\delta \to K_T(A)$. For $\delta < \delta_T$, $D_\delta = C_\delta$, and for $\delta > \delta_T$, D_δ decreases as $1/\Delta$ with $\Delta = \delta - \delta_T$. This appears on the log-log scale of Figure 9.16 as identical with the line of slope -1 (corresponding to $1/\delta$): for δ large compared with δ_T, $\delta - \delta_T$ is not significantly different from δ.

Why is it so? Because of the *particular* type of perturbations chosen. The family $A(\delta)$ contains only one singular matrix, that is, $A(\delta_T) = S$. So D_δ exists for $\delta > \delta_T$ and decreases because the perturbation takes $A(\delta)$ *away* from the singularity S. $\quad\triangle$

Example 9.1 shows an exact unfolding of singularity around $\delta_T = 10^{-11}$. We now turn to its computer realization. In Figure 9.17, we show the results of the following experiment on the matrix A of Example 9.1, with the family of perturbed matrices

$$A(t) = A + t\Delta A = A + 2^{-p} F \, |A\|, \quad t = 2^{-p},$$

where F is a random matrix with ± 1 entries. We have superimposed on Figure 9.17 the statistical estimations $K_s(A(0))$ and $K_s(A(t))$ for six values

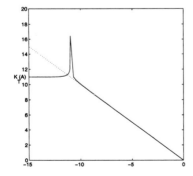

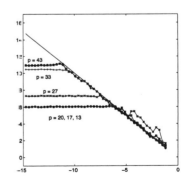

FIG. 9.16.   *The maps* $\delta \longmapsto D_\delta$ *and* $\delta \longmapsto 1/\delta$ *for the* 3×3 *matrix* A.

FIG. 9.17.   *Unfolding the singularity associated with* A: *normwise.*

of t: 10^{-13}, 10^{-10}, 10^{-8}, 10^{-6}, 10^{-5}, and 10^{-4} (corresponding to $p = 43$, 33, 27, 20, 17, and 13) and s varying, as usual, from 10^{-16} to 1. They conform to Conjecture 8.1 for $t \leq \hat{t} = 10^{-6}$. For $t \geq \hat{t} = 10^{-6}$ (that is, for $p = 20$, 17, 13), $K_s(A(t))$ remains constant at the value 10^6 (for $s \leq 10^{-6}$). The superimposition of the map $s \longmapsto 1/s$ shows that Conjecture 4.2 also is satisfied.

We complement this computer verification by normwise and component-wise experiments on the map $A \longmapsto A^{-1}$ for the Lotkin matrix.

Example 9.2

The unfolding shown in Figure 9.18 has been realized on Lotkin of order 8. For $t = 2^{-p}$, the values taken for p are 35, 25, 20, 15, 10, and 5. Then, on the same graph, we have plotted the six maps $s \longmapsto K_s^{\mathcal{N}}(A(t))$ for matrix inversion, as well as the curve $s \longmapsto 1/s$.

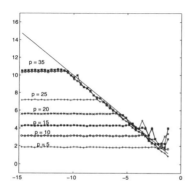
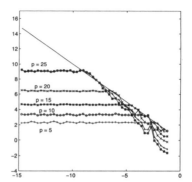

FIG. 9.18.   *Unfolding of singu-larity: Lotkin, normwise.*   FIG. 9.19.   *Unfolding of singu-larity: Lotkin, componentwise.*

The condition number estimate $K_s^{\mathcal{N}}(A)$ of the matrix A is constant at the value 3×10^{10}, and $K_s^{\mathcal{N}}(A)$ starts decreasing like $1/s$ as s increases from the value $t_0 = 1/(3 \times 10^{10}) \sim 3.3 \times 10^{-11}$. The matrix $A(35)$ is a normwise relative perturbation of A of size $2^{-35} \sim 3 \times 10^{-11} < t_0$: the condition number estimate $K_s^{\mathcal{N}}(A(35))$ varies exactly like $K_s^{\mathcal{N}}(A)$. This remains true for any matrix $A(t)$ with $t = 2^{-p} \leq t_0$, where $t_0 = t_0(A)$ measures the distance of A to singularity.

Perturbations greater than t_0 have the effect of taking away the matrix from the singularity: as 2^{-p} increases, the condition number estimate of the matrices $A(p)$ decreases in the following way. Let q be such that $2^{-q} > t_0 = t_0(A)$. We define B as a particular $A(2^{-q})$ corresponding to a given realization of F. The map $t \longmapsto K_t^{\mathcal{N}}(B)$ is constant at the value $K_\sharp(B) \leq K_\sharp(A)$, for $t \leq t_0(B) \sim 2^{-q}$, and matches the curve $t \longmapsto 1/t$ afterwards. B is farther from the singularity than A: the distance to singularity of B is of order of 2^{-q}. Such a construction can be carried out again with any r such that $2^{-r} > 2^{-q}$. When A is the Lotkin matrix of order 8, $t_0(A)$ corresponds to $p = 35$. The construction can be interpreted as the unfolding of the singularity associated with A. (Such a singularity would be achieved if the machine precision Ψ was larger than $2^{-35} \sim 10^{-10}$.)   △

Example 9.3

For the same Lotkin matrix A, we define the family of matrices $A(t) = A + \Delta A(t)$, where $\Delta A(t)_{ij} = \pm t a_{ij}$: $\Delta A(t)$ is a random componentwise perturbation of size $t = 2^{-p}$ of the matrix A. In Figure 9.19, we have superimposed the mappings for various values of p. We can see that each mapping has the same behaviour: for $t < t_0(p)$, $K_s^{\mathcal{C}}(A(t))$ is constant. For $t = t_0(p)$, $K_s^{\mathcal{C}}(A(t))$ reaches the curve $1/s$; as s increases, $K_s^{\mathcal{C}}(A(t))$ decreases but does not stay exactly on the curve $1/s$ as was the case in the normwise experiments (see Figure 9.18). This example illustrates Conjectures 4.2 and 8.1, since it appears clearly in this case that the map $s \longmapsto 1/s$ is the envelope of all the curves $s \longmapsto K_s^{\mathcal{C}}$. $\triangle$

9.3.2   Nonlinear problems

Of course, such an unfolding is not restricted to matrix inversion $A \longmapsto A^{-1}$. It can be realized for any process in the neighbourhood of a singularity. For example, Figure 9.20 shows the unfolding of the singularity associated with the double root of a polynomial.

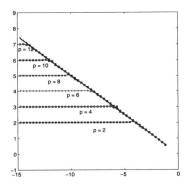

FIG. 9.20.   *Unfolding of the singularity associated with the double root of $(x-7)^2$.*

Example 9.4

We take for the polynomial $\pi(x) = x^2 - 14x + 49$, which has the double root $x = 7$. The family of perturbed polynomials is defined by $\pi(x,t) = x^2 - 14x + 49 - t$. This amounts to an absolute perturbation of size t for the constant term 49. When $t = 0$, $\pi(x,0) = \pi(x)$ and the map $s \longmapsto K_s(\pi(x))$ exactly matches the curve $t \longmapsto 1/\sqrt{t}$ (a line of slope $-1/2$ in the log-log scale of Figure 9.20). On the same plot we have superimposed the maps $s \longmapsto K_s(\pi(x,t))$ associated with polynomials obtained by varying the parameter t. Setting $t = 10^{-p}$, we have taken successively the six values $p = 12$, 10, 8, 6, 4, and 2. The computation of the solutions is done with Newton's method with a stopping criterion chosen such that no method error appears ($|x_{k+1} - x_k|/|x_k| \le 10^{-8}$). One sees only the mathematical effects, not the algorithmic ones. Therefore, one gets the behaviour described by Conjecture 4.2 for nonlinear problems with $\gamma = 2$. The reference curve is therefore $1/\sqrt{t}$. $\triangle$

These experiments with PRECISE illustrate how Conjectures 4.2 and 8.1, valid in exact arithmetic, are realized in finite precision on a computer. The main difference is that the peak at infinity that exists in exact arithmetic for $\delta = \delta_s$ does not appear when the simulation uses a sample of random matrices, because matrices taken at random cannot realize the singularity exactly.

9.4 Dangerous border and distance to singularity

The aforementioned experiments also confirm the strong connection between the dangerous border and the distance to singularity viewed by the computer, which we wish to explore further.

9.4.1 Experiments on matrix inversion $A \longmapsto A^{-1}$

Theorems 4.3 (Turing) and 4.4 (Rohn) give characterizations of the normwise and componentwise distances of a matrix A to singularity, respectively denoted δ_T and δ_B. Turing's theorem is particularly simple and appealing: it states that $\delta_T = 1/K_T$. However, Rohn's formula for δ_B does not allow us to relate δ_T with K_B^{-1} easily, and Poljak and Rohn (1993) prove that the computation of δ_B is NP-complete. Can PRECISE help design experiments to gain some insight about δ_B?

We recall (from Chapter 4) that

$$\delta_B \geq \frac{1}{\rho(|A^{-1}|E)} = \frac{1}{\rho_B} \geq \frac{1}{\||A^{-1}|E\|_\infty} = \frac{1}{M_B},$$

with equality $\delta_B = 1/\rho_B$ whenever A^{-1} has a checkerboard sign pattern. These lower bounds are easier to compute than δ_B, but we do not know how sharp they are. On the other hand,

$$K_B(A) \leq L_B = \frac{\||A^{-1}|E|A|\|_\infty}{\|A^{-1}\|_\infty} \leq M_B = \||A^{-1}|E\|$$

with $K_B = L_B$ in certain cases such as when there exist two signature matrices D_1 and D_2 such that $|A^{-1}| = D_1 A^{-1} D_2$.

What is the relationship between K_B and δ_B^{-1}? Because the computation of δ_B using Rohn's formula is NP-complete, and because L_B can be computed in polynomial time, δ_B and L_B cannot be exactly reciprocal.

We want to investigate further the order relationship between the four quantities K_B, L_B, M_B, and ρ_B and δ_B^{-1}. We choose four matrices taken from Higham (1991a): Hilbert, IPJ, Kahan, and Jordan, for which the quantities are exactly computable, either in a closed form or with Mathematica. We perform a componentwise analysis with $E = |A|$ and compare the exact quantities with the estimations provided by PRECISE for inversion $A \longmapsto A^{-1}$.

Example 9.5 Hilbert (Figure 9.21).

A is Hilbert order 7 defined by $a_{ij} = 1/(i+j-1)$. An exact inverse is known and can be compared with the computed inverse.

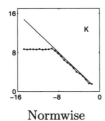

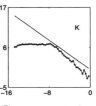

Normwise   Componentwise

FIG. 9.21. *Matrix inversion on Hilbert.*

A^{-1} has a checkerboard sign pattern so that

$$\delta_B^{-1} = \rho(|A^{-1}||A|) \; = \; K_B = L_B = \frac{|||A^{-1}||A||A^{-1}|||_\infty}{||A^{-1}||_\infty}.$$

We compute

$$\begin{cases} \delta_B = 8.5 \times 10^{-9}, \\ K_B = L_B = 1.18 \times 10^8, \\ M_B = 3.6 \times 10^8. \end{cases}$$

PRECISE estimation for K_B can be seen on the right-hand graph: $\mathsf{K}_\sharp^\mathcal{C} = 0.8 \times 10^8$, which is close to K_B. Moreover, $t_0 = 1/\mathsf{K}_\sharp^\mathcal{C} \sim 10^{-8}$, where t_0 is the size of the largest perturbation for which $\mathsf{K}_t^\mathcal{C}$ remains constant. The left-hand graph gives $t \longmapsto \mathsf{K}_t^\mathcal{N}$, for comparison. We see that $\mathsf{K}_\sharp^\mathcal{N} \sim 10^9$ to be compared with $K_T = 9.9 \times 10^8$.   △
Example 9.6 IPJ (Figure 9.22).
A^{-1} has a checkerboard sign pattern, and again

$$\delta_B^{-1} = \rho(|A^{-1}||A|) > \; K_B = L_B = \frac{|||A^{-1}||A||A^{-1}|||_\infty}{||A^{-1}||_\infty}.$$

We compute

$$\begin{cases} \delta_B \sim \dfrac{1}{6 \times 10^8} \sim 1.7 \times 10^{-9}, \\[2mm] K_B \sim 4.28 \times 10^8 \implies \dfrac{1}{K_B} \sim 2.3 \times 10^{-9}, \\[2mm] M_B \sim 5.9 \times 10^{14}. \end{cases}$$

Here, M_B is a large upper bound for K_B. This case is interesting because, although δ_B and $1/K_B$ are very close, we have

$$K_B < \frac{1}{\delta_B} \quad \text{and} \quad K_B = L_B \ll M_B.$$

The values of δ_B and K_B have been computed exactly by Mathematica.

A lower bound for the backward error is $\max_{ij} |R_{ij}|/(|A||X|)_{ij} \sim 7.9 \times 10^{-14}$. What does PRECISE say in Figure 9.22? It shows a backward error of order $s = 10^{-13}$, a value for which I_t stabilises at 1. $\mathsf{K}_\sharp^\mathcal{C} \sim 10^8$ and $t_0 \sim 10^{-8}$: PRECISE cannot distinguish between δ_B and $1/K_B$.   △
Example 9.7 Kahan (Figure 9.23).
This example is about the Kahan matrix of order 20 with $\theta = 0.25$. Since A is a triangular matrix, we know (Demmel (1987, p. 16)) that

$$\delta_B = \frac{1}{\rho(|A^{-1}||A|)} = 1.$$

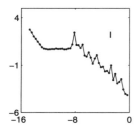
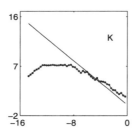
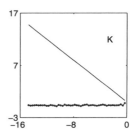

FIG. 9.22. *Matrix inversion on IPJ: componentwise.*

FIG. 9.23. *Matrix inversion on Kahan: componentwise.*

Furthermore, all the entries of A^{-1} are positive real numbers, and $|A^{-1}| = D_1 A^{-1} D_2$ with $D_1 = D_2 = I$. Therefore, $K_B = L_B$. We compute

$$\left\{ \begin{array}{l} \delta_B = 1, \\ K_B = L_B = 20.6, \\ M_B = 7.8 \times 10^5. \end{array} \right.$$

M_B is a very large upper bound of the condition number K_B. Consequently, $1/M_B$ underestimates the distance to singularity, whereas $1/K_B$ is a close lower bound for it. We have

$$\frac{1}{\delta_B} < K_B = L_B \ll M_B.$$

What does the statistical analysis of PRECISE provide? $K_{\sharp}^C$ is about 3, which is a slight underestimation of K_B (Figure 9.23), and t_0 is of the order of 1. The graph confirms that M_B is not relevant for the analysis of the componentwise distance to singularity.

This example is interesting because it shows that we must not expect to obtain a fixed unique ordering between δ_B and $1/K_B$. $\triangle$

Example 9.8 Jordan (Figure 9.24).

The last example in the series deals with the bidiagonal Jordan matrix defined by

$$\left\{ \begin{array}{l} a_{ii} = a_{ii+1} = 1, \ i = 1, \ldots n, \\ a_{ij} = 0 \ \forall j \neq i, \ j \neq i + 1. \end{array} \right.$$

A is a triangular matrix; therefore, $\delta_B = 1$, A^{-1} has a checkerboard sign pattern, and

$$K_B = L_B = \frac{\||A^{-1}||A||A^{-1}|\|_\infty}{\|A^{-1}\|_\infty}.$$

A^{-1} is an upper triangular matrix such that all entries of the upper part are ± 1. Therefore, K_B and M_B can be computed explicitly, and we obtain

$$K_B = n \text{ and } M_B = 2n - 1.$$

The Jordan matrix is an interesting case, because $1/K_B$ can be made arbitrarily smaller than δ_B, and M_B is not a large overestimation of K_B. We get, for large n,

$$\frac{1}{\delta_B} \ll K_B = L_B < M_B.$$

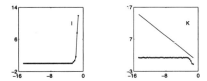

FIG. 9.24. *Matrix inversion on Jordan: componentwise, $n = 500$.*

Here, PRECISE experiments are not conclusive, as can be seen in Figure 9.24. We have performed a componentwise analysis on a Jordan matrix of order 500. The estimated condition number $K_{\#}^{\mathcal{C}} = 20$ is an underestimation of $K_B = 500$ in this case, and the dangerous border $t_0 \sim 10^{-2}$ is smaller than $1/K_{\#}^{\mathcal{C}} = 5 \times 10^{-2}$. In this example, $1/K_B \ll t_0 < 1 = \delta_B$.　△

9.4.2　Distance to singularity viewed by the computer

What is the difference between the mathematically defined distance to singularity and the distance to singularity *seen by the computer*? We look at this question in the simple framework of linear systems. A linear system $Ax = b$ is regular as long as its matrix A is not singular: the mathematical condition for the singularity of the system $Ax = b$ does not involve the right-hand side b. However, we know that in practice b may play a role in dampening the effects of instability in A^{-1}. So the question naturally arises, does t_0 reflect the mathematical distance to singularity, depending on A and A^{-1} only, or may it depend on b?

To this end, we consider the three following processes:

$$\begin{cases} (P_1) \ A \longmapsto A^{-1}, \\ (P_2) \ A \longmapsto x = A^{-1}b, \\ (P_3) \ A, b \longmapsto x = A^{-1}b. \end{cases}$$

It is reasonable to expect that the role of b may show for componentwise perturbations since $K_S(P_2)$ and $K_S(P_3)$ depend on b by means of $x = A^{-1}b$. For normwise perturbations, however, $K_T(P_1) = K_T(P_2)$ and $K_T(P_1) \le K_T(P_3) \le 2K_T(P_1)$, so in this case, we cannot expect the role of b to be very important.

In the mathematical definition of the componentwise distance to singularity, δ_B depends on A only. What is the situation for $t_0^{\mathcal{C}}$?

It is possible that $t_0^{\mathcal{C}}$ depends on b as illustrated in the next example: this happens when the potential singularity of a matrix may not be excited at all by a particular right-hand side.

Example 9.9

This happens with the Kahan matrix. For (P_1) (Figure 9.23) and for (P_2) with $b = e$ (Figure 9.12, bottom), the dangerous border is $t_0^{\mathcal{C}} \sim 1$, but with $b = A\xi$, a dangerous border $t_0^{\mathcal{C}} \sim 10^{-4}$ appears (Figure 9.12, top). As shown by Higham, a linear system involving a triangular M-matrix (as in Kahan) *and* a right-hand side with positive entries is more stable than predicted since the potential instability of the matrix A is not excited. This happens also for matrix inversion: the implicit right-hand sides are the canonical vectors and have positive entries. Therefore, we obtain a relative distance to singularity of 1 in Figures 9.23 and 9.12 (bottom). But the potential instability in A can be excited in other cases; see Figure 9.12 (top). PRECISE provides a rather accurate picture of this situation by means of $t_0^{\mathcal{C}}$.   △

However, in general, $t_0^{\mathcal{C}}$ does not depend on b. The example below describes such a situation where the role of the right-hand side b is either to lower or to increase the condition number.

Example 9.10

Comparing Figure 9.22 for (P_1), Figure 9.4 for (P_2) with $x = e_1$, and Figure 9.25 for (P_2') with $x = e_7$ shows that the same dangerous borders appear at $t_0 \sim 10^{-8}$, corresponding to $K_S(P_1) = 4.28 \times 10^8$, estimated in Figure 9.22 by $K_\sharp \sim 10^7$. But the condition numbers for (P_2) and (P_2') are different from $K_S(P_1)$:

	$K_S(P_2)$	$<$	$K_S(P_1)$	$<$	$K_S(P_2')$
exact values	1.3×10^5	$<$	4.28×10^8	$<$	10^{11}
estimation by PRECISE	10^5	$<$	10^7	$<$	10^{11}

Whatever the right-hand side b for IPJ, the distance to singularity $t_0^{\mathcal{C}}$ viewed by the computer is invariant; only the condition number can vary with b.   △

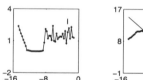

FIG. 9.25.   *IPJ with $x = e_7$/GEPP: componentwise perturbations of A.*

9.5   Roots of polynomials

9.5.1   Computation of a simple root

We consider the quadratic polynomial $\pi(x) = x^2 - 2bx + c$, where $b = 2$ and $c = 3$, admitting two simple roots 1 and 3. We study the computation of the root $x = 3$ by the standard Newton's method (see Example 5.1).

Figure 9.26 shows the behaviour of $\mathbf{I}_{\alpha\varepsilon t}$ and K_t for the threshold $\alpha = 10^{-2}$. K_t estimates the stability of π^{-1} at the computed point $(\zeta_{\alpha\varepsilon}, x_{\alpha\varepsilon}) = (\tilde{\zeta}_\alpha, \tilde{x}_\alpha)$. $\mathbf{I}_{\alpha\varepsilon t}$ becomes constant in t for $s = 10^{-4}$. Why do we observe such a large backward error? The finite Newton method is an algorithm that produces an approximation solution x_α in exact arithmetic and $x_{\alpha\varepsilon}$ in finite precision

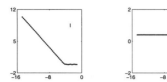

FIG. 9.26. *Indicators of stability* $I_{\alpha\varepsilon t}$ *and* K_t *for a simple root* $(\alpha = 10^{-2})$.

arithmetic, different from x when α is significantly larger than Ψ: this induces a large bias $\|\mu_t\|$ for the solution sample X_t, which reflects itself on the computation of the image sample $Y_t = p(X_t)$. We then also have a large bias $\|\nu_t\|$. It is only for $t \geq s$ that the estimation is reliable.

Although K_t is constant on the whole interval $[\Psi, 1]$, it should be considered only on the reliability interval $\mathbf{R}$ for $I_{\alpha\varepsilon t}$, which here is $\mathbf{R} = [s, 1]$.

The behaviour of $I_{\alpha\varepsilon t}$ (resp., K_t) is similar to that described in Figure 8.1 (resp., Figure 8.2) in the case $t_0 > 1$: the computation of a simple root is a regular mathematical problem. If we decrease the threshold α, we compute a solution of better quality ($\|x - x_\alpha\|$ smaller), and the bias gets smaller. Therefore, we reduce the interval of backward instability and s gets closer to Ψ. The interval of reliability increases accordingly (see Figure 9.27). We find experimentally that $s \sim \Psi$ for $\alpha \sim 10^{-4}$.

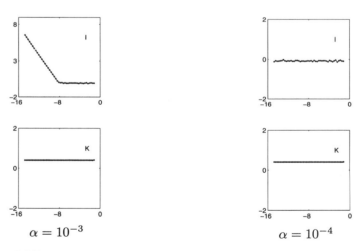

$$\alpha = 10^{-3} \qquad\qquad \alpha = 10^{-4}$$

FIG. 9.27. *Indicators of stability* $I_{\alpha\varepsilon t}$ *and* K_t *for a simple root.*

9.5.2 Necessity of a separate assessment for the arithmetical stability

We already mentioned the difficulty that arises when one wants to assess the arithmetic stability of an iterative method. The indicator $I_{\alpha\varepsilon t}$ allows assessment of the *global* reliability, taking into account the two parameters

α and ε. In order to assess the *arithmetic* reliability, one needs to compute the indicator

$$\mathbf{I}_{\varepsilon t} = \frac{\sqrt{v_t^2 + |\rho_t - \zeta_\alpha|^2}}{t \sum_{i=0}^n |a_i||x_\alpha|^i},$$

where $\zeta_\alpha = p(x_\alpha)$ is generally unknown since x_α is the solution given by the algorithm in exact arithmetic. Since ζ_α is unavailable, we can think of using the computed value $\zeta_{\alpha\varepsilon} = p(x_{\alpha\varepsilon})$. Is such an approximation legitimate in $\mathbf{I}_{\varepsilon t}$? The following experiment shows the contrary.

Example 9.11

We have written an unstable version of the Newton's iteration by introducing in each iteration an artificial cancellation. The scheme is the following:

$$x_0, \quad x_{k+1} = \frac{(10^{13} + x_k) - 10^{13}}{x_k} + x_k - \frac{p(x_k)}{p'(x_k)} - 1, \quad k \geq 0. \tag{9.1}$$

We apply it to the polynomial $p(x) = (x-1)(x-3) = x^2 - 4x + 3$ with a starting point $x_0 = -3$ and a threshold $\alpha = 10^{-2}$. In exact arithmetic, the scheme is equivalent to the classical Newton's iteration and will converge toward $x = 1$, but in finite precision arithmetic, the artificial cancellation becomes more and more influent as x_k approaches 1.

We compute x_α and $\zeta_\alpha = p(x_\alpha)$ in exact arithmetic with Mathematica (applying the iteration scheme as many steps as were necessary to compute $\tilde{x}_\alpha = x_{\alpha\varepsilon}$). We then compare $\mathbf{I}_{\varepsilon t}$ with its approximation $\hat{\mathbf{I}}_{\varepsilon t} = \sqrt{v_t^2 + |\rho_t - \zeta_{\alpha\varepsilon}|^2}/(t \sum_{i=0}^n |a_i||x_\alpha|^i)$. One sees clearly in Figure 9.28 that $\mathbf{I}_{\varepsilon t}$ exposes the existence of an important backward instability for (9.1). On the contrary, $\hat{\mathbf{I}}_{\varepsilon t}$ remains constant at the value 1 for all t and suggests the misleading conclusion that the algorithm (9.1) is backward stable to compute the root $x = 1$. $\quad \triangle$

This example shows that the arithmetic stability of the computation needs to be assessed separately by using different techniques such as extended precision. Unless otherwise stated, we use below the notation $\theta = (\alpha, \varepsilon)$.

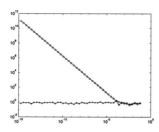

FIG. 9.28. *Assessment of the arithmetic reliability:* $\mathbf{I}_{\varepsilon t}$ (ooo) *and* $\hat{\mathbf{I}}_{\varepsilon t}$ (+ + +).

9.5.3 Evolving from a simple root to a double root

Example 9.12

We now consider the polynomial $\pi(x) = x^2 - 2bx + c$, where $b = 7$ and $c = 49 - \beta$ with $\beta > 0$. The two roots are $7 \pm \sqrt{\beta}$. The standard Newton's iteration (see Example 5.1) is used to compute the largest root $7 + \sqrt{\beta}$; it is stopped when $|x_{k+1} - x_k|/|x_k| < \alpha$.

We study the behaviour of the statistical indicators as β tends to zero so that the two simple roots become double. We display the indicators $I_{\theta t}$, K_t, $K_{t(1/2)}$ and the error estimations E_t and $E_{t(1/2)}$.

Figures 9.29–9.31 correspond to the threshold $\alpha = 10^{-5}$ and three decreasing values $\beta = 10^{-5}$, 10^{-7}, and 10^{-9}. The map $t \longmapsto 1/\sqrt{t}$ is superimposed on $t \longmapsto K_t$.

$I_{\theta t}$ has the same behaviour: it decreases linearly with t (slope -1) until $t = s$ and then stabilises to a value close to 1. The value s is the backward error; it depends on α, and on the machine precision Ψ. We observe that $t_0 < r$, so that the reliability interval $\mathbf{R} = [s, r]$ is always larger than the interval $\mathbf{S} = [s, t_0]$ where the problem is regular. We note again that *even if K_t is constant on the whole interval $[\Psi, t_0]$, its analysis is meaningful* by definition *only in the reliability interval $\mathbf{R} = [s, r]$.*

$\alpha = 10^{-5}$		
β	s	t_0
10^{-5}	10^{-11}	10^{-7}
10^{-7}	10^{-11}	10^{-9}
10^{-9}	10^{-11}	10^{-11}

In Figure 9.29, the behaviour of K_t is exactly the same as the general one shown in Figure 8.1. If we compare it with Figure 9.26, we observe the presence now of the dangerous border t_0; this is due to the fact that we approach a double root which is a Hölder singularity. On the interval $[t_0, 1]$, K_t decreases like $1/\sqrt{t}$; this corresponds to a singularity of order $1/2$. Indeed, the initial data is submitted to a perturbation of size t, which results on the double root in a perturbation of size $\sqrt{t}$. The condition number, which is the ratio of these perturbations behaves like $\sqrt{t}/t = 1/\sqrt{t}$.

As c becomes closer to b^2, the interval $\mathbf{S} = [s, t_0]$ gets smaller or even nonexistent (as in Figure 9.31); that is, t_0 decreases toward s and s remains approximately constant around 10^{-11}. The interval $\mathbf{S} = [s, t_0]$ is the regularity interval: it corresponds to the interval of perturbations where the computation "sees" the problem as regular (the computation of a simple root). For c close enough to b^2, the level of resolution $\alpha = 10^{-5}$ is too coarse to distinguish between the two roots $7 \pm \sqrt{\beta}$.

Simultaneously, $K_{t(1/2)}$ becomes the relevant condition number. In Figure 9.29, we can see that $K_{t(1/2)}$ increases until t reaches t_0 and then becomes constant for $t \geq t_0$. We see how K_t and $K_{t(1/2)}$ are complementary: K_t deals with the *simple root*

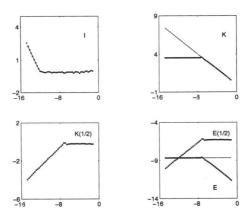

FIG. 9.29. *Evolving from a simple root to a double root: $\beta = 10^{-5}$, $\alpha = 10^{-5}$.*

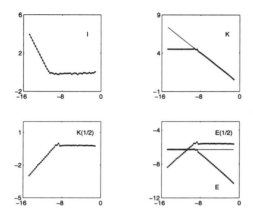

FIG. 9.30. *Evolving from a simple root to a double root:* $\beta = 10^{-7}$, $\alpha = 10^{-5}$.

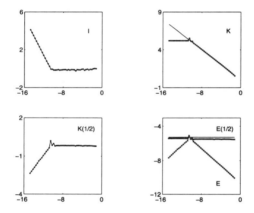

FIG. 9.31. *Evolving from a simple root to a double root:* $\beta = 10^{-9}$, $\alpha = 10^{-5}$.

computation and is valid on $[s, t_0]$, and $K_{t(1/2)}$ deals with the *double root* computation and is valid on the interval $S_{(1/2)} = [t_0, 1]$.

The constant value of $K_{t(1/2)}$ in the interval $[t_0, 1]$ first leads to an overestimation of the error, but as c gets closer to b^2, the quality of the estimation becomes better. It is remarkable that this estimation using $K_{t(1/2)}$ becomes good as soon as the estimation with K_t ceases to be feasible, i.e., when the problem becomes undiscernable from an exact double root problem to working machine precision. As long as the interval $S = [s, t_0]$ is nonempty ($t_0 \geq s$), the error estimation E_t is better when the linear condition number K_t is used, but when this interval does not exist anymore, the error estimation $E_{t(1/2)}$ based on $K_{t(1/2)}$ becomes the only one that is correct.

In Figure 9.31, there are only two intervals $[\Psi, t_0]$ and $[t_0, 1]$ because $s = t_0$: $S = [s, t_0]$ is empty. Analysing the problem as the computation of a simple root is impossible because K_t is not constant on $\mathbf{R}$. The only possibility is to consider the solution as a double root in the interval $[t_0, 1]$. The interval $S_{1/2} = [t_0, 1]$ is the reliability interval for the estimation by a Hölder condition number of order $1/2$. $\triangle$

One sees from this simple nonlinear problem that PRECISE can resolve satisfactorily the difficulties created by the existence of a *large bias* resulting from a large consistency error, often present for iterative solvers or numerical methods. The indicator $I_{\theta t}$ now describes the backward stability with respect to the global perturbation induced by a *numerical method and finite precision*. The computed solution $x_\theta = x_{\alpha\varepsilon}$ solves $F(x_\theta) = y_\theta$ instead of $F(x) = y$: x_θ is the solution associated with the particular perturbation of the right-hand side $y - y_\theta$, where θ is a vector of two parameters here, $\theta = (\alpha, \varepsilon)$. The indicator $I_{\theta t}$ is the key parameter to extend to numerical analysis the backward error analysis of Wilkinson that has proved so successful for numerical software.

In linear problems, the singularity observed is very strong because it corresponds to the transition between an existing unique solution to no solution at all (or possibly an infinity if the right-hand side satisfies the conditions of compatibility). Here we observe a much milder singularity, which corresponds to a change in the Hölderian regularity: the order of regularity decreases from 1 (simple root) to 1/2 (double root). However, the behaviours of the various indicators of stability have a strong degree of resemblance, and general laws for computation in the neighbourhood of singularities are emerging. One noticeable difference, however, is that for linear problems, the reliability interval **R** does not extend beyond t_0 ($t_0 = r$), while here we can get $t_0 \ll r$.

9.5.4 Conditional stability

We have indicated in Chapter 2 that the numerical stability of a method can become conditional to the arithmetic. This may happen in the neighbourhood of a singularity. If this is the case, a numerical method that converges in exact arithmetic when $\alpha \to 0$ may converge in finite precision ε only if some condition between α and ε is satisfied.

For example, Newton's method applied to compute a double root is convergent with an arithmetic of precision ε only if the threshold α for convergence is such that $\alpha \geq O(\sqrt{\varepsilon})$. Can we analyse this phenomenon with PRECISE?

Example 9.13

We apply Newton's method to $\pi(x) = x^2 - 14x + 49 = (x - 7)^2$ and plot $\alpha \longmapsto t_0(\alpha)$, when t_0 is the observed dangerous border for α ranging from 10^{-8} to 10^{-1}. The experimental map (—) fits the theoretical map (- - -) $\alpha \longmapsto \alpha^2$ as shown in Figure 9.32 with a log-log scale. $\triangle$

FIG. 9.32. *Conditional stability: computation of a double root for $\pi(x) = 0$.*

9.6 Eigenvalue problems

In this section, we study eigenvalues through four distinct basic cases:
1. a simple eigenvalue,
2. a semisimple eigenvalue,
3. a multiple defective eigenvalue,
4. the transition from a simple to a defective eigenvalue.

For each example, we define a triangular or diagonal matrix M of order 3, then we analyse with PRECISE the computation of an eigenvalue of the matrix $A = QMQ^T$, where Q is provided by the MATLAB routine ORTHOG taken from Higham's collection of test matrices. The exact eigenvalues of A, which are known, are used to validate the error estimation. On the graphs, the exact error Ex is shown as a continuous line, whereas the estimated error E_t is displayed with "oooo." All graphs use a logarithmic scale on both axes. The x-axis bears the perturbation size, and the y-axis shows the statistical estimate as indicated in the caption. The algorithm used to compute the eigenvalues is the QR algorithm, which is backward stable. The formulae for the statistical estimates can be found in Table 8.4. In what follows, the indicators $I_{\varepsilon t}$ and $E_{\varepsilon t}$ are respectively denoted by I_t and E_t for the sake of simplicity.

9.6.1 Computation of eigenvalues

Example 9.14 A simple eigenvalue.
Let M be the diagonal matrix $\mathrm{diag}(1, 2, 3)$. The behaviour of the estimated condition number K_t and of the estimated error E_t are shown respectively in Figure 9.33. As expected, we observe that K_t is constant for the whole range of perturbations at the value 1. The resulting estimate of the error is good.　△
Example 9.15 A semisimple eigenvalue.
M is the diagonal $(-1, -1, -1)$, and the eigenvalue -1 has an algebraic multiplicity of order $m = 3$ and an ascent equal to $l = 1$: -1 is triple and semisimple.

As explained in Chapter 3, the application $A \longmapsto \lambda$ when λ is semisimple is Lipschitz continuous. Therefore, we can use K_t as an estimate of the condition number. The behaviour of the statistical indicator K_t and the error estimation is shown in Figure 9.33. The classical condition number K_t conforms to the expected theoretical behaviour, and the estimated error is very close to the exact one. As expected, the computation of a semisimple eigenvalue has the same behaviour as that of a simple eigenvalue because $l = 1$ in both cases.　△
Example 9.16 A defective eigenvalue.
Let M be the Jordan block

$$M = \begin{pmatrix} -1 & 1 & 0 \\ 0 & -1 & 1 \\ 0 & 0 & -1 \end{pmatrix}.$$

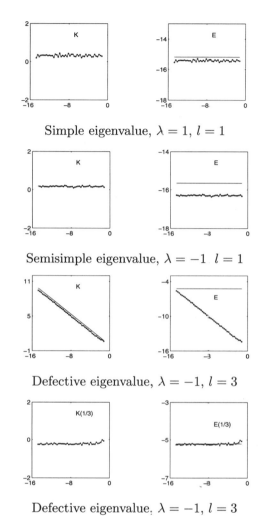

Simple eigenvalue, $\lambda = 1$, $l = 1$

Semisimple eigenvalue, $\lambda = -1$ $l = 1$

Defective eigenvalue, $\lambda = -1$, $l = 3$

Defective eigenvalue, $\lambda = -1$, $l = 3$

FIG. 9.33.

The eigenvalue -1 has an algebraic multiplicity $m = 3$ and an ascent equal to $l = 3$: -1 is triple and defective. As $l = 3$, the expected theoretical slope for the statistical indicator K_t is $(1 - l)/l = -2/3$. In such a case, the relevant condition number is the Hölder condition number estimated by $K_{(1/3)}$.

The behaviour of the statistical indicators K_t and $K_{t(1/3)}$ together with the corresponding error estimations E_t and $E_{t(1/3)}$ in Figure 9.33. The theoretical map $t \longmapsto t^{-2/3}$ is overimpressed on K_t.

We do not observe a dangerous border $t_0 < \Psi$, and we see that $K_{t(1/3)}$ is constant for the whole range of perturbations. The estimated error $E_{t(1/3)}$, built from $K_{t(1/3)}$, is very close to the exact error Ex. The estimated error E_t, constructed on K_t is not relevant since there is no range of perturbations for which K_t is constant and hence no reliability interval S.

The behaviour of a defective problem is better described by its Hölderian condition number than by its linear condition number. $\triangle$

9.6.2   Transition from a simple to a multiple defective eigenvalue

Example 9.17 (Chatelin, Fraysse, and Braconnier (1995)).
Define the matrix M by

$$M(a,b) = \begin{pmatrix} -1-a & 1 & 0 \\ 0 & -1 & 1 \\ 0 & 0 & -1+b \end{pmatrix}.$$

When $a \neq -b$, the spectrum of $A = QMQ^T$ is $\sigma = \{-1-a, -1, -1+b\}$ and the three eigenvalues are simple. All indicators are computed for $\lambda = -1$.

We are interested in three cases:

1. $b = -1$: the spectrum of $M(a,-1)$ is $\sigma = \{-1-a, -1, -2\}$. As $a \to 0$, the eigenvalue -1 tends to become a double defective eigenvalue with $m = l = 2$.
2. $b = a$: the spectrum of $M(a,a)$ is $\sigma = \{-1-a, -1, -1+a\}$. As $a \to 0$, the eigenvalue -1 tends to become a triple defective eigenvalue with $m = l = 3$.
3. $b = a^{1/2}$: the spectrum of $M(a, a^{1/2})$ is $\sigma = \{-1-a, -1, -1+a^{1/2}\}$. As $a \to 0$, $-1-a$ approaches -1 faster than $-1+a^{1/2}$.

The theoretical map $t \longmapsto t^{(1-l)/l}$ is shown by a continuous line for $l = 3$ and a dashed line for $l = 2$ in Figures 9.34–9.36.

1) $M(a,-1)$ and $M(a,a)$.

For both matrices, we observe in Figure 9.34 that the change of regularity occurs for a distance to singularity that is proportional to the reciprocal of the *square* ($b = -1$) or of the power *three halves* ($b = a$) of the condition number. Indeed one has

- for $(a,b) = (10^{-4}, -1)$: $t_0(a,b) = 10^{-9}$ and $K_\sharp = 3 \times 10^4$, that is, $t_0(a,b) \sim 1/K_\sharp^2$.
- for $(a,b) = (10^{-3}, 10^{-3})$: $t_0(a,b) = 10^{-10}$ and $K_\sharp = 2 \times 10^6$, that is, $t_0(a,b) \sim 1/K_\sharp^{3/2}$.

For a decreasing from 10^{-1} to 10^{-7}, the values of the dangerous borders $t_0(a,-1)$ and $t_0(a,a)$ are listed in Table 9.5.

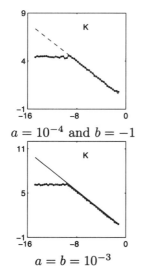

$a = 10^{-4}$ and $b = -1$

$a = b = 10^{-3}$

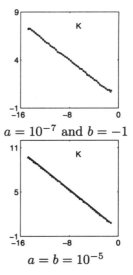

$a = 10^{-7}$ and $b = -1$

$a = b = 10^{-5}$

FIG. 9.34. K_t *for* $M(a,a)$ *and* $M(a,-1)$.

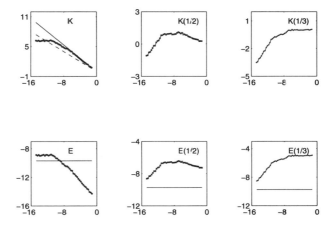

FIG. 9.35. *Transitory case for* $M(a, a^{1/2})$, $a = 10^{-4}$.

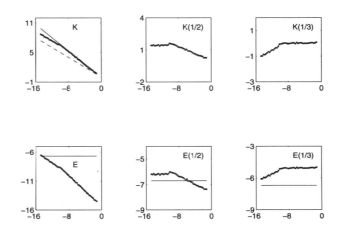

FIG. 9.36. *Transitory case for* $M(a, c^{1/2})$, $a = 10^{-6}$.

These two examples confirm Conjecture 4.2: $t_0 \sim K_\sharp^{l/(1-l)}$, where l is the ascent of the eigenvalue, is equivalent to $K_\sharp \sim t_0^{1/l-1}$. This confirms the fact that the degree of regularity h ($h = 1/l$ here) plays a role in the distance to singularity that is seen by the computer (see Chapter 4).

2) $M(a, a^{1/2})$.

For $a = 10^{-4}$ (resp., $a = 10^{-6}$), the behaviours of the statistical indicators K_t, $K_{t(1/2)}$, $K_{t(1/3)}$ are shown in Figure 9.35 (resp., Figure 9.36), together with the error estimations E_t, $E_{t(1/2)}$, $E_{t(1/3)}$.

i) For $a = 10^{-4}$, the map $t \longmapsto K_t$ presents three areas:

- area (1): for $\Psi \le t \le t_0 \sim 10^{-11}$, K_t is constant.
- area (2): for $t_0 \le t \le t_1 \sim 10^{-8}$, K_t decreases and is parallel to $t \longmapsto t^{-1/2}$ ($l = 2$).
- area (3): for $t \ge t_1$, K_t decreases and is parallel to $t \longmapsto t^{-2/3}$ ($l = 3$).

In area (2), $K_{t(1/2)}$ is constant and $K_{t(1/3)}$ is constant in area (3). The estimated values for the three condition numbers are $K_\sharp = 10^6$, $K_{\sharp(1/2)} = 10$, and $K_{\sharp(1/3)} = 1$. We observe *two dangerous borders*, t_0 and t_1.

a	10^{-1}	10^{-2}	10^{-3}	10^{-4}	10^{-5}	10^{-6}	10^{-7}
$t_0(a, -1)$	10^{-3}	10^{-5}	10^{-7}	10^{-9}	10^{-11}	10^{-13}	$\leq \Psi$
$t_0(a, a)$	10^{-4}	10^{-7}	10^{-10}	10^{-13}	$\leq \Psi$	$\leq \Psi$	$\leq \Psi$

TABLE 9.5

Dangerous borders $t_0(a, -1)$ and $t_0(a, a)$

- for $\Psi \leq t \leq t_0$, the ascent of -1 is $l = 1$: -1 is simple.
- for $t_0 \leq t \leq t_1$, $-1 - a$ is viewed by the computer as part of a Jordan block of size 2 associated with -1: -1 becomes double defective with an ascent $l = 2$.
- for $t \geq t_1$, $-1 + a^{1/2}$ is viewed by the computer as part of a Jordan block of size 3 associated with -1: -1 becomes triple defective with an ascent $l = 3$.

The study of E_t, $E_{t(1/2)}$, $E_{t(1/3)}$ confirms this point of view. However, the best error estimation is obtained in area (1) using K_t. This observation remains valid for all our experiments: the best error estimation is always obtained in the first large enough area where the condition number estimate associated with the largest possible order of regularity is constant. Here, $1/l$ is largest for $l = 1$.

We can say that the computer "sees" the problem as the computation

- of a simple eigenvalue in area (1),
- of a defective eigenvalue of ascent $l = 2$ in area (2).
- of a defective eigenvalue of ascent $l = 3$ in area (3).

ii) For $a = 10^{-6}$, the map $t \longmapsto K_t$ presents two areas:

- area (1): for $\Psi \leq t \leq t_0 \sim 10^{-9}$, K_t decreases and is parallel to $t \longmapsto t^{-1/2}$.
- area (2): for $t \geq t_0$, K_t decreases and is parallel to $t \longmapsto t^{-2/3}$.

In area (1), $K_{t(1/2)}$ is constant and $K_{t(1/3)}$ is constant in area (2). The estimated values for the two Hölder condition numbers are $K_{\sharp(1/2)} \sim 50$ and $K_{\sharp(1/3)} = 1$. Only one *dangerous border* t_1 remains visible; t_0 is smaller than Ψ.

- For $\Psi \leq t \leq t_1$, $-1 - a$ is viewed by the computer as part of a Jordan block of size 2 associated with -1: -1 is seen as double defective with an ascent $l = 2$.
- For $t \geq t_1$, $-1 + a^{1/2}$ is viewed by the computer as part of a Jordan block of size 3 associated with -1: -1 is seen as triple defective with ascent $l = 3$.

The study of the error estimation shows that E_t is far from Ex in the whole range of perturbations. $E_{t(1/2)}$ is close to Ex in (1), and $E_{t(1/3)}$ is close to Ex in (2). (If we extrapolate (2), $E_{t(1/2)}$ decreases and goes far from Ex, but $E_{t(1/3)}$ remains constant and close to Ex.) Here, it is not possible to obtain a reliable error estimate with K_t since there is no area where K_t is constant. The largest possible order of regularity is $1/2$ here, and we observe again that we obtain a better error estimation with $K_{t(1/2)}$ than with $K_{t(1/3)}$.

The dangerous border t_0 that occurs in the case $a = 10^{-4}$ (i.e., associated with K_t) also takes place for the case $a = 10^{-6}$ for a perturbation size less than Ψ, but it is not visible because the current machine precision is not sufficient. For a computer providing a high enough accuracy, such a dangerous border could become visible because there would possibly be a range of perturbations where the eigenvalue $-1 - a$ could appear as simple.

We can say that the computer "sees" the problem as the computation
- of a defective eigenvalue of ascent $l = 2$ in the area (1),
- of a defective eigenvalue of ascent $l = 3$ in the area (2).

The fact that the same eigenvalue is "seen" in a variable way by the computer is the reason for the existence of *two* dangerous borders t_0 and t_1: there are two successive changes in the law of errors.   △

9.6.3   Comparison with theoretical bounds

For a simple eigenvalue, there are explicit formulae for the condition numbers (see Chapter 3): PRECISE estimates agree satisfactorily with these formulae. In this paragraph, we wish to study eigenvalues with large Hölder condition numbers. Let $A = Q^*MQ$, where M is the diagonal matrix $\mathrm{diag}(1, 10, 20)$. We define the matrix $A_\beta = V_\beta A V_\beta^{-1}$, $V_\beta = (q_1, q_2, q_2 + \beta q_3)$, where q_i, $i = 1, 2, 3$, are the columns of the orthogonal matrix Q. Therefore, as β tends to zero, the third eigenvector tends to have the same direction as the second one, and the eigenbasis associated with the portion of the spectrum $\{10, 20\}$ becomes more and more ill conditioned.

Figure 9.37 shows PRECISE estimates (normwise analysis) obtained for the second eigenvalue $\lambda = 10$ and $\beta = 10^{-6}$. As expected, this eigenvalue has a large condition number of order 10^{12}. For perturbations of amplitude larger than 10^{-13}, this eigenvalue is seen as double by the computer, as indicated by $\mathrm{K}_{t(1/2)}$, which remains constant on $[10^{-13}, 1]$. This is due to the fact that this eigenvalue tends to cluster with the third one, and the corresponding eigenbasis is ill conditioned for β small. Seen as a double eigenvalue, λ has a large Hölder condition number around $\mathrm{K}_{\sharp(1/2)} \sim 10^6$.

We can compare this estimation with the upper bound given in Theorem 4.1, written here in relative norms:

$$\frac{|\lambda' - \lambda|}{|\lambda|} \leq \underbrace{\frac{2}{|\lambda|} \left(\mathrm{cond}_2(V_\beta)\|X_*\|_2 \|A_\beta|_2\right)^{1/l} \frac{\|\Delta A_\beta\|_2^{1/l}}{\|A_\beta\|_2^{1/l}}}_{\Gamma_{1/l}(\beta)} \quad \text{with } l = 2.$$

Computing the upper bound $\Gamma_{(1/l)}(\beta)$ for the Hölder condition number for $l = 2$ and $\beta = 10^{-6}$, we find 1.23×10^6, which is in agreement with PRECISE

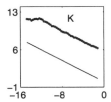
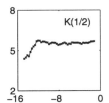
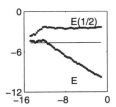

FIG. 9.37.   *Normwise analysis of $\lambda = 10$: ill conditioned eigenbasis ($\beta = 10^{-6}$).*

estimation. Table 9.6 compares PRECISE estimation $\kappa_{\sharp(1/2)}$ of the Hölder condition number with the upper bound $\Gamma_{1/2}(\beta)$ for decreasing values of the parameter β.

These examples show the ability of PRECISE for analysing a wide range of eigenvalue problems. They tend also to indicate that the upper bound of Theorem 4.1 can be realistic.

Although PRECISE is a rather costly method, its use need not be restricted to matrices of small orders, as our examples might suggest. Let us suppose that we want to analyse the spectrum of a large matrix, which is ill conditioned only in a subspace of moderate size $m \ll n$. It is easy to determine *with satisfactory accuracy and backward stability* the invariant subspace M associated with the well-conditioned eigenvalues. (Classical theoretical tools for checking the numerical quality are available in this case and are cheap to compute.) Let Q be an orthonormal basis for the invariant subspace M and $\underline{Q}$ be an orthonormal basis for the complementary subspace. We denote by $n - m$ the dimension of the invariant subspace; thus $m \times n$ is the size of $\underline{Q}$. In the basis $[Q, \underline{Q}]$, the matrix A can be written

$$\begin{pmatrix} Q^* \\ \underline{Q}^* \end{pmatrix} A \begin{pmatrix} Q & \underline{Q} \end{pmatrix} = \begin{pmatrix} Q^*AQ & Q^*A\underline{Q} \\ \underline{Q}^*AQ & \underline{Q}^*A\underline{Q} \end{pmatrix} = \begin{pmatrix} B & C \\ 0 & \underline{B} \end{pmatrix}.$$

$\underline{B}$ is the projection of A on the supplementary subspace of the invariant subspace M and contains information about the Jordan structure. Since M is associated with the stable part of the spectrum, $\underline{B}$ retains only the information of the Jordan structure corresponding to the ill-conditioned part of the spectrum. This matrix $\underline{B}$ is of order m, which we expect to be much smaller than n: $\underline{B}$ can now be handled very easily by PRECISE at a lower cost. Therefore, PRECISE can be used to analyse locally the spectral stability of large matrices, provided that it is preceded by a projection step on a stable invariant subspace.

β	10^{-1}	10^{-2}	10^{-3}	10^{-4}
Upper bound	1.24×10^1	1.23×10^2	1.23×10^3	1.23×10^4
PRECISE	10^1	10^2	10^3	10^4

β	10^{-5}	10^{-6}	10^{-7}	10^{-8}
Upper bound	1.23×10^5	1.23×10^6	1.23×10^7	1.23×10^8
PRECISE	10^5	10^6	10^7	10^8

TABLE 9.6
Estimations of the Hölder condition number

9.7   Conclusion

Through a variety of examples, we showed how helpful a perturbation method such as PRECISE can be to analyse the stability of algorithms/methods and mathematical problems. We recall in this conclusion the three most important features of PRECISE.

i) The first property of PRECISE is its ability to assess the reliability of an algorithm or a numerical method by means of an arithmetic or numerical quality indicator.

ii) The second property concerns the estimation K_t of the δ-sensitivity via a statistical analysis of samples of perturbed solutions or residuals. For perturbations of size smaller than a threshold t_0, K_t appears to be almost constant to the value $K_\sharp$, whereas when $t \geq t_0$, K_t decreases. The value $K_\sharp$ is the estimation of the asymptotic condition number. We have checked on a wide range of examples that the value $K_\sharp$ is a good estimation for the theoretical condition numbers. For many applications, the theoretical condition number is not known: this occurs, for instance, for defective eigenvalues, where only upper bounds are available. PRECISE can provide the order of magnitude for condition numbers of nonlinear problems when the theoretical formulae are lacking.

iii) The third characteristic of PRECISE is its ability to determine the *dangerous border*, which we interpret as the *the distance to singularity viewed by the computer*. For nonlinear problems that are not smooth but remain well posed, the dangerous border t_0 indicates the change into a less regular problem. The dangerous border can be interpreted as the size of perturbation for which the process is seen as singular by the computer. There may exist more than one dangerous border. This shows the ability of PRECISE to describe accurately the subtle and complex reality of finite precision computations.

9.8   Bibliographical comments

It is common wisdom among numerical analysts not to attempt to compute a Jordan form because it is a difficult ill-posed problem. However, there are important applications—in mechanics, for example—where the knowledge of the structure of the underlying exact Jordan form is important (Sanchez-Hubert and Sanchez-Palencia (1989)). The basic reference about the unfolding in exact arithmetic of a Jordan form is Arnold (1971).

Chapter 10

Robustness to Nonnormality

It has long been known that nonnormal matrices can exhibit spectral instability (Henrici (1962a), van der Sluis (1975), Chatelin (1988c, 1993a, 1993b)). However, nonnormality was not until recently considered seriously by practitioners, but in the past few years, problems arising from high technology (Braconnier, Chatelin, and Dunyach (1995)) and theoretical physics (Reddy (1991), Kerner (1989)) have emerged and display a departure from normality that can be exponentially growing with some parameter. The question of their computational treatment therefore requires attention. In this chapter, we address in turn the following four questions:

   i) what is a measure of nonnormality?
   ii) where do highly nonnormal matrices come from?
   iii) what is the influence of nonnormality on numerical stability in exact arithmetic?
   iv) what is its influence on the reliability of numerical software?

10.1 Nonnormality and spectral instability

10.1.1 Spectral instability

A *normal* matrix is the most general matrix enjoying a diagonal Schur form. Therefore, all its eigenvalues and eigenvectors are well conditioned: a normal matrix is stable with respect to spectral representation. A *nonnormal* matrix, on the other hand, has a triangular Schur form S, which can be derived from its Jordan form J in the following way. Let $A = XJX^{-1}$, where the Jordan form J is diagonal whenever A is diagonalizable. Consider the QR factorization of X; then

$$A = Q(RJR^{-1})Q^* = QSQ^*.$$

Therefore, the spectral instability of A depends on the ascents of the multiple defective eigenvalues and the condition of the Jordan basis X (or equivalently $\operatorname{cond}(R) = \|R\|\|R^{-1}\|$).

159

The matrices that occur in practice often depend, implicitly or explicitly, on one or several parameters, which can be the order n, the matrix A itself, or a physical parameter such as the Reynolds number or the Péclet number. Whenever the spectral instability of the family of matrices under consideration is such that the ascent of at least one eigenvalue is unbounded[1] and/or the condition number of the Jordan basis is unbounded under the parameter variation, we shall say—in a somewhat loose sense—that this family of matrices is *highly nonnormal*.

10.1.2   Measures of nonnormality

Nonnormal matrices with well-conditioned eigenvalues are computationally easy to handle, so a good measure of nonnormality should reflect how ill conditioned the spectral decomposition is. This is not easy. The two following indicators have been proposed by Henrici (1962a):

   i) $\nu(A) = \|AA^* - A^*A\|$, directly computable from A,

   ii) $\Delta(A) = \|N\|$, where N is the strictly triangular part of the Schur form $S = D + N$, which is of theoretical interest.

They have been related to the conditioning of the eigenbasis when A is diagonalizable (Smith (1967)). Let λ be a *simple* eigenvalue of the diagonalizable matrix A. We denote the distance of λ to the rest of the spectrum of A by $d = \min_i |\lambda - \lambda_i|$. If x (resp., x_*) is the right (resp., left) eigenvector associated with λ, then the absolute spectral condition number of λ is

$$C(\lambda) = \frac{\|x\|_2 \|x_*\|_2}{|x_*^* x|}.$$

Smith (1967) proved that

$$C(\lambda) \leq \left[1 + \frac{1}{n-1} \left(\frac{\|N\|_F}{d} \right)^2 \right]^{(n-1)/2} \leq e^{(1/2)(\|N\|_F/d)^2}.$$

Therefore, the more ill conditioned λ, the larger the ratio $\|N\|_F/d$, which means that $\|N\|_F$ increases and/or the distance d to the rest of the spectrum decreases (λ tends to be a multiple eigenvalue).

Moreover, if *all* the eigenvalues λ_j of A are *simple*, Wilkinson (1965) proved that

$$\inf_X \operatorname{cond}_F(X) = \sum_{j=1}^n C(\lambda_j) = \gamma;$$

then we have

$$\gamma = \sum_{j=1}^n C(\lambda_j) \leq \left(1 + \frac{1}{n-1} \|N\|_F^2 \sum_{j=1}^n \frac{1}{d_j^2} \right)^{(n-1)/2} \leq \prod_{j=1}^n e^{(1/2)(\|N\|_F/d_j)^2}.$$

---

[1]The ascent of an eigenvalue can grow without limit only for matrices of unlimited order n, $n \to \infty$.

Then the quantity γ is large if and only if the Frobenius condition number of the eigenbasis is large, and if γ is large, then one $\tilde{a}_j$ (at least) is small and/or $\|N\|_F$ is large.

The quantity $\nu(A)$ is computable but not homogeneous in A. Since $\nu(A) \leq 2\|A^*A\| \leq 2\|A\|^2$, only the homogeneous ratio $\nu(A)/\|A^2\|$ is possibly unbounded. We introduced in Chatelin and Fraysse (1993c) the following definition.

Definition 10.1 *The quantity*

$$\text{He}(A) = \frac{\nu(A)}{\|A^2\|}$$

is the Henrici number *associated with* A.

Whenever $\text{He}(A)$ is large, A exhibits spectral instability. Indeed, if A is diagonalizable, then (Smith (1967))

$$\text{cond}(X) \geq \left(1 + \frac{1}{2}\text{He}(A)\right)^{1/4}.$$

Examples of linear growth for $\text{He}(A)$ are the Schur matrix (Example 6.2) and the Tolosa matrix (Duff, Grimes, and Lewis (1992)). This inequality shows that when He increases, the condition number of the eigenbasis also increases, but it is important to realize that, conversely, for a diagonalizable matrix A, a large condition number for the *eigenbasis may not be* an indication of a *large* departure from normality. If $\text{cond}(X)$ is large for a diagonalizable matrix, this may indicate only that the eigenvalue problem is at the edge of singularity. At least two simple eigenvalues with almost parallel eigenvectors coalesce into a double defective eigenvalue. A is close to a defective matrix. This does not require that A is pathologically nonnormal. The following example illustrates this point.

Example 10.1 (Chatelin (1988c)).
Consider the matrix

$$A = \begin{pmatrix} a & c \\ 0 & b \end{pmatrix}.$$

Its departure from normality is $|c|$, and both $\nu_F(A) = \sqrt{2}|c|\sqrt{c^2 + (b-a)^2}$ and $\text{He}^2(A) = \frac{2c^2(c^2+(b-a)^2)}{a^2+b^2+(a+b)^2c^2}$ are increasing functions of c. If b is distinct from a, we can write the eigendecomposition

$$A = XDX^{-1} = \begin{pmatrix} 1 & 1 \\ 0 & \dfrac{b-a}{c} \end{pmatrix} \begin{pmatrix} a & 0 \\ 0 & b \end{pmatrix} \begin{pmatrix} 1 & \dfrac{c}{a-b} \\ 0 & \dfrac{b-a}{c} \end{pmatrix}.$$

If $b = a$, the Jordan decomposition of A is

$$A = X'JX'^{-1} = \begin{pmatrix} 1 & 1 \\ 0 & \dfrac{1}{c} \end{pmatrix} \begin{pmatrix} a & 1 \\ 0 & a \end{pmatrix} \begin{pmatrix} 1 & -c \\ 0 & c \end{pmatrix}.$$

We then have

$$
\begin{aligned}
\mathrm{cond}_2^2(X) &\leq \mathrm{cond}_F^2(X) = \left[2 + \left(\frac{b-a}{c}\right)^2\right]\left[1 + \left(\frac{c}{a-b}\right)^2 + \left(\frac{b-a}{c}\right)^2\right] \\
&\leq n^2\mathrm{cond}_2^2(X), \\
\mathrm{cond}_2^2(X') &\leq \mathrm{cond}_F^2(X') = \left[2 + \frac{1}{c^2}\right][1 + 2c^2] \leq n^2\mathrm{cond}_2^2(X').
\end{aligned}
$$

1) If c is fixed, and b tends to a, we see that $\mathrm{cond}_2(X)$ tends to be infinite, although $\nu_F(A)$ decreases towards its limit $\sqrt{2}c^2$ and He tends to $\frac{c^2}{|a|}\frac{1}{\sqrt{1+2c^2}}$. The matrix A has a very ill conditioned eigenbasis but a *bounded* departure from normality.

2) If $|c|$ increases, $\mathrm{cond}(X)$ for $b \neq a$ or $\mathrm{cond}(X')$ for $b = a$ increases, as does $\nu_F(A)$. He increases like $\frac{\sqrt{2}c}{a+b}$ if $a \neq b$ and like $\frac{c^2}{|a|}$ if $a = -b$. $\triangle$

However, the above indicators $\nu(A)$, $\Delta(A)$, and $He(A)$ may fail to fully reflect the spectral instability as illustrated here.

Example 10.2

Consider the family of matrices $A_n = QJ_nQ^*$, where J_n is a Jordan block of order n defined by

$$
J_n = \begin{pmatrix}
0 & 1 & 0 & 0 & 0 \\
\vdots & 0 & 1 & \ddots & 0 \\
\vdots & & \ddots & \ddots & 0 \\
\vdots & & \cdots & 0 & 1 \\
0 & 0 & \cdots & 0 & 0
\end{pmatrix}
$$

and Q is a unitary $n \times n$ matrix. J_n is the Jordan form of A_n and has the eigenvalue 0 with ascent n. Therefore, the sensitivity of this eigenvalue to perturbations of size ε in A_n is $\varepsilon^{1/n}$: it increases exponentially with n. However, $\nu(A_n) = \|A_nA_n^* - A_n^*A_n\|_2 = 1$ and $\Delta(A_n) = \|A_n\|_2 = 1$ for all n. Moreover, $\|A_n^2\|_2 = 1$, so $He(A_n)$ is also constant at 1 as $n \to \infty$. We illustrate the high sensitivity of the zero eigenvalue by computing the eigenvalues of A_n by QR for $n = 10, 50, 200$, and 500. It is known that the Toeplitz operator J, which is the limit in l^2 of J_n as $n \to \infty$, has a continuous spectrum which consists of the closed unit disk (Chatelin (1983)). The computed spectra are plotted in Figure 10.1. The difference that we see between the exact eigenvalue 0 and the n computed ones is only the effect of spectral instability because QR is backward stable, and the backward error is of order of machine precision. It is clear that as n increases, most of the computed eigenvalues tend first to cluster on a circle centered at 0, with radius converging to 1 as n increases, and gradually to fill the interior for much larger values of n. $\triangle$

The exponential spectral instability exhibited above by A_n may seem overwhelming for large n. However, any property is two sided, and a more optimistic view can be derived from a look at the alternate perspective: use the computed eigenvalues of A_n to approximate the continuous spectrum of the Toeplitz operator J. In exact arithmetic, the task is hopeless for any finite n: 0 is always at distance 1 from the border of the unit disk, but in finite precision, the spectral information delivered by a reliable software converges toward the

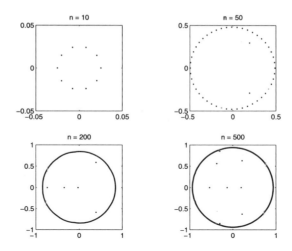

FIG. 10.1. *Eigenvalues of A_n computed with QR.*

continuous spectrum as $n \to \infty$. The spectral information computed from A_n is already qualitatively very good for $n = 500$ (which is small when compared with infinity!).

10.1.3 A look at the Harwell–Boeing collection

Listed in Table 10.1 are the values of the three quantities $\|A\|$, $\nu(A)$, and He(A) (computed with the Frobenius norm) for a sample of 10 matrices taken from the Harwell–Boeing collection (Duff, Grimes, and Lewis (1992)).

It should be clear from a look at this sample that the question of getting a reliable measure of the nonnormality without computing the spectral decomposition can be hard. Indeed for half of the matrices, the Henrici number He(A) is small or moderate, whereas all values of $\nu_F(A)$ and $\|A\|_F$ are significantly large, but the perturbed spectra confirm that all spectra are unstable.

Matrix Id	Size	$\|A\|_F$	$\nu_F(A)$	He$_F(A)$
MCCA	180	2.3×10^{19}	4.5×10^{32}	0.1×10^{-5}
IMPCOL E	225	1.58×10^{4}	1.11×10^{8}	95
WEST0497	497	1.22×10^{6}	9.5×10^{11}	281
WEST0655	655	7.10×10^{5}	2.7×10^{11}	1016
FS 183 1	183	1.1×10^{9}	8.6×10^{13}	4.5×10^{7}
LNS 511	511	1.0×10^{11}	2.7×10^{21}	7.6×10^{8}
LNSP 131	131	1.5×10^{10}	1.6×10^{20}	3×10^{9}
GRE 216B	216	14.3	13.9	0.8
PORES 1	30	3.7×10^{7}	7.1×10^{14}	0.8
ARC 130	130	4.9×10^{5}	1.5×10^{11}	1.5×10^{5}

TABLE 10.1

10.1.4   Perturbed spectra, pseudospectra, and spectral portraits

One reliable way to investigate computationally spectral instability is to test the sensitivity of the eigenvalues to perturbations ΔA on A, i.e., to compute the spectrum of $A + \Delta A$ by means of a *backward stable* algorithm such as QR or Arnoldi–Tchebycheff, as already illustrated in Example 10.2. In this example, the perturbation ΔA is not imposed a priori but results from the finite precision.

Such a technique is in the module of PRECISE for sensitivity analysis, where ΔA are real random perturbations of A. The perturbed spectra are related to the theoretically defined set

$$\sigma_\varepsilon(A) = \{z \in \mathbb{C};\ z \text{ is an eigenvalue of } A + \Delta A,\ \|\Delta A\| \le \varepsilon\|A\|\},$$

which is known as the *ε-pseudospectrum* of A (Varah (1979)). Clearly, the larger this set in $\mathbb{C}$, the more unstable the eigenvalues. It will be proved in Chapter 11 that

$$\sigma_\varepsilon(A) = \left\{z \in \mathbb{C};\ \|(A - zI)^{-1}\| \ge \frac{1}{\varepsilon\|A\|}\right\}.$$

The contour line $\{z \in \mathbb{C};\ \|(A - zI)^{-1}\| = \frac{1}{\varepsilon\|A\|}\}$ is then the border of the ε-pseudospectrum, and for nonnormal matrices, $\|(A - zI)^{-1}\|$ can be large even at points z that are far from eigenvalues. This appears clearly on the map $z \longmapsto \log_{10}(\|(A - zI)^{-1}\|\|A\|)$, which is called the spectral portrait of the matrix A (Godunov (1992b)). Reliable algorithms to compute spectral portraits for large matrices are devised in Marques and Toumazou (1995a, 1995b).

In concluding this section, we can say that the question of defining a reliable measure of nonnormality is still largely open. It may be necessary in practice to turn to more expensive tools such as perturbed spectra or spectral portraits to analyse the spectral instability of highly nonnormal matrices. Such tools can be found in the second module of PRECISE, to be presented in Chapter 11.

It is now time to look at the basic question, where do the highly nonnormal matrices that emerge in science and technology come from?

10.2   Nonnormality in physics and technology

The matrices that occur in physics are often discretizations of a partial differential operator, and their nonnormality can be inherited from the one of the operator. In the physical and mechanical examples cited below, the essential ingredient is that the *spectrum* of a family of operators depending on a parameter exhibits a *severe discontinuity* as the parameter varies. This can occur when the model describes a strong coupling between two physical phenomena, giving rise to physical instabilities.

Example 10.3 A one-dimensional convection-diffusion operator (Reddy and Trefethen (1994).
Consider the one-dimensional convection-diffusion operator defined in $L^2(0, d)$ by

$$T_d u = u'' + u, \qquad u(0) = u(d) = 0.$$

For any finite d, the spectrum of T_d consists of real eigenvalues with finite multiplicity $\lambda_n = -\frac{1}{4} - \frac{\pi^2}{d^2} n^2$, $n = 1, 2, \ldots$. The limiting case $d = \infty$ is set in $L^2(0, \infty)$ and corresponds to the single boundary condition $u(0) = 0$. It can be shown that the spectrum of T_∞ is now the region Π of $\mathbb{C}$ enclosed by the parabola $P = \{z \in \mathbb{C}; \ z = -\alpha^2 + i\alpha, \ \alpha \in \mathbb{R}\}$. This shows that the spectrum $\sigma(T_d)$ of T_d is highly discontinuous in the limit when $d \to \infty$. As a result, for z inside the parabola P, $\|(T_d - zI)^{-1}\|$ can be large even for z far away from eigenvalues. Indeed Reddy and Trefethen (1994) show that the ε-pseudospectrum of T_d is such that

$$\sigma_\varepsilon(T_d) \subseteq \sigma_\varepsilon(T_\infty) = \Pi + \Delta_\varepsilon \text{ with } \Delta_\varepsilon = \{z; \ |z| \leq \varepsilon\}.$$

The spectra are discontinuous as $d \to \infty$, but the ε-pseudospectra are shown to be continuous. The same analysis carries over to the operator with explicit convection and diffusion parameters—that is, $S(\delta, \nu, c)u = \nu u'' + cu'$, $u(0) = u(\delta)$—provided that the previous parameter d is replaced by the Péclet number $\text{Pe} = \delta c / \nu$. Note that Pe is large for a fixed δ when c is large and/or ν is small.

The consequence is that even on a finite interval $[0, \delta]$, when convection is dominant (c/ν large), predictions of numerical behaviour, such as $\|(S(\delta, \nu, c) - zI)^{-1}\|$ small for z different from an eigenvalue, based on the exact spectrum that lies on the real axis, are likely to be misleading for z inside the parabola, as illustrated in Reddy and Trefethen (1994).   △

Example 10.4 Controlled fusion of plasma (Kerner (1986, 1989)).
The resistive magnetohydrodynamics theory combines fluid equations and Maxwell's equation, where the resistivity is a parameter that ideally tends to 0. The ideal nondissipative magnetohydrodynamics spectrum has three completely different branches: the fast and slow magnetoacoustic and the Alfvén waves. With a small resistivity the spectrum is drastically changed, and in addition, new instabilities cause the plasma to break away from the magnetic field. Kerner (1986, 1989) deals with the computation of such unstable spectra associated with highly nonnormal matrices. △

Example 10.5 Flutter (Braconnier, Chatelin, and Dunyach (1995)).
The flutter phenomenon occurs in structural mechanics combined with aerodynamics. It is a dynamic instability that can occur in structures in motion subject to aerodynamic loading. It is a self-induced vibrational motion initiated by a source of energy external to the structure. For a wing, it occurs when a torsional vibration is in phase with the flexion motion. This coupling may occur during particular flight conditions (dependent on such things as the speed of the plane and the air density). This is the type of phenomenon that aircraft designers seek to eliminate as much as possible. Much of their work is concerned with ensuring stability of airplanes at all times, speeds, and altitude ranges. The modelling of the flutter phenomenon also gives rise to highly nonnormal matrices, described in Bennani, Braconnier, and Dunyach (1994)

and Braconnier, Chatelin, and Dunyach (1995). One of such matrices, known as Tolosa, is in the Harwell–Boeing collection (Duff, Grimes, and Lewis (1992)). △

10.3 Convergence of numerical methods in exact arithmetic

The coupling between physical phenomena is often transferred in the numerical approximation of evolution equations as a requirement for a coupling between parameters such as time and space mesh sizes to ensure numerical stability. Without a proper restriction on the discretization sizes, the numerical method can be unstable. Thus we expect that nonnormality in physics may have an impact on the numerical stability of the approximation methods whenever this stability is conditional to the parameters of the method.

This is indeed the case. For example, it has long been well known that for fully discrete evolution equations, the condition that requires that the spectrum of the spatial discretization matrix lies in the stability region for the time-stepping formula is only a *necessary* condition for stability whenever the continuous operator is nonnormal. Recently, Reddy and Trefethen (1990, 1992) have proposed a *necessary and sufficient* condition by means of the ε-pseudospectra.

More generally, the realization that when there is spectral discontinuity with respect to a parameter, there can be nevertheless continuity for the pseudospectra, led Trefethen (1992) to propose what can be called the *Trefethen principle*:

> Conditions for convergence of numerical methods should be based on *pseudospectra* rather than on exact spectra.

Trefethen applies his principle to the analysis of the convergence, in *exact arithmetic*, of numerical methods for various partial differential equations, mainly in computational fluid dynamics (Trefethen, et al. (1993)). Trefethen's principle is also well popularized in a *SIAM News* article, "Are Eigenvalues Overvalued?" (Cipra (1995)).

An area of computational physics where nonnormality is encountered not infrequently is computational fluid dynamics. For example, it occurs in the study of parallel shear flows in fluid dynamics, whose behaviour is governed by the Orr–Sommerfeld operator (see Drazin and Reid (1981)). The discretization of this nonnormal operator leads to a nonnormal matrix whose departure from nonnormality increases with the Reynolds number of the flow (Reddy (1991)).

There are interesting consequences of nonnormality for hydrodynamic stability (Trefethen, et al. (1993)). In order to explain the discrepancy between the computational predictions of the eigenvalue analysis and laboratory experiments in certain flows, called "subcritical transition to turbulence," one traditionally blames it on a failure of the linearization about the laminar solution, recommending that we look closer at the nonlinear terms or linearize about another solution ("secondary instability"). Recently, the complementary view that the cause might sometimes be found also in the high nonnormality of the linearized problem has emerged. Schmid and Henningson (1992) and Gustavsson (1991) proved that the operators that arise in Poiseuille and Couette flows are in a sense *exponentially* far from normal. Hence the stability analysis cannot be based on the exact spectrum, but should be based on the pseudospectra (Trefethen, et al. (1993)). This seems to be a very promising new direction in computational turbulence.

When the nonnormality is not in the mathematical equation but in the approximation method, one should also be cautious, as is illustrated by the fully discrete spectral approximation of a first-order mixed initial boundary value problem devised by Trefethen and Trummer (1987). With the Chebyshev collocation method in space, they show that the numerical stability of the discretization in space coupled with the discretization in time is at risk because the differentiation matrix is nonnormal: it is a low-rank perturbation of a fully defective Jordan block. (See Example 2.10 for numerical illustrations.) Numerical stability in exact arithmetic is guaranteed only with an appropriate coupling between time and space steps.

10.4   Influence on numerical software

The negative influence of nonnormality on the numerical stability of approximation methods in *exact arithmetic* has been known for a long time (see Godunov and Ryabenki (1964), for example). In comparison, the influence of nonnormality on the reliability of numerical methods in *finite precision* seems to be much less widely appreciated.

This should not be the case because the underlying phenomenon is essentially of the same mathematical nature in both cases. It is rooted in the spectral instability of the problem and therefore in the sensitivity of the spectrum of the corresponding operator or matrix.

The perturbations generated by numerical methods in *exact arithmetic* arise from the approximation of $F(x) = y$ by $F_i(x_h) = y_h$. The perturbations in *finite precision* take into account, in addition, the parameter ε of the arithmetic. The two situations can be analysed in the unified framework presented in Chapter 2 by adding the arithmetic parameter ε to the list of convergence parameters for the numerical method.

The essential role of the spectral decomposition in the analysis of evolution equations implies that spectral sensitivity can be a crucial issue for numerical stability in exact as well as in finite precision. Spectral instability often comes from the discontinuity of the spectrum with respect to some parameter. The parameter can come from physics (convection in Example 10.3), the numerical method (Example 2.10), or the arithmetic (Example 10.8, on the Schur matrix).

However, we saw in Chapter 6 that finite precision can affect the convergence of numerical methods in two ways: i) the condition for convergence and ii) the quality of convergence. There is ample theoretical and experimental evidence that both *algorithms and iterative solvers* can be affected by high nonnormality when run in finite precision: their reliability can decrease severely.

This is a new phenomenon in finite precision: it does not take place in exact arithmetic (Chaitin-Chatelin and Gratton (1995)).

In addition, iterative methods can also be affected when the condition for convergence is not robust enough to perturbations generated by finite precision, resulting in a divergence in finite precision arithmetic even though the condition for convergence is well satisfied in exact arithmetic. Then, Trefethen's principle is also often the key to analysis of the convergence condition of numerical methods in *finite precision*, as we illustrate in Chapter 11, Example 11.4.

10.4.1 Reliability

The reliability or backward stability of algorithms and iterative methods can be analysed by means of the backward error at the computed solution. The backward stability follows usually from a bound of the type

$$\text{backward error} \leq C(n, A) \, \Psi,$$

where C is a constant that depends on the details of the arithmetic, the order n, and possibly on the matrix A.

1) When the constant C does not depend on A, then the reliability of the method is unaffected by nonnormality. This is the case for

  i) algorithms for $Ax = b$, such as LU with complete pivoting, QR factorization, and Hessenberg–Arnoldi implemented with H/G transformations or with iterative MGS (IMGS),

  ii) iterative methods for $Ax = \lambda x$, such as the QR algorithm.

Remark: This empirical result for the QR algorithm can be challenged by mathematical counterexamples. To be mathematically founded, it would require a complete proof of unconditional convergence for the multishifted algorithm. A 3×3 counterexample that makes QR diverge has been given in Batterson (1990) (see also the footnote on page 8). A complete theory of global convergence for QR is lacking. We must content ourselves with the overwhelming practical evidence of convergence to machine precision.

2) When the constant C depends on A, the above factorizations could be affected by high nonnormality. This is the case for finite algorithms such as QR factorization and Hessenberg–Arnoldi decomposition when they are implemented with MGS. This is also the rule for most iterative methods that converge under some condition on A.

The influence of the presence of A in the convergence condition is discussed later (§ 10.4.2). We present an example of the role of A in the backward stability of an algorithm: the Hessenberg decomposition of A by the Arnoldi scheme. It has been known since their introduction by Saad (1992) that nonsymmetric Krylov-based methods are sensitive to the quality of the orthogonal basis in the Krylov subspace. Recently, the backward stability of several implementations of the Hessenberg–Arnoldi factorization has been analysed (Arioli and Fassino (1994), Bennani and Braconnier (1994b), Drkosova, et al. (1995), Greenbaum and Strakoš (1994), Greenbaum, Ptak, and Strakoš (1995)). We illustrate the numerical behaviour of three variants on the Schur matrix introduced in Example 6.2.

Example 10.6 Hessenberg–Arnoldi decomposition on Schur (Bennani and Braconnier (1994b), Braconnier (1994b)).

For S_ν, $\nu_F(S_\nu) = O(\nu^2)$ and $\|S_\nu\|_F^2 = O(\nu)$, so $\text{He}(\nu) = O(\nu)$ as $\nu \to \infty$. We set $A = QS_\nu Q^*$. The Arnoldi scheme for the Hessenberg decomposition of A computes an orthonormal basis V_m of size $m \times n$ for the Krylov subspace based on $u \neq 0$ of dimension m (see Example 6.2 for the notations). We let the dimension m increase from 1 to n. We define $H^{(m+1)}$ as the $(m+1) \times m$ matrix obtained by adding to H_m the $(m+1)$st row $(0, \ldots, 0, h_{m+1m})$. Then (6.1) can be rewritten as $AV_m = V_{m+1}H^{(m+1)}$. We now define $A^{(m+1)}$ as the $n \times (m+1)$ matrix defined by $[u, AV_m]$, where u is the starting vector for the Krylov subspace. It can be verified that Arnoldi is equivalent to the QR factorization of $A^{(m+1)}$, that is, $A^{(m+1)} = V_{m+1}R^{(m+1)}$, where $R^{(m+1)} = [\|u\|_2 e_1, H^{(m+1)}]$ is the $(m+1) \times (m+1)$ triangular factor of $A^{(m+1)}$. It is therefore understandable that the Arnoldi scheme and the QR factorization have the same numerical behaviour. We illustrate this fact in the three implementations:

  i) Householder (H),
  ii) MGS,
  iii) IMGS.

We choose $n = 100$, $\nu = 10^{-7}$, 10, 150, and 10^5 and apply the Arnoldi scheme with the three different orthogonalization strategies iteratively for $m = 1, 2, \ldots$ up to $n = 100$. For each m, the eigenvalues of H_m are computed by the QR algorithm to produce the four eigenvalues of largest modulus as approximations of λ_j, $\bar{\lambda}_j$, $j = 1, 2$. We make a comparative study, for varying values of ν, of the loss of orthogonality, the backward stability of the Hessenberg decomposition, and the backward error on the four computed eigenvalues as m increases from 1 to 100.

Each property is quantified respectively by

- $\omega_m = \|\widetilde{V}_m^* \widetilde{V}_m - I\|_2$ for the loss of orthogonality,
- $\beta_m = \|A\widetilde{V}_m - \widetilde{V}_{m+1}\widetilde{H}^{(m+1)}\|_F / \|A\|_F$ for the backward stability[2] of the incomplete Hessenberg decomposition (proof in Bennani and Braconnier (1994b)),
- $\eta_m = \max_{j=1,2} \|A\tilde{x}_j - \tilde{\lambda}_j \tilde{x}_j\|_2 / (\|A\|_F \|\tilde{x}_j\|_2)$ for the backward error associated with $(\tilde{\lambda}_j, \tilde{x}_j)$, $j = 1, 2$.

A look at Figures 10.2–10.4 confirms the following three facts:

1. The loss of orthogonality for MGS increases with ν, whereas H and IMGS offer a comparable quality of orthogonality at machine precision.
2. Implementations with H and IMGS are equally backward stable (only the results for $\nu = 10^5$ are displayed). One cannot make any conclusions for MGS because β_m is only a lower bound for the backward error when $\widetilde{V}_m$ is not orthogonal (see the footnote below and Figure 10.2 for $\nu = 10^5$).
3. The convergence (with respect to m) of the four dominant computed eigenvalues is delayed when ν increases for H and IMGS. Divergence occurs for MGS for $\nu = 150$ and 10^5. $\triangle$

---

[2]If $\widetilde{V}_m$ is not orthonormal to working accuracy, β_m is a *lower bound* for the backward error; cf. MGS.

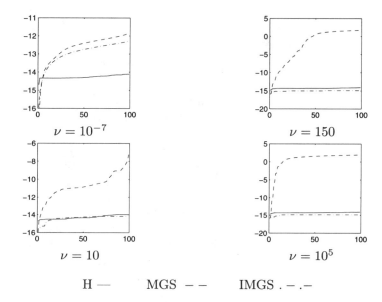

H —   MGS − −   IMGS . − .−

FIG. 10.2.   *Loss of orthogonality:* $m \longmapsto \log_{10} \omega_m$.

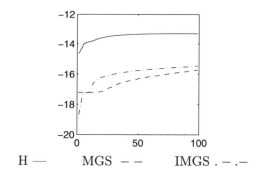

H —   MGS − −   IMGS . − .−

FIG.   10.3.   *Backward stability analysis*
for the Hessenberg decomposition for $\nu = 10^5$:
$m \longmapsto \log_{10} \beta_m$.

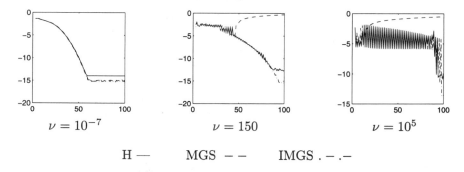

H —   MGS − −   IMGS . − .−

FIG. 10.4.   *Backward error on eigenelements* $m \longmapsto \log_{10} \eta_m$.

We complete the comparative study of the performance of the three implementations of the orthogonalization of the Krylov basis by displaying the computed spectra of the Schur matrix by the QR algorithm (as a reference) and by Arnoldi (in its three variants) plus the exact spectrum.

Example 10.7 Exact and computed spectra for Schur (Braconnier (1994b)). As before, we choose $n = 100$ and $\nu = 10$, 150, and 10^5. For $\nu = 10$, the exact spectrum of S_ν (o), the spectra computed by Arnoldi with H (+), IMGS (*), and MGS ($\times$) are shown in Figure 10.5. Figure 10.6 shows on the left (resp., right) for $\nu = 150$ (resp., $\nu = 10^5$) the exact spectrum of S_ν (o), the spectrum computed by Arnoldi with H (+) and IMGS (*). Displayed below are the spectrum of S_ν computed by Arnoldi with MGS ($\times$) together with the exact spectrum (o) for $\nu = 150$ and $\nu = 10^5$, respectively. From these illustrations, we conclude that

- Arnoldi with H or IMGS is almost as backward stable as QR. There is no significant difference between H and IMGS.
- As for Arnoldi with MGS, it is increasingly unreliable as ν increases.   △

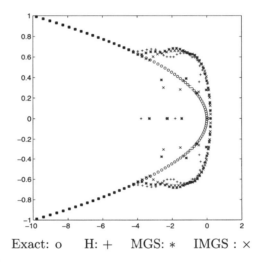

Exact: o   H: +   MGS: *   IMGS : ×

FIG. 10.5.   *Exact and computed spectra for Schur, $n = 100$, $\nu = 10$.*

10.4.2   Convergence condition for iterative methods

The convergence condition often takes the form of a requirement on the spectrum of A to lie in some stability region. If A has a high spectral sensitivity, the condition may not remain satisfied under the perturbations on A generated by finite precision computations.

An example of diverging successive iterations on a matrix A such that $\rho(A) < 0.41$ in exact arithmetic is given in Example 6.4. We complement this example with an illustration of the spectral instability of the Schur matrix.

Example 10.8 Perturbed spectra for Schur (Chatelin (1993a)). Figure 10.7 displays the perturbed spectra, that is, for $A = S_\nu$, the computed spectra of $A + \Delta A$, where ΔA is the family of normwise perturbations given by PRECISE, $t = 2^{-p}$, $p = 40$ to 50 by a step of 2. The sample size is 10, $n = 20$, and $\nu = 1$, 10,

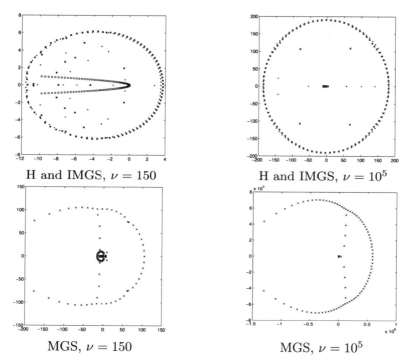

FIG. 10.6. *Exact (o) and computed spectra: H (+), IMGS (*), and MGS (×).* $\nu = 150$ *and* $\nu = 10^5$, $n = 100$.

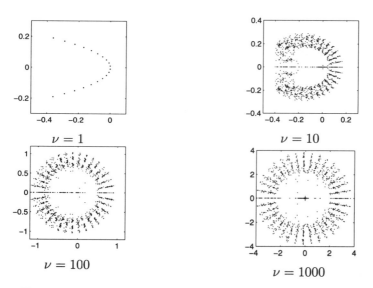

FIG. 10.7. *Normwise perturbed spectra for Schur,* $n = 20$.

100, and 1000. The results with componentwise perturbations are similar. The high spectral instability of Schur is spectacular. △

For $Ax = \lambda x$, subspace iteration converges under a separation condition on the spectrum (Chatelin (1988c, 1993a)). The influence of nonnormality on the convergence of Tchebycheff-subspace iteration is exposed in Bennani and Braconnier (1994a).

10.4.3 Conclusion

We have shown that high nonnormality can occur in physics and technology whenever there is a strong coupling between phenomena giving rise to physical instabilities. Therefore, high nonnormality should be taken seriously in numerical software since it may affect the reliability and the convergence of numerical methods when run on a computer in finite precision arithmetic.

10.5 Bibliographical comments

As a rule, the influence of nonnormality has been mostly ignored in both exact and floating-point arithmetic, with two major exceptions. In exact arithmetic, Trefethen's principle gives a necessary and sufficient condition for the convergence of certain numerical methods for evolution equations (Trefethen, et al. (1993).

In finite precision, Chatelin and her co-workers were the first to point out and analyse the decrease in the convergence quality of numerical software in the presence of nonnormality (Chatelin (1993a, 1993b), Chaitin-Chatelin (1994a, 1995b), Bennani and Braconnier (1994a), Braconnier, Chatelin, and Dunyach (1995), Braconnier (1994b), Chaitin-Chatelin and Fraysse (1995), Chaitin-Chatelin and Gratton (1995)).

Chapter 11

Qualitative Computing

The first module of PRECISE is well suited for study of computations in the neighbourhood of a singularity. It allows us to describe the *local evolution* from a regular to a singular problem when perturbations increase in size. However, we have seen that under the influence of some parameter such as high nonnormality, the "computational diffusion" of a singularity may not remain local. It can become *global* by affecting the whole spectrum, as was illustrated by the evolution, with ν, of the computed spectrum of the Schur matrix (Chapter 10, Examples 10.7 and 10.8). Another extreme example is the computed logistic equation (Chapter 2), where, for some values of the evolution parameter, all digits of the computed iterates are wrong after as few as 100 steps.

In these extreme situations—so extreme that they have been called chaotic—the mathematical or numerical instability is so high that we cannot hope for a conventional control of the computation error, as was possible in less ill conditioned situations. Classical computation becomes meaningless because none of the digits in the results are correct. Such computations are so challenging that they have been called "impossible" (Ekeland (1984), Chatelin (1989a)). However, there exists a broad spectrum of intermediate situations between right and wrong on the computer. In *qualitative computing*, the aim is no longer to control the computing error (it does not tend to zero) but rather to extract meaning from results that appear classically as "wrong." When the computation cannot deliver full information on the exact solution because the problem is singular, then the computation—by means of a backward stable method—can still deliver relevant *partial information* about the singularity.

The second module of PRECISE, the module for sensitivity analysis, consists of tools that can be helpful in the extreme situations faced by qualitative computing. They include sets of pseudosolutions and sensitivity portraits, spectral portraits, pseudospectra, and perturbed spectra that we describe here.

11.1   Sensitivity and pseudosolutions for $F(x) = y$

The backward error $B(\tilde{x})$ at the approximate solution $\tilde{x}$ for the equation $F(x) = y$ has been defined as the size of the perturbation of F and y such that $\tilde{x}$ is the exact solution for the perturbed equation. The explicit formula for $B(\tilde{x})$ depends on the type of norms and perturbations that are chosen to define (τ).

Definition 11.1 *The set of ε-pseudosolutions for $F(x) = y$ is given by*

$$\Sigma_\varepsilon(x) = \{z; \ B(z) \leq \varepsilon\}.$$

Two examples of pseudosolutions have already been encountered:
- pseudotrajectories for the logistic (Chapter 6),
- pseudospectra for matrices (Chapter 10).

The set of ε-pseudosolutions represents all the solutions of $F(x) = y$ that can be computed by an algorithm or a method that produces a backward error less than ε when solving $F(x) = y$. In particular, if the computed solution $\tilde{x}$ is such that $B(\tilde{x}) = \varepsilon$, then $\Sigma_\varepsilon(x)$ represents the set of points z in the neighbourhood of x that are indistinguishable from x by the computation. The notion is related to that of *domain of uncertainty* for the root x (van der Sluis (1970)). The larger the set $\Sigma_\varepsilon(x)$ around x, the more unstable the equation $F(x) = y$ at x. The knowledge of x is not required; it is sufficient that the set $\Sigma_\varepsilon(x)$ be "fat."

It may be interesting to look at the border $\partial\Sigma_\varepsilon(x)$ of $\Sigma_\varepsilon(x)$ and determine whether it encloses a large region. When the border $\partial\Sigma_\varepsilon(x)$ is not computable because, for example, one has no explicit formula for the backward error or because each component of $B(\tilde{x})$ depends on the whole vector $\tilde{x}$, one can alternatively plot the sample of perturbed computed solutions obtained by random perturbations of the data of amplitude less than ε.

Example 11.1

Consider a linear system $Ax = b$. The componentwise backward error at $\tilde{x}$ can be taken as the vector $B(\tilde{x}) = (|r_i|/(|A||\tilde{x}| + |b|)_i)_{i=1,\dots,n}$. Here, the ith component of $\partial\Sigma_\varepsilon$ depends on the whole vector $\tilde{x}$. Figure 11.1 shows how the first computed entry of the solution of the system $Ax = b$ evolves under componentwise perturbations of A. The matrix A is IPJ of order 7 (see Chapter 9), and the right-hand side b is such that the exact solution is $x = [1 + i, -3 - 2i, 5 + 4i, 8, -7 + 3i, -10, 4 - 2i]^T$. The amplitude of the perturbations is $t = 2^{-p}$, p ranging from 40 to 50. For each perturbation size, we take a sample size of 20. We notice that the computed values are not uniformly distributed around the exact value $1 + i$. They tend to stay in alignment. $\triangle$

There are two problems that lend themselves very naturally to a graphical display of $\partial\Sigma_\varepsilon$. They consist of the computation of the spectrum $\sigma = \{\lambda_i\}_{i=1,\dots,n}$ of matrices, and of the set $Z = \{x_i\}_{i=1,\dots,n}$ of roots of polynomials, because both sets are in $\mathbb{C}$. We treat these two problems successively.

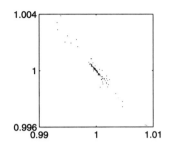

FIG. 11.1. *Perturbed solutions of a linear system (first component).*

11.2 Pseudospectra of matrices

11.2.1 Definitions

We consider the eigenproblem $Ax = \lambda x$. Associated with the approximate eigenpair $(\tilde{\lambda}, \tilde{x})$, one defines the residual $r = A\tilde{x} - \tilde{\lambda}\tilde{x}$. Formulae for the normwise and componentwise *relative* backward errors at $(\tilde{\lambda}, \tilde{x})$ have been given in Chapter 5.

Definition 11.2

i) *The* normwise ε-pseudospectrum *of A is defined as*

$$\sigma_\varepsilon^{\mathcal{N}}(A) = \left\{ z \in \mathbb{C}; \ \exists y \neq 0, \ B^{\mathcal{N}}(z) = \frac{\|r\|}{\alpha\|y\|} \leq \varepsilon \right\}$$

with $r = Ay - zy$.

ii) *The* componentwise ε-pseudospectrum *of A is defined as*

$$\sigma_\varepsilon^{\mathcal{C}}(A) = \left\{ z \in \mathbb{C}; \ \exists y \neq 0, \ B^{\mathcal{C}}(z) = \max_{i=1,\dots,n} \frac{|r_i|}{(E|y|)_i} \leq \varepsilon \right\}$$

with $r = Ay - zy$.

The following characterization for $\sigma_\varepsilon^{\mathcal{N}}(A)$ and $\sigma_\varepsilon^{\mathcal{C}}(A)$ is straightforward.

Proposition 11.1

i) $\sigma_\varepsilon^{\mathcal{N}}(A) = \{z$ eigenvalue of $A + \Delta A$ for all ΔA such that $\|\Delta A\| \leq \varepsilon\alpha\}$.

ii) $\sigma_\varepsilon^{\mathcal{C}}(A) = \{z$ eigenvalue of $A + \Delta A$ for all ΔA such that $\max_{i,j} \frac{|\Delta a_{ij}|}{e_{ij}} \leq \varepsilon\}$.

Proof: The proof follows immediately from the definition of the backward error. $\square$

Another characterization can be given by means of the following distances to singularity:

i) normwise: $\delta_T(A - zI) = \min\{\omega; \ \|\Delta A\| \leq \omega\alpha$ such that $A + \Delta A - zI$ is singular$\}$,

ii) componentwise: $\delta_B(A - zI) = \min\{\omega; \ |\Delta A| \leq \omega E$ such that $A + \Delta A - zI$ is singular$\}$.

Proposition 11.2

i) $\sigma_\varepsilon^{\mathcal{N}}(A) = \{z \in \mathbb{C}; \ \delta_T(A - zI) \leq \varepsilon\} = \{z \in \mathbb{C}; \ \|(A - zI)^{-1}\| \geq (\varepsilon\alpha)^{-1}\}$,

ii) $\sigma_\varepsilon^{\mathcal{C}}(A) = \{z \in \mathbb{C}; \ \delta_B(A - zI) \leq \varepsilon\}$.

Proof:

i) From the characterization of $\sigma_\varepsilon^N(A)$ given in Proposition 11.1, one sees that σ_ε^N consists of all z in $\mathbb{C}$ such that $A + \Delta A - zI$ is singular for $\|\Delta A\| \leq \varepsilon\alpha$. This means that the distance to singularity $\delta_T(A - zI)$ is less than or equal to ε.

Because $A + \Delta A - zI$ is singular, there exists $y \neq 0$ such that $(A + \Delta A - zI)y = 0$ or $(A - zI)y = -\Delta Ay$. Set $(A - zI)y - t$ with $\|y\| = 1$; then $\|t\| \leq \varepsilon\alpha$. Hence $y = (A - zI)^{-1}t$ and $\|(A - zI)^{-1}\| \geq \|y\|/\|t\| = 1/(\varepsilon\alpha)$. The reciprocal follows easily from $\delta_T(A - zI) = (\|(A - zI)^{-1}\|\alpha)^{-1}$ (Theorem 4.3).

ii) This part is similar to i). The quantity $\delta_B(A - zI)$ is no more easily computable (Theorem 4.4). $\square$

The borders $\partial\sigma_\varepsilon^N(A)$ and $\partial\sigma_\varepsilon^C(A)$ are defined by the curves $\{z \in \mathbb{C}; \alpha\|(A - zI)^{-1}\| = 1/\varepsilon\}$ and $\{z \in \mathbb{C}; \delta_B(A - zI) = 1/\varepsilon\}$, respectively. The border $\partial\sigma_\varepsilon^C(A)$ is not easy to compute, whether by means of Proposition 11.2ii) or of Definition 11.2ii) (y unknown), but the border $\partial\sigma_\varepsilon^N(A)$ is easily computable by means of the above characterization, using the $\| . \|_2$ norm, for example, and $\alpha = \|A\|_2$. This is our choice in the next section on spectral portraits.

11.2.2   Spectral portraits of matrices

The eigenvalues of A are the poles of the resolvent $(A - zI)^{-1}$ for z in $\mathbb{C}$; that is, they are the singular points of the map $A \longmapsto A - zI$.

The way by which $\|(A - zI)^{-1}\|_2$ decreases from infinity as z moves away from an eigenvalue λ is of theoretical and practical importance. Because the variation of $\|(A - zI)^{-1}\|_2$ in the neighbourhood of an eigenvalue is extremely steep, the level curves of $z \longmapsto \|A\|_2\|(A - zI)^{-1}\|_2$ corresponding to a uniform scale are not very informative. To circumvent this difficulty, one can consider instead an *exponential* scale, that is, a uniform scale for $\log_{10}\|A\|_2\|(A - zI)^{-1}\|_2 = \Phi(z)$.

Definition 11.3 *The graphical display of the map* $z \longmapsto \Phi(z)$ *around the eigenvalues of A is the* spectral portrait *of the matrix A.*

The spectral portrait provided by PRECISE uses colours or shades of grey to parameterize the values of $\Phi(z)$ at z. There is an option to plot the level curves $z \longmapsto \Phi(z) = $ constant.

The computation of $\Phi(z) = \log_{10}\sigma_{\max}(A)/\sigma_{\min}(A - zI)$ can be done by singular value decomposition for small matrices or by a complex Hermitian Lanczos algorithm on the augmented matrix

$$\begin{pmatrix} 0 & A - zI \\ A^H - \bar{z}I & 0 \end{pmatrix}$$

or with shift and invert on the normal formulation (Marques and Toumazou (1995a, 1995b)).

Example 11.2 Rose.

Figure 11.2 displays, in shades of grey (scale of 10 levels), the spectral portrait of Rose, the companion matrix associated with the monic polynomial $p(x) = (x -$

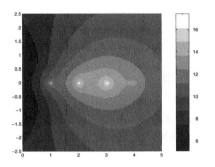

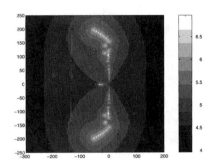

FIG. 11.2. *Spectral portrait of Rose.*

FIG. 11.3. *Spectral portrait of Tolosa.*

$1)^3(x-2)^3(x-3)^3(x-4) = x^{10} + \sum_{i=0}^{9} a_i x^i$. The 10 coefficients are $a_0 = 864$, $a_1 = -4968$, $a_2 = 12492$, $a_3 = -18086$, $a_4 = 16703$, $a_5 = -10290$, $a_6 = 4287$, $a_7 = -1194$, $a_8 = 213$, and $a_9 = -22$.

z varies in the square $[0,5] \times [-2.5, 2.5]$, and $\Phi(z)$ varies between 6 and 15. Although the triple roots play a symmetric role in $p(x)$, the corresponding triple eigenvalues have increasing Hölder condition numbers. The computational drift of the three singularities towards the simple eigenvalue 1 is clear.   △

Example 11.3 Tolosa.

The spectral portrait of Tolosa of order 135 from the Harwell–Boeing collection is displayed in Figure 11.3. z varies in a square $[-250, 250] \times [-300, 200]$, and $\Phi(z)$ varies in $[4, 7]$. All the eigenvalues of Tolosa are simple, but the eigenvalues of largest imaginary part are the most unstable. They are the one of interest to engineers. For $n = 135$, He(Tolosa) $= 7 \times 10^2$.   △

11.2.3   Normwise versus componentwise pseudospectra

For matrix computations whose asymptotic behaviour is ruled in *exact* arithmetic by the eigenvalue distribution, it may happen, in the case of high spectral instability, that in finite precision the asymptotic behaviour is no longer ruled by the exact eigenvalues but by the pseudoeigenvalues. Depending on the type of perturbations generated by the computation in finite precision, the pseudoeigenvalues may belong to the normwise or the componentwise pseudospectra. We now give an example to illustrate each case.

Example 11.4 Richardson's iteration (Trefethen (1990)).

We consider the system $Ex = b$, where $E = Q^*TQ$ is called Eccen in Trefethen. The matrix Q is orthonormal, and T is an upper triangular Toeplitz matrix defined by

$$T = T_n = \begin{bmatrix} 1 & \frac{3}{4} & \frac{3}{8} & \frac{3}{16} & \cdots & \frac{3}{2^n} \\ & 1 & \frac{3}{4} & \frac{3}{8} & \cdots & \cdots \\ & & 1 & \frac{3}{4} & \cdots & \cdots \\ & & & \ddots & \vdots & \vdots \\ & & & & \ddots & \frac{3}{4} \\ & & & & & 1 \end{bmatrix}_{n \times n}$$

In the computations, we choose a matrix of order $n = 200$ and the right-hand side b such that the exact solution x is the vector of all ones. Taking x_0 as the null vector, we compute the following Richardson iteration depending on the parameter α:

$$x_0 = 0, \qquad x_{k+1} = x_k + \alpha(b - Ex_k) = (I - \alpha E)x_k + \alpha b, \quad k \geq 0.$$

For $\alpha = 1$, the iteration matrix $I - E$ has a spectral radius equal to zero; thus fast convergence is ensured in exact arithmetic. Figure 11.4 shows the relative forward error $\|x - \tilde{x}_k\|/\|x\|$ obtained in finite precision for $\alpha = 1$ (left) and $\alpha = 2/3$ (right). We notice that the computed solution diverges almost immediately for $\alpha = 1$. Such a result is all the more unexpected that the spectral radius of the iteration matrix is zero! A hint is that the computed spectral radius of the iteration matrix $I - E$ is 1.0873 instead of zero.

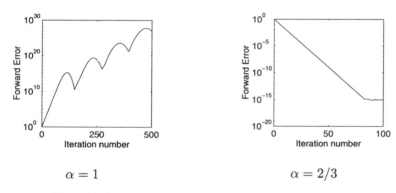

$$\alpha = 1 \qquad\qquad\qquad\qquad \alpha = 2/3$$

FIG. 11.4. *Richardson iterations on Eccen, $n = 200$.*

This can be explained by the spectral instability of $I - E$, which derives from that of the triangular Toeplitz matrix: T_n has a spectral instability that increases exponentially with n. Reichel and Trefethen (1992) show that $\lim_{n\to\infty} \sigma(T_n) = \mathcal{D} = \{z; \, |z - 3/2| \leq 1\}$, and $\mathcal{D}$ is the continuous spectrum of the compact Toeplitz operator that is the limit of T_n, in l^2, as $n \to \infty$. Since $\sigma(T_n) = \{1\}$ for all n, we conclude that $\sigma(T_n)$ is discontinuous in the limit $n \to \infty$. But the pseudospectra are continuous, and $\sigma_\varepsilon(T_n) \subseteq \sigma_\varepsilon(T) = \mathcal{D} + \Delta_\varepsilon$, where $\Delta_\varepsilon = \{z; \, |z| \leq \varepsilon\}$.

Figure 11.5 displays the perturbed spectra of E for normwise relative perturbations, $t = 2^{-p}$, and p varies from 40 to 50 by steps of 2. Using the information provided by the pseudospectrum, it appears that the value $\alpha = 2/3$ (and not $\alpha = 1$)

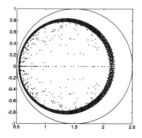

FIG. 11.5. *Perturbed spectra of Eccen, $n = 200$, in the disk $\mathcal{D}$.*

should ensure optimal convergence. With $\mathcal{D} = \lim_{n\to\infty} \sigma_\varepsilon(T_n)$ for E, the corresponding limit for the matrix $I - \alpha E$ is $\mathcal{D}' = \{z; \ |z - \frac{3}{2}\alpha| \leq \alpha\}$. This corresponds to a rate of convergence defined as $\rho_\alpha = \max\{|1 - \frac{5}{2}\alpha|, |1 - \frac{1}{2}\alpha|\}$. A simple computation shows that the value of α that minimizes ρ_α is $\alpha = 2/3$. Figure 11.4 (right) confirms that with $\alpha = 2/3$ convergence to the exact solution occurs within fewer than 100 iterations. $\triangle$

The Eccen matrix provides a good example for which the information given by the normwise limit pseudospectrum is the key for understanding the convergence condition on α and therefore improving the computation.

We now give an example which shows the possible difference between the roles of normwise and componentwise pseudospectra.

Example 11.5 A nonlinear recurrence (Brugnano and Trigiante (1990)).
We consider the LU factorization of the family of tridiagonal matrices of varying order $n = 1, 2, \ldots$, defined by

$$
B_n(\beta, \gamma) = \begin{bmatrix} \gamma & \beta & & & \\ 1 & \ddots & \ddots & & \\ & \ddots & \ddots & \ddots & \\ & & \ddots & \ddots & \beta \\ & & & 1 & \gamma \end{bmatrix}_{n\times n},
$$

where β and γ are real parameters. The LU factorization of $B_n(\beta, \gamma)$ is chosen under the form

$$
L = \begin{bmatrix} \alpha_1 & & & \\ 1 & \ddots & & \\ & \ddots & \ddots & \\ & & 1 & \alpha_n \end{bmatrix}_{n\times n} \quad \text{and} \quad U = \begin{bmatrix} 1 & x_1 & & \\ & \ddots & \ddots & \\ & & \ddots & x_{n-1} \\ & & & 1 \end{bmatrix}_{n\times n},
$$

where $\alpha_i = \gamma - \beta/\alpha_{i-1}$ and $x_i = \beta/\alpha_i$. As the order n of the matrix increases, the actual computation of the nonlinear iteration

$$
\alpha_1 = \gamma, \qquad \alpha_i = \gamma - \frac{\beta}{\alpha_{i-1}}, \ 2 \leq i \leq n, \tag{11.1}
$$

becomes "chaotic" for some values of γ, in the following sense.

If $|\gamma| \geq 2\sqrt{\beta}$, there exists a unique limit for α_i as $i \to \infty$, but if $|\gamma| < 2\sqrt{\beta}$, α_i may have a periodic behaviour for some values of γ: it can be proved that the values $\gamma_{r,p} = 2\sqrt{\beta}\cos\frac{r\pi}{p}$ for $r = 1, \ldots p-1$ lead to oscillations of period p (Brugnano and Trigiante (1990)).

Let $\Sigma_n(\beta)$ be the spectrum of the matrix $A_n(\beta) = B_n(\beta, 0) = B_n(\beta, \gamma) - \gamma I$. The parameter β controls the nonnormality of $A_n(\beta)$. $B_n(\beta, \gamma)$ is singular when $-\gamma$ is an eigenvalue of $A_n(\beta)$. $\Sigma_n(\beta) = \{2\sqrt{\beta}\cos\frac{r\pi}{n+1}, \ r = 1, \ldots n\}$, and in the limit when $n \to \infty$, $\Sigma(\beta) = \overline{\bigcup_n \Sigma_n(\beta)} = [-2\sqrt{\beta}, 2\sqrt{\beta}]$. It has been shown (Bakhvalov (1977, pp. 356–361)) that the limit as $n \to \infty$, $\varepsilon \to 0$ of the normwise ε-pseudospectra of A_n is the domain limited by the ellipse $\mathcal{E}_\beta$ of major horizontal axis $\beta + 1$ and minor vertical axis $\beta - 1$. This is the *spectrum of the family of matrices* A_n, $n = 1, 2, \ldots$ (Godunov and Ryabenki (1964)). The ellipse $\mathcal{E}_\beta$ encloses Σ_β.

Figure 11.6 displays the normwise perturbed spectra of $A_n(\beta)$ for $n = 30, 50, 120,$ and 170, with $\beta = 10$. They correspond to normwise perturbations of relative size $t = 2^{-p}$ (p ranging from 50 to 40 by steps of 2). We see that the shape of the exact spectrum $\Sigma_n(\beta)$ (indicated by $+$) is lost and that, as n increases, the perturbed spectra tend to occupy the interior of the ellipse $\mathcal{E}_\beta$, which is also drawn. Such a spectral instability leads us to expect that the computation of the α_i by (11.1), which is convergent in exact arithmetic for $|\gamma| \geq 2\sqrt{\beta}$, might show instabilities in finite precision for γ in the intervals $\left[2\sqrt{\beta}, \beta + 1\right]$ and $\left[-\beta - 1, -2\sqrt{\beta}\right]$, because of the perturbations generated by the finite precision arithmetic. If this happened, this would signal that the behaviour of (11.1) in finite precision is ruled by the normwise ε-pseudospectrum.

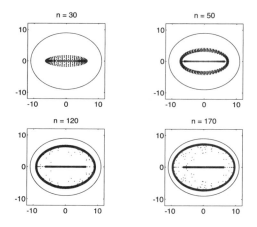

FIG. 11.6.   *Exact and normwise perturbed spectra of $A_n(\beta)$, $n = 30, 50, 120, 170$; $\beta = 10$.*

The experiment shown in Figure 11.7 (corresponding to $\beta = 1, 100, 10^4,$ and 10^8) rules out this possibility. The computation for 100 values of γ regularly spaced in the interval indicated on the picture. Each interval in centered on $2\sqrt{\beta}$. For each value of γ we compute the first 500 iterates of α_i and plot the 25 computed iterates $i = 501$ to 525. We can see the apparently chaotic behaviour of the iterates for $\gamma < 2\sqrt{\beta}$ and the good convergence as soon as $\gamma \geq 2\sqrt{\beta}$.

In this example, the key for the analyzing the reliability of the iteration (11.1) is the limit *componentwise* pseudospectrum, which is the interval $\Sigma = [-2\sqrt{\beta}, 2\sqrt{\beta}]$ and is much smaller that the region enclosed by $\mathcal{E}_\beta$ for large values of β. $\triangle$

11.3   Pseudozeroes of polynomials

11.3.1   Definitions

We consider the polynomial $p(x) = \sum_{i=0}^{n} a_i x^i$, $x \in \mathbb{C}$. To the approximate zero z is associated the residual $r = p(z) = a^T \underline{z}$ with $a = (a_0, \ldots, a_n)^T$

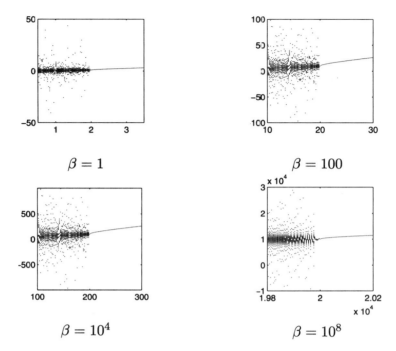

$\beta = 1$ $\qquad\qquad\qquad\qquad$ $\beta = 100$

$\beta = 10^4$ $\qquad\qquad\qquad\qquad$ $\beta = 10^8$

FIG. 11.7. *Iteration* (11.1) α_i, $i = 501$ *to* 525, *versus* γ.

and $\underline{z} = (1,\ z,\ \ldots,\ z^n)^T$. Formulae for the normwise and the componentwise relative backward error at z have been given in Chapter 5. We choose $\beta = \|a\|$ and $f = |a|$.

Definition 11.4

i) *The* set of normwise ε-pseudozeroes *of* $p(x) = 0$ *is defined by*

$$Z_\varepsilon^{\mathcal{N}}(p) = \left\{ z \in \mathbb{C};\ B^{\mathcal{N}}(z) = \frac{|r|}{\|\underline{z}\|_* \|a\|} \le \varepsilon \right\}.$$

ii) *The* set of componentwise ε-pseudozeroes *of* $p(x) = 0$ *is defined by*

$$Z_\varepsilon^{\mathcal{C}}(p) = \left\{ z \in \mathbb{C};\ B^{\mathcal{C}}(z) = \frac{r|}{\sum_{i=0}^n |a_i||z^i|} = \frac{|a^T \underline{z}|}{|a|^T |\underline{z}|} \le \varepsilon \right\}.$$

As was the case for the pseudospectra, the pseudozeroes have the following characterizations, where we define $(p+\Delta p)(z) = \sum_{i=0}^n (a_i + \Delta a_i) z^i = (a + \Delta a)^T \underline{z}$ with $\Delta a = (\Delta a_0,\ \ldots,\ \Delta a_n)^T$.

Proposition 11.3

i) $Z_\varepsilon^{\mathcal{N}}(p) = \{z$ such that $(p + \Delta p)(z) = 0$ for all Δp satisfying $\|\Delta a\| \le \varepsilon \|a\|\}$.

ii) $Z_\varepsilon^{\mathcal{C}}(p) = \{z$ such that $(p + \Delta p)(z) = 0$ for all Δp satisfying $\max_{i=0,\ldots,n} |\Delta a_i|/|a_i| \le \varepsilon\}$.

Proof: The proof follows immediately from the definition of the backward error. □

11.3.2 The maps $z \longmapsto 1/B(z)$

In order to study the sensitivity of the computation of zeroes of polynomials, it is informative to consider, as for eigenvalues, the maps $z \longmapsto 1/B(z)$ in the normwise and/or the componentwise case, using an exponential scale. Such curves represent the border of Z_ε if $B(z) = \varepsilon$. Note that for zeroes of polynomials, both $B^{\mathcal{N}}(z)$ and $B^{\mathcal{C}}(z)$ are computable.

Example 11.6

We consider again the polynomial $p(x) = (x-1)^3(x-2)^3(x-3)^3(x-4)$ of Example 11.2. Figure 11.8 shows the maps $z \longmapsto \log_{10} B^{\mathcal{N}}(z)$ with $\| . \|_2$ and $z \longmapsto \log_{10} B^{\mathcal{C}}(z)$, respectively, as well as a representation in shades of grey. Such pictures can be called the *sensitivity portrait of polynomial zeroes*, analogous with the spectral portraits of matrices.

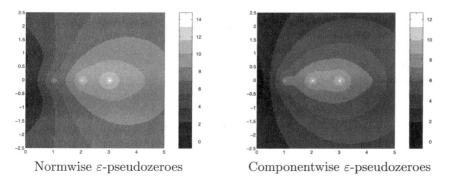

Normwise ε-pseudozeroes   Componentwise ε-pseudozeroes

FIG. 11.8. *Sensitivity portraits of the roots of* $p(x) = (x-1)^3(x-2)^3(x-3)^3(x-4)$.

Rose is the companion matrix associated with $p(x)$. Figure 11.9 displays the level curves for the maps $z \longmapsto \|(A - zI)^{-1}\|_2 = 1/\varepsilon$, $z \longmapsto B^{\mathcal{N}}(z) = \varepsilon$, and $z \longmapsto B^{\mathcal{C}}(z) = \varepsilon$, corresponding to $A = $ Rose, and $p(x) = 0$. Qualitatively, the three upper plots look similar, but one should not forget that they correspond respectively to the *different* intervals [6, 18], [1, 13], and [0, 12] for the variation of $\log_{10} \varepsilon$. In order to make it easier to perceive the difference in sensitivity for the roots of $p(x)$ when they are considered as eigenvalues of Rose or as roots of $p(x)$, we draw the seven level curves corresponding to a uniform discretization of the common interval [6, 12], that is $\varepsilon = 10^{-6}$, 10^{-7} up to 10^{-12}. See Figure 11.9 (bottom). As expected, the three pictures look now very different from their counterparts. △

11.3.3 Zeroes of a polynomial as eigenvalues of the associated companion matrix

The roots of a polynomial $p(x) = x^n + \sum_{i=0}^{n-1} a_i x^i$ are identical in exact arithmetic to the eigenvalues of the companion matrix Comp(p). This is true

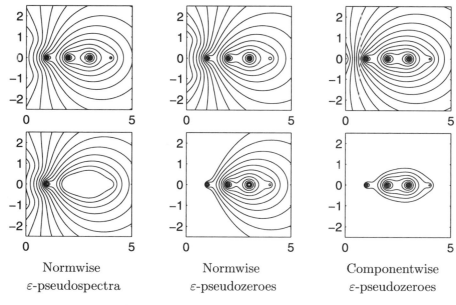

Normwise	Normwise	Componentwise
ε-pseudospectra	ε-pseudozeroes	ε-pseudozeroes

FIG. 11.9. $p(x) = (x-1)^3(x-2)^3(x-3)^3(x-4)$.

in the absence of perturbations. Is this property still true under perturbations; that is, how does the sensitivity of the solution as a root of p compare with its sensitivity as an eigenvalue of $\mathrm{Comp}(p)$? Because of the sparsity pattern of $\mathrm{Comp}(p)$, the answer clearly depends on the type of perturbations of $\mathrm{Comp}(p)$ generated by the algorithm chosen to compute the roots of p.

In order to investigate this question, we first look at the computed spectra of companion matrices $A = \mathrm{Comp}(p)$, taking the point of view of *eigenvalues*. The companion matrices are perturbed in four fashions:

a) The matrix $A = \mathrm{Comp}(p)$ is subject to normwise or componentwise perturbations:

$$A = (a_{ij}) \quad \begin{cases} \text{n1) normwise } \dfrac{\|\Delta A\|}{\|A\|}, \\[2mm] \text{c1) componentwise } \max_{ij} \dfrac{|\Delta a_{ij}|}{|a_{ij}|}. \end{cases}$$

b) The matrix $A = \mathrm{Comp}(p)$ is subject to structured perturbations; only the polynomial $p(z) = a^T \underline{z}$ is subject to normwise or componentwise perturbations:

$$\begin{cases} \text{n2) normwise } \dfrac{\|\Delta a\|}{\|a\|}, \\[2mm] \text{c2) componentwise } \max_i \dfrac{|\Delta a_i|}{|a_i|} \end{cases}$$

with $a = (a_0, \ldots, a_{n-1})^T$.

The four figures to follow display the spectra of the companion matrices associated respectively with the four polynomials:

1. $p_1(x) = (x-1)(x-2)^2(x-3)^3(x-4)^4$ in Figure 11.10,
2. $p_2(x) = (x-1)(x-2)^4(x-3)^4(x-4)$ in Figure 11.11,
3. p_3 in Figure 11.12 is the monic polynomial associated with the polynomial of degree 16 defined by Wilkinson (1963, p. 63),
4. p_4 in Figure 11.13 is the monic polynomial deduced from another polynomial of degree 16 defined in Wilkinson (1963, p. 75).

Each figure shows three plots corresponding to the perturbed spectra for three possible ways of perturbing the matrix; they are displayed according to the format n1 – n2 – c1. The case c2, being similar to c1, is not displayed here. For each plot, the perturbation size is t^{-p}, where p varies from 30 to 50; for each p the sample size is 10.

The main conclusion that can be drawn is that, despite the amount of freedom offered by arbitrary perturbations over structured perturbations,

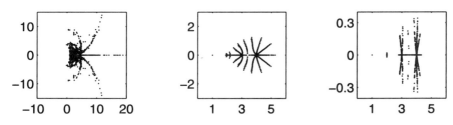

FIG. 11.10. *Perturbed spectra for* $\mathrm{Comp}(p_1)$.

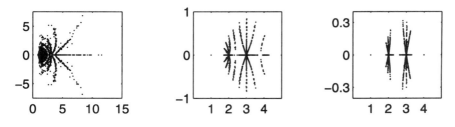

FIG. 11.11. *Perturbed spectra for* $\mathrm{Comp}(p_2)$.

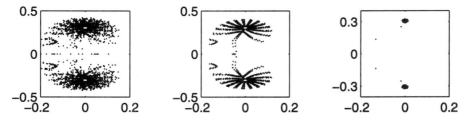

FIG. 11.12. *Perturbed spectra for* $\mathrm{Comp}(p_3)$.

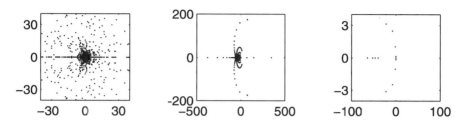

FIG. 11.13. *Perturbed spectra for* Comp(p_4).

the perturbed spectra exhibit similar patterns: the effects of structured perturbations of a given level are qualitatively similar to the effects derived from arbitrary perturbations for a smaller level.

11.3.4 Eigenvalues of a matrix as roots of the characteristic polynomial

The dual point of view of the preceding discussion is now taken: the eigenvalues of a matrix A can be regarded as the eigenvalues of the companion matrix Comp(A) associated with the characteristic polynomial of A. Now the characteristic polynomial, which is defined by the eigenvalues only, contains no information about the departure from normality of A, for example. The consequence is illustrated Schur of order $n = 20$ with $\nu = 10^3$. Figure 11.14 shows six plots.

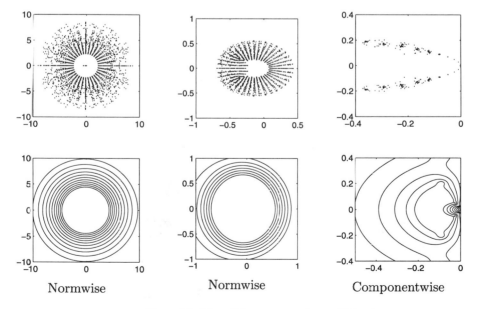

FIG. 11.14. *Schur versus* Comp*(Schur)*.

1. The two leftmost plots correspond to Schur; the upper plot displays the normwise perturbed spectra and the lower plot shows the borders of the ε-pseudospectrum for ε in $[10^{-5},\ 10^{-10}]$.

2. The remaining four plots correspond to Comp(Schur), that is, the companion matrix associated with the characteristic polynomial $\pi(x)$ of Schur, with the same characteristics: $n = 20$ and $\nu = 10^3$.

The upper plots display the perturbed roots associated respectively with normwise and componentwise perturbations of $\pi(x)$ (see § 11.3.3). The lower plots display the borders of the ε-pseudozeroes of $\pi(x)$ for ε in $[10^{-1},\ 10^{-4}]$.

We again see that pseudospectra and pseudozeroes are different. The difference in these behaviours comes mainly from the fact that the parameter ν, which rules the departure from normality, has no influence on the characteristic polynomial of Schur but does influence the sensitivity of the eigenvalues of Schur. In addition, this example shows clearly by how much componentwise and normwise pseudozeroes can differ.

11.4   Divergence portrait for the complex logistic iteration

We have seen that the logistic iteration (2.27), $x_0 = 1/2$, $x_{k+1} = rx_k(1 - x_k)$, $k \geq 0$, for r taking real values, converges or remains bounded for $-2 \leq r \leq 4$. We now consider the similar iteration for the parameter λ and the sequence of iterates $\{z_k\}$ taking *complex* values:

$$z_0 = 1/2, \qquad z_{k+1} = \lambda z_k(1 - z_k), \quad k \geq 0. \tag{11.2}$$

Depending on λ, this iteration may either converge, remain bounded, or diverge. To study this dependence on λ, we can plot for λ in $\mathbb{C}$ the map $\lambda \longmapsto k_\lambda$, defined as the index of the first iteration such that $|z_k(z_k - 2)| \geq 8$, where $\{z_k\}$ are computed by (11.2). Such a map can be called the *divergence portrait* of the complex iteration (11.2). We have used a maximum number of iterations equal to 32. The result is displayed in Figure 11.15. The 32 regions corresponding to $k_\lambda = 1$ up to 32 are displayed according to a scale of nine levels of grey. Black corresponds to $k_\lambda > 32$. One recognizes the celebrated Mandelbrot set in black. This set defined as $\{\lambda; |z_k| \nrightarrow \infty\}$ corresponds to the

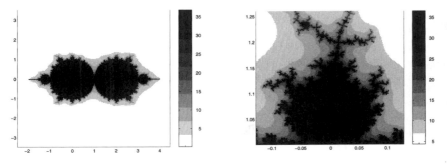

FIG. 11.15. *Divergence portrait of* (11.2).

largest values k_λ. The left (resp., right) divergence portrait corresponds to the region $[-2, 4] \times [-3, 3]$ (resp., $[-0.13, 0.13] \times [1, 1.26]$) in $\mathbb{C}$.

11.5   Qualitative assessment of a Jordan form

If A is a complex or real matrix of order n, then there exists a nonsingular matrix X and a block diagonal matrix J with blocks J_{k_i} of the form

$$J_{k_i} = \begin{pmatrix} \lambda_i & 1 & \\ & \ddots & 1 \\ & & \lambda_i \end{pmatrix}$$

satisfying $A = X^{-1}JX$. This matrix J is unique modulo the ordering of the diagonal blocks. Such a problem is mathematically *ill posed*. As a result, the computation of the Jordan form of a matrix is ill conditioned. The basic methods for determining the Jordan decomposition are
- the method proposed by Golub and Wilkinson (1976), using deflation and singular value decomposition,
- the method of Kågström and Ruhe (1981), based on similarity transformations and orthogonal deflation.

Both methods are facing the same two difficulties. The first arises when one has to group the computed eigenvalues corresponding to the same multiple eigenvalue. (The computation of an eigenvalue of multiplicity m, in finite precision arithmetic, gives m different simple eigenvalues.) The second difficulty is that both methods require the computation of the rank of the matrix, which is a difficult numerical problem: it is mathematically ill posed.

In order to assess the Jordan structure, Chatelin (1989b) has proposed a qualitative approach based on statistical estimation of the most probable Jordan structure of the matrix. Given a matrix A, one computes the eigenvalues of various matrices obtained by random normwise perturbations of A. From the superimposition of these perturbed spectra, one can infer which Jordan form is the most likely to occur. A more detailed presentation of this technique can be found in Chatelin and Braconnier (1994).

The principle for the interpretation of the perturbed spectra is the following. Suppose that the matrix A possesses a unique real eigenvalue λ with multiplicity m. The characteristic polynomial $\pi(z) = \det(A - zI)$ is given by $\pi(z) = (z - \lambda)^m$. But in finite precision arithmetic, one never solves the exact problem $\pi(z) = 0$ but a slightly perturbed problem. Let the computed eigenvalue $\tilde{\lambda}$ be such that $\pi(\tilde{\lambda}) = r$. Then $\tilde{\lambda}$ satisfies the equation

$$\pi(\tilde{\lambda}) - r = (\tilde{\lambda} - \lambda)^m - r = 0.$$

One gets m computed eigenvalues

$$\tilde{\lambda} = \lambda + |r|^{1/m} e^{(i2k\pi)/m} \text{ or } \tilde{\lambda} = \lambda + |r|^{1/m} e^{(i(2k+1)\pi)/m}, \qquad k = 1, \ldots, m,$$

depending on whether r is a *positive* or a *negative* real number.

The perturbations t corresponding to a positive r are, in average, as frequent as those corresponding to a negative r. For $m = 6$ for instance, the perturbed eigenvalues are located at the vertices of the two hexagons shown in Figure 11.16. Varying the size t of the perturbation, one then obtains two families of hexagons that create a star with twelve branches.

When the Jordan structure corresponds to an even number of blocks of the same size, then we observe additional perturbations associated with a complex value for t: for two blocks, the computed eigenvalues are the zeroes of the minimal polynomials $(\tilde{\lambda} - \lambda)^{m/2} = r$ or $(\tilde{\lambda} - \lambda)^{m/2} = \bar{r}$, with m even. Since r and $\bar{r}$ are complex conjugate, $(\tilde{\lambda} - \lambda)^m = r\bar{r}$ represents the characteristic polynomial, where $r\bar{r}$ is real again. These eigenvalues can be seen between the rays obtained with real perturbations. Figure 11.17 shows the location of the computed eigenvalues λ_1 to λ_6 obtained when, for $m = 6$ and $l = 3$, there exist two blocks of size 3. These eigenvalues are at the vertices of two triangles, symmetric with respect to the real axis.

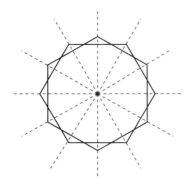

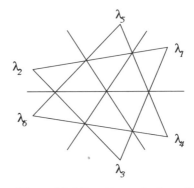

FIG. 11.16. *Perturbation of λ, $m = 6$, $l = 6$, r real, positive and negative.*

FIG. 11.17. *Perturbation of λ, $m = 6$, $l = 3$, complex.*

We illustrate this in four different examples for which we know in advance the exact Jordan structure. For each eigenvalue under study, we show two perturbed spectra: one corresponds to normwise relative perturbations ranging from $2^{-50} \sim 9 \times 10^{-16}$ to $2^{-40} \sim 9 \times 10^{-13}$, and the second one corresponds to smaller perturbations ranging from $2^{-53} \sim 10^{-16}$ to $2^{-50} \sim 9 \times 10^{-16}$.

All the following experiments in §§ 11.5 and 11.6 correspond to *normwise* perturbations of the matrix. The percentages given in the comments correspond to the relative number of occurrences of *real* perturbations on the eigenvalues for a sample of size 25.

Example 11.7 (Ruhe (1970)).

$$A_1 = \begin{pmatrix} 1 & 1 & 1 & -2 & 1 & -1 & 2 & -2 & 4 & -3 \\ -1 & 2 & 3 & -4 & 2 & -2 & 4 & -4 & 8 & -6 \\ -1 & 0 & 5 & -5 & 3 & -3 & 6 & -6 & 12 & -9 \\ -1 & 0 & 3 & -4 & 4 & -4 & 8 & -8 & 16 & -12 \\ -1 & 0 & 3 & -6 & 5 & -4 & 10 & -10 & 20 & -15 \\ -1 & 0 & 3 & -6 & 2 & -2 & 12 & -12 & 24 & -18 \\ -1 & 0 & 3 & -6 & 2 & -5 & 15 & -13 & 28 & -21 \\ -1 & 0 & 3 & -6 & 2 & -5 & 12 & -11 & 32 & -24 \\ -1 & 0 & 3 & -6 & 2 & -5 & 12 & -14 & 37 & -26 \\ -1 & 0 & 3 & -6 & 2 & -5 & 12 & -14 & 36 & -25 \end{pmatrix}.$$

The spectrum of A_1 is $\sigma = \{1, 2, 3\}$, with the Jordan structure $(1)^1$, $(2)^2$, $(2)^3$, $(3)^2$, and $(3)^2$.

Figure 11.18 shows the perturbed spectra of A_1 in the neighbourhood of $\lambda = 2$. We observe that most eigenvalues are located either on a six-branch star (see left figure) or on one small cross (see right figure): this structure appears in 97.5% of the cases and corresponds to the decomposition into one block of size 3 and one block of size 2. We notice that other Jordan structures (which would correspond to only one block of size 5, for instance) are more likely to occur with high enough perturbations: they appear in about 8% of the cases for perturbations between 10^{-15} and 10^{-12} and in fewer than 2.5% of the cases for perturbations between 10^{-16} and 10^{-15}. The exact Jordan structure is predicted by looking for the perturbed spectra with highest frequency.

Similarly, in Figure 11.19 for $\lambda = 3$, one observes one cross corresponding to two blocks of size 2: 89.5% of the computed eigenvalues are on this cross, and they

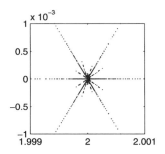 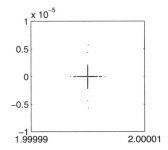

FIG. 11.18. *Matrix A_1. $\lambda = 2$, $m = 5$, $l = 3$.*

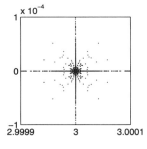 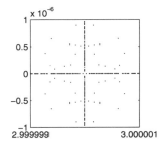

FIG. 11.19. *Matrix A_1. $\lambda = 3$, $m = 4$, $l = 2$.*

correspond to a real value for r. The other eigenvalues that can be seen outside the cross correspond, as explained earlier, to complex conjugate values for r. However, all cases (r either complex or real) correspond to the exact Jordan structure of two blocks of size 2. △

Example 11.8 (Brunet (1989)).

$$A_2 = \begin{pmatrix} 8.1 & 0.8 & -2.7 & -2.4 & -0.8 & 4.5 & -2.4 & -1.5 \\ 1.5 & 3.4 & 2 & 0.8 & 3.6 & 0 & 0.8 & -4.5 \\ -2.7 & -3.6 & 3.4 & 0.8 & 3.6 & 0 & 0.8 & 2.5 \\ -4.5 & 0.8 & 1.5 & 4.6 & -0.8 & -2.5 & -2.4 & -1.5 \\ -0.8 & 0.8 & 3.6 & 4.1 & 6.2 & 2.8 & -2.9 & 2.4 \\ 2.4 & 2.8 & -2.8 & 3.1 & 2.8 & 3.4 & -1.1 & -0.8 \\ -2.4 & 2.9 & 0.8 & -1.7 & 4.1 & 2.4 & 5.3 & -0.8 \\ -0.8 & -3.1 & -2.4 & 1.3 & -1.1 & -0.8 & -4.3 & 4.6 \end{pmatrix}.$$

The spectrum of A_2 is $\sigma = \{-1, -2, 7\}$, with the Jordan structure $(-1)^1$, $(-2)^1$, and $(7)^6$.

We study the eigenvalue $\lambda = 7$. Figure 11.20 shows the perturbed spectra in the neighbourhood of 7. We observe very clearly a 12-branch star (two possible hexagons) corresponding to a unique Jordan block of size 6. This structure, which occurs in 97% of the cases, corresponds to the exact mathematical structure. △

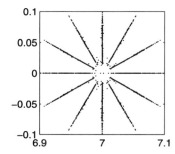 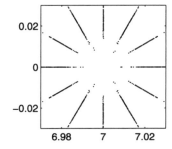

FIG. 11.20. *Matrix A_2. $\lambda = 7$, $m = 6$, $l = 6$.*

Example 11.9 (Brunet (1989)).

$$A_3 = \begin{pmatrix} 7.4 & 1.15 & -3.05 & -1.7 & -0.45 & 4.15 & -3.1 & -0.8 \\ 0.1 & 4.1 & 1.3 & 2.2 & 4.3 & -0.7 & -0.6 & -3.1 \\ -1.3 & -4.3 & 4.1 & -0.6 & 2.9 & 0.7 & 2.2 & 1.1 \\ -3.8 & 0.45 & 1.85 & 3.9 & -1.15 & -2.15 & -1.7 & -2.2 \\ 0.6 & 0.1 & 4.3 & 2.7 & 5.5 & 3.5 & -1.5 & 1 \\ 3.8 & 2.1 & -2.1 & 1.7 & 2.1 & 4.1 & 0.3 & -2.2 \\ -1.7 & 2.55 & 1.15 & -2.4 & 3.75 & 2.75 & 6 & -1.5 \\ -0.1 & -3.45 & -2.05 & 0.6 & -1.45 & -0.45 & -3.6 & 3.9 \end{pmatrix}.$$

$\sigma(A_3) = \{-1, -2, 7\}$, with the Jordan structure $(-1)^1$, $(-2)^1$, $(7)^3$, and $(7)^3$.

We observe in Figure 11.21 a six-branch star that reveals the two blocks of size 3, instead of the 12-branch star observed in Figure 11.20. Here again, the eigenvalues that are between the branches of the star are associated with complex conjugate values of t. △

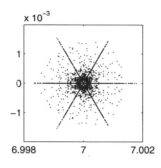
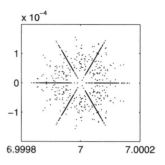

FIG. 11.21. *Matrix A_3. $\lambda = 7$, $m = 6$, $l = 3$.*

Example 11.10 (Brunet (1989)).

$$A_4 = \begin{pmatrix} 6.7 & 0.8 & -3.4 & -2.4 & -0.8 & 3.8 & -2.4 & -0.1 \\ -1.3 & 3.4 & 0.6 & 0.8 & 3.6 & -1.4 & 0.8 & -1.7 \\ 0.1 & -3.6 & 4.8 & 0.8 & 3.6 & 1.4 & 0.8 & -0.3 \\ -3.1 & 0.8 & 2.2 & 4.6 & -0.8 & -1.8 & -2.4 & -2.9 \\ -0.8 & -0.6 & 3.6 & 1.3 & 4.8 & 2.8 & -0.1 & 2.4 \\ 2.4 & 1.4 & -2.8 & 0.3 & 1.4 & 3.4 & 1.7 & -0.8 \\ -2.4 & 2.2 & 0.8 & -3.1 & 3.4 & 2.4 & 6.7 & -0.8 \\ -0.8 & -3.8 & -2.4 & -0.1 & -1.8 & -0.8 & -2.9 & 4.6 \end{pmatrix}.$$

$\sigma = \{-1, -2, 7\}$ with Jordan structure $(-1)^1$, $(-2)^1$, $(7)^3$, $(7)^2$, and $(7)^1$.

Figure 11.22 shows the perturbed spectra of A_4 in the neighbourhood of $\lambda = 7$. Most of the eigenvalues are located either on a six-branch star corresponding to the block of size 3 or on a cross at the center of the star (see right figure and Figure 11.23 for a zoom) corresponding to the block of size 2. The block of size 1 would appear as a point located at $\lambda = 7$. We notice that here the exact Jordan structure appears in 99.5% of the cases. $\triangle$

In concluding our discussion of these examples, we observe that by means of a very simple analysis of the perturbed spectra of a matrix, we are able to determine the Jordan form occurring with the highest probability.

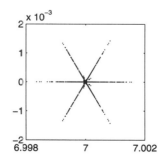
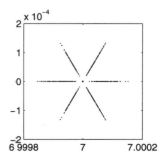

FIG. 11.22. *Matrix A_4. $\lambda = 7$, $m = 6$, $l = 3$.*

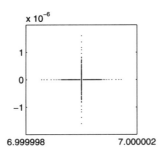

FIG. 11.23. *Matrix A_4. Zoom on $\lambda = 7$, $m = 6$, $l = 2$.*

11.6   Beyond linear perturbation theory

For small enough perturbations, a linear perturbation theory can be established
for multiple defective eigenvalues by means of Puiseux series (Kato (1976) and
Chatelin (1983)). For larger perturbations, however, nonlinear effects have to
be taken into account. There is to date no general theory, and we present three
examples that exhibit some nonlinear effects.
Example 11.11
The matrix under consideration is the following:

$$B_1(\alpha) = Q^* \begin{pmatrix} -1+\alpha & 1 & 0 \\ 0 & -1 & 1 \\ 0 & 0 & -1-\alpha \end{pmatrix} Q,$$

where Q is the orthonormal matrix of order 3 provided by the MATLAB routine taken
from Higham (1991a). $\sigma(B_1(\alpha)) = \{-1, -1-\alpha, -1+\alpha\}$. When the parameter α tends
to zero, then the simple eigenvalue -1 tends to become triple and defective.

Figure 11.24 shows the perturbed spectra of $B_1(\alpha)$ for three different values of
the parameter α: 10^{-4}, 10^{-5}, and 0 and for normwise relative perturbations ranging
from $2^{-50} \sim 9 \times 10^{-16}$ to $2^{-40} \sim 9 \times 10^{-13}$. For $\alpha = 10^{-3}$, one can see that the
eigenvalues are well separated and considered as three distinct eigenvalues by the
computer. (The perturbed spectra are a dot for each eigenvalue.) For $\alpha = 10^{-4}$,
we observe the presence of rays that are not straight lines as in the previous section
(qualitative computation of a Jordan form) but are bent. Furthermore, these rays

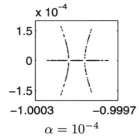

$\alpha = 10^{-4}$

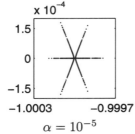

$\alpha = 10^{-5}$

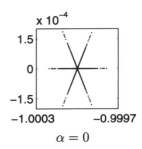

$\alpha = 0$

FIG. 11.24. *Perturbed spectra for the matrix B_1.*

are not centered on the exact eigenvalues but are located in between. This is where the linear perturbation theory for defective multiple eigenvalues ceases to be valid. The same phenomenon appears for even smaller perturbations when $\alpha = 10^{-5}$ and is more and more visible when the eigenvalues are less and less separated, i.e., as $\alpha \to 0$. When $\alpha = 0$, one retrieves the classical perturbed spectra for a defective triple eigenvalue, as already noted in the previous section: they correspond to the classical linear perturbation theory. $\triangle$

Example 11.12

We consider the matrix presented in Example 9.1[7]:

$$B_2(\alpha) = Q^* \begin{pmatrix} -1-\alpha^2 & 1 & 0 \\ 0 & -1 & 1 \\ 0 & 0 & -1+\alpha \end{pmatrix} Q,$$

$\sigma(B_2(\alpha)) = \{-1, -1-\alpha^2, -1+\alpha\}$. When the parameter α tends to zero, then the simple eigenvalue -1 tends first to become double and defective and then to become triple and defective.

Figure 11.25 shows the perturbed spectra of $B_2(\alpha)$ for three different values of the parameter α: 10^{-4}, 10^{-5}, and 0 and for normwise relative perturbations ranging from $2^{-50} \sim 9 \times 10^{-16}$ to $2^{-40} \sim 9 \times 10^{-13}$. We can see that for the perturbed spectra has the shape of a cross, revealing that the eigenvalues $-1-\alpha^2$ and -1 are seen as a unique defective double eigenvalue. For smaller values of α, we observe, as in the previous example, the presence of bent rays. Again, when $\alpha = 0$, one retrieves the perturbed spectra associated with a defective triple eigenvalue, as expected. $\triangle$

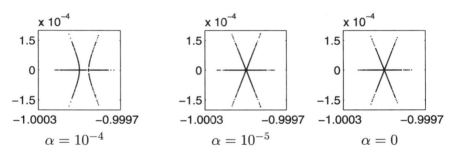

FIG. 11.25. *Perturbed spectra for the matrix B_2.*

Example 11.13 (Kågström and Ruhe (1981)).

The matrix of order 8 has a structure defined by

$$A(a) = \begin{pmatrix} 0 & I_4 \\ C(a) & D(a) \end{pmatrix}$$

with

$$C(a) = \begin{pmatrix} 1-2a^2 & -a+a(a^2+2b^2) & -2a^2b^2 & ab^2(a^2+b^2) \\ -2a & a^2+2b^2 & -2cb^2 & b^2(a^2+b^2) \\ -1 & 0 & 0 & 0 \\ 0 & -1 & 0 & 0 \end{pmatrix} \quad \text{of order 4}$$

and

$$D(a) = \begin{pmatrix} -3a & 1+a^2+2b^2 & -a(1+2b^2) & b^2(a^2+b^2) \\ -2 & 0 & 0 & 0 \\ 0 & -2 & 0 & 0 \\ 0 & 0 & -2 & 0 \end{pmatrix}.$$

The spectrum of this matrix is $\sigma = \sigma_0 \cup \sigma_i \cup \sigma_{-i}$ with

$$\begin{aligned}
\sigma_0 &= \{0, -a\}, \\
\sigma_i &= \left\{i, \sqrt{-1-2a-a^2}, (-2a + \sqrt{4a^2 - 4(1+2a+2a^2)})/2\right\}, \\
\sigma_{-i} &= \left\{i, -\sqrt{-1-2a-a^2}, (-2a - \sqrt{4a^2 - 4(1+2a+2a^2)})/2\right\}.
\end{aligned}$$

When $a = 0$, $A(0)$ has the Jordan structure $(0)^1$, $(0)^1$, $(i)^2$, $(i)^1$, $(-i)^2$, and $(-i)^1$. In this case, the qualitative approach also permits us to retrieve this structure. The interesting cases occur when the parameter a gradually approaches zero. Figure 11.26 presents some perturbed spectra (in the neighbourhood of the point $-i$) obtained by componentwise random perturbations of the matrices $A(10^{-8})$ (left) and $A(10^{-7})$ (right). For each matrix, the upper plot is associated with perturbations of relative size ranging from 2^{-50} to 2^{-40}, and the lower plot, with smaller perturbations ranging from 2^{-53} to 2^{-50}. This figure shows that the perturbed spectra can look fuzzier than the one presented previously. This is because the matrices here under study do not have exactly the same structure as the matrix $A(0)$. In particular, if we apply perturbations that are too small, it becomes difficult to infer the underlying structure. (The cross is not well drawn, and one sees three spots instead.) The cross shows clearly when one allows larger perturbation sizes. In addition, when a tends to zero, the cross corresponding to the block of size 2 appears more and more distinctly. △

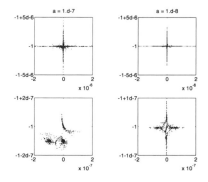

FIG. 11.26. *Kågström–Ruhe matrix. Componentwise perturbed spectra for $a = 10^{-7}$ and $a = 10^{-8}$.*

Example 11.14 The Rose revisited.
This last example involves the companion matrix Rose associated with the polynomial $p(x) = (x-1)^3(x-2)^3(x-3)^3(x-4)$ studied in Example 11.2. The perturbed spectra correspond to perturbations ranging from $2^{-30} \sim 9 \times 10^{-10}$ to $2^{-50} \sim 9 \times 10^{-16}$ on the left plot, from $2^{-40} \sim 9 \times 10^{-13}$ to 2^{-50} on the central plot, and from 2^{-50} to $2^{-53} \sim 10^{-16}$ on the right plot.

As in the previous examples, two types of effects are visible:

1. For small perturbations, the spectra behave according to the asymptotic linear perturbation theory, and the multiplicities 1 or 3 are clearly visible.

2. For larger perturbations, nonlinear and long distance phenomena occur. The curves described by the individual eigenvalues are no longer linear; they bend more or less, depending on the condition number of the eigenvalues. Moreover, spurious eigenvalues appear as a result of the connection between separate eigenvalues realized through large enough perturbations. This is an emerging collective behaviour that cannot be predicted by the linear asymptotic perturbation theory. The spurious roots between 2 and 3 and between 3 and 4 are visible for p between 40 and 50, but the spurious roots between 1 and 2 are visible only for larger perturbations (p between 30 and 40).

It is striking to see, in Figure 11.27, that the three triple eigenvalues of Rose have very different condition numbers (they "diffuse" differently), whereas the expression for $p(x)$ is symmetric in these three roots. The same phenomenon could already be seen on the spectral portrait for Rose given in Figure 11.2. In particular, the simple root 4 belongs to the influence zone of the triple root 3, which creates the spurious curve on the right, corresponding to the appearance of a spurious double root at approximately 3.8. This is an emerging collective phenomenon arising for large enough perturbations.   △

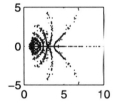 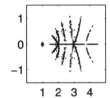 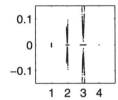

FIG. 11.27. *Perturbed spectra for Rose.*

11.7   Bibliographical comments

The general definition of sets of pseudosolutions of $F(x) = y$ by means of the backward error seems new. However, it is similar to the classical notion of domain of uncertainty for x (see van der Sluis (1970)). Two particular cases have been often considered in numerical analysis: pseudospectra for matrices and pseudozeroes for polynomials.

The first use of pseudospectra in numerical analysis is attributed to Varah (1979). This idea is closely related to the earlier notion of spectrum of a family of matrices (Godunov and Ryabenki (1964)). The normwise ε-pseudospectrum corresponds to the choice of a *relative* norm to bound ΔA. Trefethen (1992) considers alternatively an *absolute* norm and defines normwise absolute ε-pseudospectra. Pseudospectra of Toeplitz matrices are studied in Reichel and Trefethen (1992). Trefethen and his co-workers have popularized plots of perturbed spectra (with *complex* normwise perturbations) in many instances—for example, Trefethen (1990, 1992).

Mosier (1986) considers sets of ε-pseudozeroes for polynomials under the name *root loci*, used in the linear control community. See also Hinrichsen and Kelb (1993) and Toh and Trefethen (1994).

Chapter 12

More Numerical Illustrations with PRECISE

In this chapter, we present supplementary illustrations of the use of the facility "perturbed spectra" in the toolbox PRECISE to study the spectral sensitivity of six matrices of various orders. Perturbations can be normwise or componentwise, according to the legend. Four plots are displayed for each experiment. The plot in the upper left corner corresponds to perturbation size varying from 1.9×10^{-6} to 1.8×10^{-15} ($p = 20$ to 50), the one in the upper right corner to perturbation sizes from 1.9×10^{-9} to 1.7×10^{-15} ($p = 30$ to 50), the one in the bottom left corner to perturbation sizes from 1.8×10^{-12} to 1.7×10^{-15} ($p = 40$ to 50), and the one in the bottom right corner to perturbation sizes from 1.7×10^{-15} to 2.2×10^{-16} ($p = 50$ to 53). By default, the sample size for each $t = 2^{-p}$ is equal to 20.

In addition to their aesthetic beauty, the displays intend to show the wide variety of spectral sensitivity exhibited by matrices submitted to normwise and componentwise perturbations.

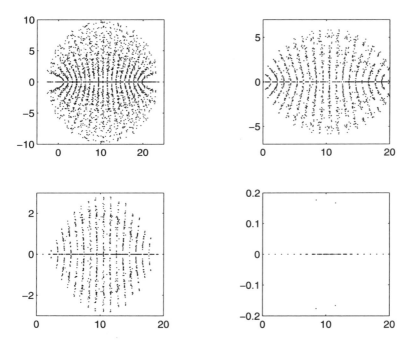

Normwise, $n = 20$

Wilkinson matrix W

The Wilkinson matrix is a bidiagonal matrix defined by

$$\left. \begin{array}{ll} w_{ii} = i, & w_{ii+1} = n, \\ w_{ij} = 0, & \text{for } j \neq i \text{ or } i + 1 \end{array} \right\} \quad \text{for } i = 1, \ldots, n.$$

$\sigma = \{i\}_{i=1,n}$ and the Jordan structure is $\{(i)^1\}_{i=1,n}$.
For $n = 50$, the sample size is 3.

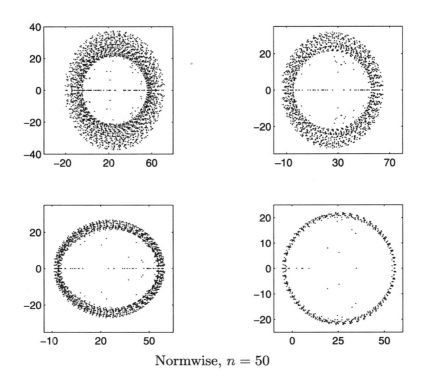

Normwise, $n = 50$

> ## Comments on W
> The center of the spectrum becomes increasingly unstable as n increases.

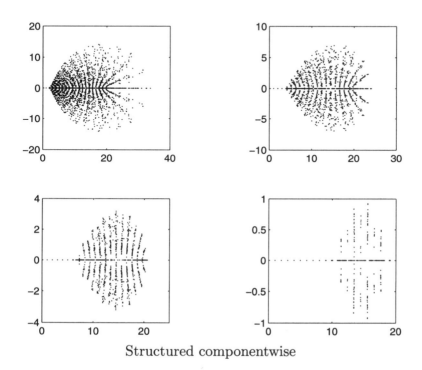

Structured componentwise

_CW_ of order 20

CW is the companion matrix associated with the Wilkinson polynomial

$$p(x) = \prod_{i=1}^{20}(x - i).$$

$\sigma = \{i\}_{i=1,20}$ and the Jordan structure is $\{(i)^1\}_{i=1,20}$.
The matrix CW is submitted to the structured perturbations c2 (left-hand page, componentwise) and n2 (right-hand page, normwise) described in § 11.3.3. CW is similar to W.

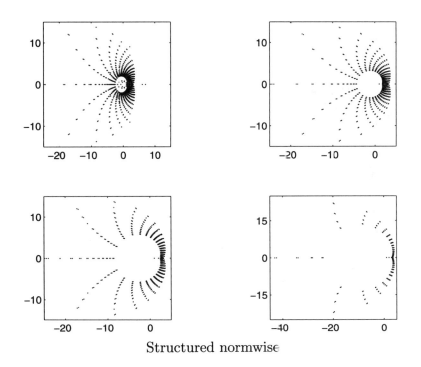

Structured normwise

Comments on *CW*

Normwise and componentwise perturbations induce a very different behaviour for the spectrum of CW. This behaviour is strikingly different from that for W of order 20, which is similar to CW.

   i) On the left-hand page, it appears that the left part of the spectrum is less sensitive to perturbations.

   ii) On the right-hand page, on the contrary, it is the left part of the spectrum that displays high instability.

In both cases, the appearance of spurious eigenvalues signals the emergence of a collective behaviour.

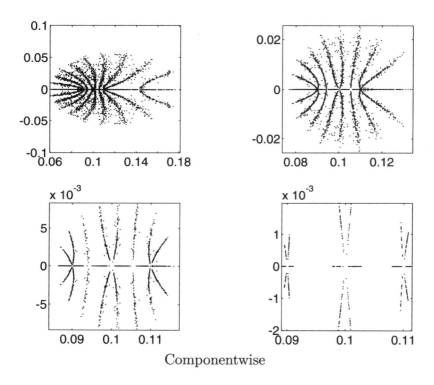

Componentwise

Cluster of order 10

Cluster is the companion matrix associated with the polynomial

$$p(x) = (x - 0.09)^3(x - 0.1)^3(x - 0.11)^3(x - 0.15).$$

$\sigma = \{0.09, 0.1, 0.11, 0.15\}$ and the Jordan structure is $(0.09)^3$, $(0.1)^3$, $(0.11)^3$, and $(0.15)^1$.

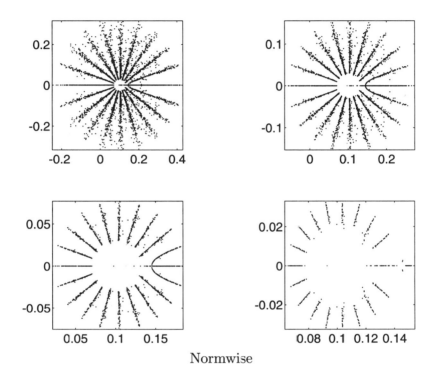

Normwise

Comments on Cluster

Again, very different effects of normwise and componentwise perturbations are visible.

i) On the left-hand page, the asymptotic behaviour of small perturbations for the triple eigenvalues conforms to the linear theory.

ii) On the right-hand page, the individual behaviour is not preserved by normwise perturbations. On the contrary, one sees a collective behaviour similar to that induced by one single Jordan block of order 10.

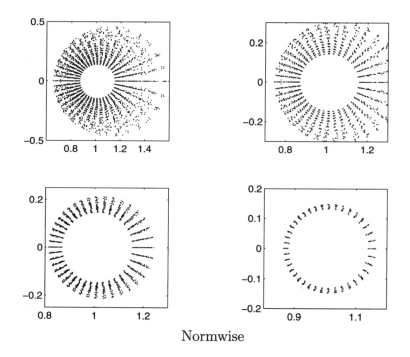

Normwise

Eccen of order 20

Eccen is the Toeplitz matrix defined in Example 11.4. $\sigma = \{1\}$, and the Jordan structure is $(1)^n$.

Comments on Eccen

Normwise perturbations of the spectrum indicate that Eccen tends to behave numerically as one single Jordan block of size 20.

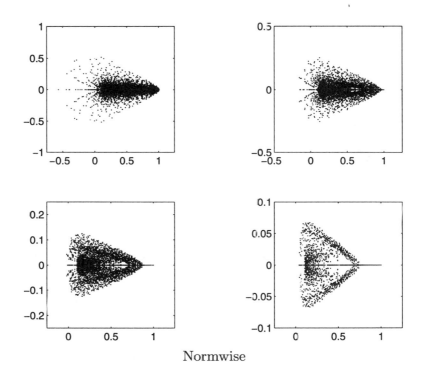

Normwise

Kahan matrix K of order $n = 150$

K is the upper triangular matrix defined by

$$\begin{pmatrix} 1 & -c & \dots & & & -c \\ & s & -sc & \dots & & -sc \\ & & s^2 & -s^2c & \dots & -s^2c \\ & & & \ddots & \dots & \vdots \\ & & & & s^{n-2} & -s^{n-2}c \\ & & & & & s^{n-1} \end{pmatrix},$$

where $s^{n-1} = 0.1$ and $s^2 + c^2 = 1$. The sample size is 5.

Comments on K

Here, the left part of the spectrum is more sensitive to normwise perturbations than the right part.

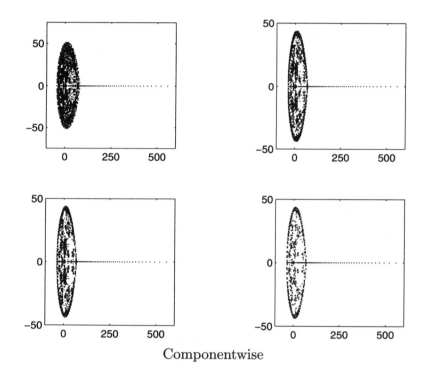

Componentwise

Frank matrix F of order 150

F is the upper Hessenberg matrix defined by

$$\begin{cases} f_{ij} = n - j + 1 & \text{for } i \leq j, \\ f_{i+1\,i} = n - i, & i = 1, \ldots, n - 1, \\ f_{ij} = 0 & \text{for } i > j + 1. \end{cases}$$

The spectrum is real for $\mathrm{Re}\lambda > 100$. The sample size is 3.

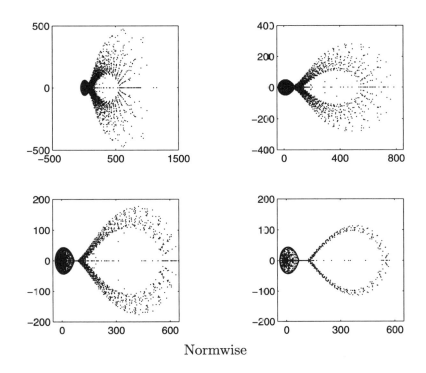

Normwise

Comments on F

Once more, one appreciates the different impact of normwise and componentwise perturbations.

i) On the left-hand page, most of the right part of the spectrum is stable under componentwise perturbations.

ii) On the right-hand page, it is, on the contrary, the right part of the spectrum that is most affected by normwise perturbations.

Annex: The Toolbox PRECISE for MATLAB

In this chapter, we give a sample of the MATLAB codes that we have used throughout a sample of this document to perform the experiments with PRECISE. They concern the following items.

Module 1

1. linear systems (GEPP) (normwise analysis).
2. eigenvalue problems (QR) (normwise analysis).

The formulae for the statistical indicators are given in Chapter 8. The graphical part is straightforward and has not been included here.

Module 2

1. perturbed spectra,
2. spectral portraits.

The routines for data perturbations used in both modules are given at the end of this annex, just before the spectral portraits. We provide here only the most significant routines. Interested readers can obtain the whole set of routines by anonymous ftp from ftp.cerfacs.fr under the directory pub/algo/software/Qualcomp/PRECISE.

Statistical study of the solution of the system $Ax = b$ solved by the LU factorization and using normwise random perturbations of A and/or b

```
%
clear all;
hold off;
clg;
% Choice of the matrix A (order n) and of the right-hand side b
% x: exact solution
%
n = 10;
A = dingdong(n);
x(1:n,1) = sqrt(1:n)';
b = A * x;
%
% Computation of the unperturbed solution
```

211

```
% xcal: computed solution
%
xcal = A \ b;
nxcal = norm(xcal,inf);
%
% Reference for the metrics
% A only --> 1,  b only --> 2,  A and b --> 3;
%
choix = 1;
if choix == 1
   alpha = norm(A,inf);
   beta = 0;
elseif choix == 2
   alpha = 0;
   beta = norm(b,inf);
else
   alpha = norm(A,inf);
   beta = norm(b,inf);
end;
ref = alpha*nxcal + beta;
%
% Computation of the corresponding error and residual
% res: infinite norm of the residual
% nerr: infinite norm of the exact error
%
nres = norm(A * xcal - b,inf);
nerr = norm(xcal - x,inf);
%
% Choice of the area of the perturbation (pmin and pmax),
% of the step size (pinter) and the sample size (nech)
%
pmin = 5;
pmax = 50;
pinter = 1;
nech = 50;
%
ind = 1;
%
% Initialisation of the perturbation
%
rand('seed',0);
%
% Main loop on the perturbation size
%
for jper = pmax:(-pinter):pmin
%
%%% Building the samples of computed solutions (EchX) and images by A (EchY)
   for i = 1:nech,
      M = rnorm(jper,A,alpha);
      w = rnorm(jper,b,beta);
```

```
        y = M \ w;
        EchX(i,:) = y';
        y = A * y;
        EchY(i,:) = y';
    end
%%% Computing the means and standard deviations of both samples
    for i = 1:n
        MeanX(i,1) = mean(EchX(:,i));
        StdX(i,1) = std(EchX(:,i));
        MeanY(i,1) = mean(EchY(:,i));
        StdY(i,1) = std(EchY(:,i));
        Rel(i,1) = sqrt(StdY(i)^2 + (MeanY(i) -b(i))^2);
    end
%%% Computing the normwise statistical indicators
    t = 2^(-jper+1);
    Absc(ind) = t;
    I(ind) = norm(Rel,inf) / (t*ref);
    L(ind) = norm(StdX,inf) /(t*nxcal);
    K(ind) = norm(StdX,inf)*ref / (nxcal*norm(StdY,inf));
    Er(ind) = norm(StdX,inf)*nres / (nxcal*norm(StdY,inf));
    Ex(ind) = nerr / nxcal;
    Ust(ind) = 1/t;
    ind = ind+1;
%
% End of the main loop
%
end
```

Statistical study of the solution of the eigenproblem $Ax = \lambda x$ using the QR factorization and using normwise random perturbations of A

```
%
clear all;
hold off;
clg;
% Choice of the matrix and of the right-hand side
% 1: exact eigenvalue
n = 3;
A = [ -1    0    0
        0   -1    0
        0    0   -1 ];
l = -1;
%
%
% Computation of the unperturbed solution
% Xcal: computed eigenvectors
% dlcal: computed eigenvalues
% Lambda: computed eigenvalues sorted by increasing modulus
%
```

```
%
[Xcal,dlcal] = eig(A);
[Lambda,k] = sort(diag(dlcal));
Lambda
%
% Choice of the eigenvalue (lcal) to be studied
% index: index of the chosen eigenvalue
% asc: ascent of  this eigenvalue (guess)
% xcal: eigenvector associated with lcal
%
index = input('index of the wanted eigenvalue = ');
asc = input('ascent of the wanted eigenvalue (guess) = ');
Xcal = Xcal(:,k);
xcal(1:n,1) = Xcal(:,index);
lcal = Lambda(index);
nxcal = norm(Xcal(1:n,index),inf);
%
% Reference for the metrics
alpha = norm(A,inf);
ref = alpha*nxcal;
%
% Computation of the corresponding error and residual
% nres: infinite norm of the residual
% nerr: infinite norm of the exact error
%
nres = norm(A * xcal - lcal*xcal,inf);
nerr = norm(lcal - l,inf);
%
% Choice of the area of the perturbation (pmin and pmax),
% of the step size (pinter) and the sample size (nech)
%
pmin = 5;
pmax = 50;
pinter = 1;
nech = 20;
%
ind = 1;
%
% Initialisation of the perturbation
%
rand('seed',0);
%
% Main loop on the perturbation size
%for jper = pmax:(-pinter):pmin
%
%%% Building the samples of computed solutions (EchX) and images by A (EchY)
    for i = 1:nech,
        M = rnorm(jper,A,alpha);
        [y,D] = eig(M);
        [Lambda,k] = sort(diag(D));
```

```
        y = y(:,k);
        EchX(i,1) = Lambda(index);
        y = A * y(:,index) - Lambda(index) * y(:,index) ;
        EchY(i,:) = y';
    end
%%% Computing the means and standard deviation of both samples
    MeanX(i,1) = mean(EchX(:,1));
    StdX(i,1) = std(EchX(:,1));
    for i = 1:n
        MeanY(i,1) = mean(EchY(:,i));
        StdY(i,1) = std(EchY(:,i));
        Rel(i,1) = sqrt(StdY(i)^2 + MeanY(i)^2);
    end
%%% Computing the normwise statistical indicators
    t = 2^(-jper+1);
    Absc(ind) = t;
    I(ind) = norm(Rel,inf) / (t*ref);
    L(ind) = norm(StdX,inf) /(t*abs(lcal));
    K(ind) = norm(StdX,inf)*ref / (abs(lcal)*norm(StdY,inf));
    Kl(ind) = (norm(StdX,inf) / abs(lcal)) * ((ref / norm(StdY,inf) )^(1/asc) );
    Er(ind) = norm(StdX,inf)*nres / (abs(lcal)*norm(StdY,inf));
    Erl(ind) = (norm(StdX,inf)/abs(lcal)) * ((nres / norm(StdY,inf) )^(1/asc) );
    Ex(ind) = nerr / abs(lcal);
    Ust(ind) = (t^(1-asc))^(1/asc);
    ind = ind+1;
%
end
%
```

Routines for perturbing the data

```
function AP = rnorm(p,A,f)
% RNORM    AP=RNORM(p,A) is a random normwise perturbation
%          of a rectangular matrix A.
%          Each element is submitted to an
%          absolute perturbation of size 2^(-p+1)*f
%          A(i,j) <- A(i,j) + r*2^(-p+1)*f
%          where pb(r=1) = pb(r=-1) = 1/2.

  v = size(A);
  for i = 1:v(1)
    for j = 1:v(2)
      if rand(1) > 0.5,
        AP(i,j) = A(i,j) + 2^(-p+1)*f;
      else
        AP(i,j) = A(i,j) - 2^(-p+1)*f;
      end
    end
  end
end
```

```
end
function AP = rcomp(p,A,E)
% RCOMP    AP=RCOMP(p,A,E) is a random componentwise perturbation
%          of a rectangular matrix A.
%          Each element is submitted to a
%          relative perturbation of size 2^(-p+1)
%          A(i,j) <- A(i,j) + r*2^(-p+1)*E(i,j)
%          where pb(r=1) = pb(r=-1) = 1/2.

  v = size(A);
  for i = 1:v(1)
    for j = 1:v(2)
      if rand(1) > 0.5,
        AP(i,j) = A(i,j) + 2^(-p+1)*E(i,j);
      else
        AP(i,j) = A(i,j) - 2^(-p+1)*E(i,j);
      end
    end
  end
end
```

Routines for computing a spectral portrait

```
function P = portrait(A,x1,x2,y1,y2,xmesh,ymesh)
%
% P = portrait(A,x1,x2,y1,y2,xmesh,ymesh)
% Computes the spectral portrait of the matrix A
% i.e. the values of z --> log10 ( ||(A -zI)^(-1)|| ||A|| )
% for z=x+iy varying in the complex plane [x1,x2] x [y1,y2].
% The region of the complex plane under study is discretized as follows
% xmesh: number of points in the interval [x1,x2] (for the x-axis)
% ymesh: number of points in the interval [y1,y2] (for the y-axis)
%

  normA = norm(A,2);
  P = 0;
  l = 0;
  xstep = (x2 - x1) / (xmesh - 1);
  ystep = (y2 - y1) / (ymesh - 1);
  j = 1;
  for ky = 0:ymesh - 1
    for kx = 0:xmesh - 1
      x = x1 + kx*xstep;
      y = y1 + ky*ystep;
      l = x + i*y;
% compute the norm of the resolvant ||inv(A-lI)||
      r = resolv(A,l,normA);
      Res(j) = r;
```

```
        j = j+1;
      end
   end
% reshape the matrix for plotting
  P = forme(Res,xmesh,ymesh);
end
%


function r = resolv(A,l,normA)
%
% function r = RESOLV(A,l,normA)
%
%   computes log10 ( || (A-l*I)^(-1) || ||A|| )
%   using the Singular value decomposition of A-l*I
%   normA = input argument such that normA = ||A||
%

  n = length(A);
  B = A - l*eye(n);
  r = log10( normA / min(svd(B)));
end

function A = forme(Res,xmesh,ymesh)
%
% A = FORME (RES, XMESH, YMESH)
%    reshapes the vector RES into a matrix that contains the values
%    at each point of the mesh in the correct order for colormap

  B = reshape(Res,xmesh,ymesh);
  B = B';
  for i = 1:ymesh
     A(i,1:xmesh) = B(ymesh+1-i,1:xmesh);
  end

end

function psnorm(B,nech,pmin,pmax,pinter,point)
%
% function PSNORM(B,nech,pmin,pmax,pinter,point);
%  computes and displays normwise perturbed spectra of B.
%  Relative perturbations varies between  2^(-pmax) to 2^(-pmin)
%  taking the intermediate values: 2^(-pmax-pinter),
%  2^(-pmax-2*pinter)...
%
%  B: matri under study
%  nech: sample size per perturbation
%  pmin: 2^(-pmin) = maximal relative amplitude of the perturbation
%  pmax: 2^(-pmax) = minimal relative amplitude of the perturbation
%  pinter: step size for the perturbation
```

```
%  point: (optional) size of the points on the figure (from 1 to 6)
%           default is 3.
%
%
hold off;
if nargin == 5
  point = 3;
end
A = B;
nA = norm(A,inf);
hold on;
for p = pmin:pinter:pmax
  for i = 1:nech
    M = rnorm(p,A,nA);
    X = eig(M);
    p1 = plot(real(X),imag(X),'.');
    set(p1,'MarkerSize',point);
  end
end
axis('square');
end
```

Bibliography

E. ANDERSON, Z. BAI, C. BISCHOF, J. DEMMEL, J. DONGARRA, J. DU CROZ, A. GREENBAUM, S. HAMMARLING, A. MCKENNEY, S. OSTROUCHOV, AND D. SORENSEN (1992), *LAPACK User's Guide*, SIAM, Philadelphia.

M. ARIOLI AND C. FASSINO (1994), *Roundoff Error Analysis of Algorithms Based on Krylov Subspace Methods*, IAN-Tech. Rep. 944, CNR, University of Pavia.

M. ARIOLI AND F. ROMANI (1992), *Stability, convergence and conditioning of stationary iterative methods of the form $x^{(i+1)} = Fx^{(i)} + q$ for the solution of linear systems*, IMA J. Numer. Anal., **12**, 21–30.

M. ARIOLI, J. DEMMEL, AND I. DUFF (1989), *Solving sparse linear systems with sparse backward error*, SIAM J. Matrix Anal. Appl., **10**, 165–190.

M. ARIOLI, I. DUFF, AND D. RUIZ (1992), *Stopping criteria for iterative solvers*, SIAM J. Matrix Anal. Appl., **13**, 138–144.

V. I. ARNOLD (1971), *On matrices depending on parameters*, Russian Math. Surveys, **26**, 29–43.

J. P. AUBIN (1972), *Approximation of Elliptic Boundary Value Problems*, Wiley, New York.

Z. BAI (1993), *A Collection of Test Matrices for the Large Scale Nonsymmetric Eigenvalue Problem*, Tech. Rep., University of Kentucky.

N. S. BAKHVALOV (1977), *Numerical Methods*, Mir, Moscow.

J. L. BARLOW (1993), *Error bounds for the computation of null vectors with application to Markov chains*, SIAM J. Matrix Anal. Appl., **14**, 798–812.

R. BARRETT, M. BERRY, T. CHAN, J. DEMMEL, J. DONATO, J. DONGARRA, V. EIJKHOUT, R. POZO, C. ROMINE, AND H. VAN DER VORST (1994), *Templates for the Solution of Linear Systems: Building Blocks for Iterative Methods*, SIAM, Philadelphia.

S. BATTERSON (1990), *Convergence of the shifted QR algorithm on 3×3 normal matrices*, Numer. Math., **58**, 341–352.

F. L. BAUER (1966), *Genauigkeitsfragen bei der Lösung linearer Gleichungssysteme*, ZAMM, **46**, 409–421.

F. L. BAUER (1974), *Computational graphs and rounding error*, SIAM J. Numer. Anal., **11**, 87–96.

F. BENFORD (1938), *On the law of anomalous numbers*, Proc. Amer. Philos. Soc., **78**, 551–572.

M. BENNANI AND T. BRACONNIER (1994a), *Comparative Behaviour of Eigensolvers on Highly Nonnormal Matrices*, Tech. Rep. TR/PA/94/23, CERFACS.

M. BENNANI AND T. BRACONNIER (1994b), *Stopping Criteria for Eigensolvers*, Tech. Rep. TR/PA/94/22, CERFACS.

M. BENNANI, T. BRACONNIER, AND J.-C. DUNYACH (1994), *Solving large-scale nonnormal eigenproblems in the aeronautical industry using parallel BLAS*, in High-Performance Computing and Networking, Lecture Notes in Computer Science 796, W. Gentzsch and U. Harms, eds., Springer, New York, 72–77.

M. BENNANI, M. C. BRUNET, AND F. CHATELIN (1988), *De l'utilisation en calcul matriciel de modèles probabilistes pour la simulation des erreurs de calcul*, C. R. Acad. Sci. Paris Série I, **307**, 847–850.

M. BENNANI (1991), *A propos de la stabilité de la résolution d'équations sur ordinateurs*, Ph.D. dissertation, Institut National Polytechnique de Toulouse.

M. V. BERRY (1978), *Les jeux de lumière dans l'eau*, La Recherche, **72**, 760–768.

M. V. BERRY (1991), *Asymptotics, singularities, and the reduction of theories*, in *Proceedings of the 9th Congress of Logic, Methodology and Philosophy of Science*, D. Prawitz, B. Skyrms, and D. Westerståhl, eds., Studies in Logic and the Foundations of Mathematics, Uppsala, Kluwer Academic Publishers, Dordrecht, the Netherlands.

Å. BJÖRCK AND V. PEREYRA (1970), *Solution of Vandermonde systems of equations*, Math. Comp., **24**, 893–903.

Å. BJÖRCK (1967), *Solving linear least squares ploblems by Gram-Schmidt orthogonalization*, BIT, **7**, 257–278.

Å. BJÖRCK (1991), *Component-wise perturbation analysis and error bounds for linear least squares solutions*, BIT, **31**, 238–244.

Å. BJÖRCK (1994), *Numerics of Gram-Schmidt orthogonalization*, Linear Algebra Appl., **197-198**, 297–316.

J. H. BLEHER, S. RUMP, U. KULISCH, M. METZGER, C. ULLRICH, AND W. WALTER (1987), *A study of FORTRAN extension for engineering/scientific computation to ACRITH*, Computing, **39**, 93–110.

B. BLISS, M. C. BRUNET, AND E. GALLOPOULOS (1992), *Automatic parallel program instrumentation with applications in performance and error analysis*, in Expert Systems for Scientific Computing, E. N. Houstis, J. R. Rice, and R. Vichnevtsky, eds., North-Holland and IMACS, Amsterdam, 235–260.

L. BLUM, M. SHUB, AND S. SMALE (1989), *On a theory of computation and complexity over the real numbers: NP-completeness, recursive functions and universal machines*, Bull. AMS, **21**, 1–46.

T. BRACONNIER, F. CHATELIN, AND J.-C. DUNYACH (1995), *Highly nonnormal eigenvalue problems in the aeronautical industry*, Japan J. Ind. Appl. Math., **12**, 1.

T. BRACONNIER (1993), *The Arnoldi-Tchebycheff Algorithm for Solving Large Nonsymmetric Eigenproblems*, Tech. Rep. TR/PA/93/25, CERFACS.

T. BRACONNIER (1994a), *The Arnoldi-Tchebycheff Algorithm for Solving Large Complex Non Hermitian Generalized Eigenproblems*, Tech. Rep. TR/PA/94/08, CERFACS.

T. BRACONNIER (1994b), *The Role of the Orthogonalization Scheme Used for Eigensolvers Applied to Nonnormal Matrices*, Tech. Rep. TR/PA/94/20, CERFACS.

T. BRACONNIER (1994c), *Sur le calcul de valeurs propres en précision finie*, Ph.D. dissertation, Université H. Poincaré, Nancy.

T. BRACONNIER (1995), *Influence of the Orthogonality on the Backward Error and the Stopping Criterion for Krylov Methods*, Tech. Rep., Department of Mathematics, University of Manchester.

D. BROUWER (1937), *On the accumulation of errors in numerical integration*, Astron. J., **46**, 149–153.

L. BRUGNANO AND D. TRIGIANTE (1990), *Sulle soluzioni di equazioni alle differenze dell'algebra lineare numerica*, Atti della Acad. Sc. Bologna, **V**, 93–108.

M. C. BRUNET (1989), *Contribution à la fiabilité de logiciels numériques et à l'analyse de leur comportement: une approche statistique*, Ph.D. dissertation, Université Paris IX Dauphine.

J. R. BUNCH, J. W. DEMMEL, AND C. F. VAN LOAN (1989), *The strong stability of algorithms for solving symmetric linear systems*, SIAM J. Matrix Anal. Appl., **10**, 494–499.

J. R. BUNCH (1987), *The weak and strong stability of algorithms in numerical linear algebra*, Linear Algebra Appl., **88/89**, 49–66.

S. L. CAMPBELL AND C. D. MEYER (1991), *Generalized Inverses of Linear Transformations*, Dover, Mineola, NY.

F. CHAITIN-CHATELIN AND V. TOUMAZOU (1995), *Possibilités et limites du calcul sur ordinateur*, Cours de formation continue, ENSTA, Paris, 25–29 Septembre.

F. CHAITIN-CHATELIN AND V. FRAYSSÉ (1995), *Qualitative computing and the robustness of numerical methods to high nonnormality*. IMACS'95 Conference on iterative methods, Blagoevgrad, Bulgaria, June 17–20, to appear in IMACS Comp. Appl. Math.

F. CHAITIN-CHATELIN AND S. GRATTON (1995), *Convergence of Successive Approximations in Finite Precision under High Nonnormality*, Tech. Rep. TR/PA/95/43, CERFACS. Submitted to BIT.

F. CHAITIN-CHATELIN (1994a), *Is Nonnormality a Serious Difficulty?*, Tech. Rep. TR/PA/94/18, CERFACS. Presented at ILAS 94, Rotterdam.

F. CHAITIN-CHATELIN (1994b), *Le calcul sur ordinateur à précision finie*, Tech. Rep. TR/PA/94/05, CERFACS. Rapport réalisé à la demande de l'Institut d'Expertise de l'Ecole Normale Supérieure pour le compte de la DGA/DRET.

F. CHAITIN-CHATELIN (1995a), *Le calcul qualitatif. Comment donner un sens à des résultats faux?*, Tech. Rep. TR/PA/95/10, CERFACS. Support de cours pour le DEA intensif Problèmes inverses en Astrophysique, Concepts mathématiques et méthodes de résolution, CIRM, Luminy, 20–24 mars 95.

F. CHAITIN-CHATELIN (1995b), *On the influence of high nonnormality on the reliability of iterative methods in computational linear algebra*, ICIAM 95, Hamburg, July 3–7.

T. F. CHAN AND D. E. FOULSER (1988), *Effectively well-conditioned linear systems*, SIAM J. Sci. Stat. Comput., **9**, 963–969.

F. CHATELIN AND T. BRACONNIER (1994), *About the qualitative computation of Jordan forms*, ZAMM, **74**, 105–113.

F. CHATELIN AND M.-C. BRUNET (1990), *A probabilistic round-off error propagation model. Application to the eigenvalue problem*, in Reliable Numerical Computation, M. G. Cox and S. Hammarling, eds., Oxford University Press, Oxford, 139–160.

F. CHATELIN AND V. FRAYSSÉ (1991), *Arithmetic reliability of algorithms*, in 2nd Symposium on High Performance Computing, M. Durand and F. El Dabaghi, eds., North-Holland, Amsterdam, 441–450.

F. CHATELIN AND V. FRAYSSÉ (1992), *Elements of a condition theory for the computational analysis of algorithms*, in Iterative Methods in Linear Algebra, R. Beauwens and P. De Groen, eds., North-Holland, Amsterdam, 15–25.

F. CHATELIN AND V. FRAYSSÉ (1993a), *About the distance to singularity for nonlinear problems*. Presented at the SCAN-93 IMACS/GAMM International Symposium on Scientific Computing, Computed Arithmetic and Validated Numerics, Technical University of Vienna, Austria, September 26–29.

F. CHATELIN AND V. FRAYSSÉ (1993b), *Distances to singularity viewed by computers*. Presented at the XII Householder Symposium on Numerical Algebra, UCLA Conference Center, Lake Arrowhead, CA, June 13–18.

F. CHATELIN AND V. FRAYSSÉ (1993c), *Qualitative computing: Elements of a Theory for Finite Precision Computation*, Lecture Notes for the Comett European Course, June 8–10, Thomson-CSF, LCR Corbeville, Orsay.

F. CHATELIN AND P. TROUVÉ (1993), *Le calcul scientifique, pour quoi faire?*, Bulletin d'information du Laboratoire Central de Recherches et des Laboratoires Electroniques de Rennes, Thomson–CSF, 1, 3–10.

F. CHATELIN, V. FRAYSSÉ, AND T. BRACONNIER (1993), *Qualitative Computing: Elements of a Theory for Finite Precision Computation*, Tech. Rep. TR/PA/93/12, CERFACS. Lecture Notes for the Workshop on Reliability of Computations, March 30–April 1, Toulouse, France.

F. CHATELIN, V. FRAYSSÉ, AND T. BRACONNIER (1995), *Computations in the neighbourhood of algebraic singularities*, Num. Funct. Anal. Opt., **16**, 287–302.

F. CHATELIN, (1970), *Méthodes d'approximation des valeurs propres d'opérateurs linéaires dans un espace de Banach. I. Critère de stabilité*, C. R. Acad. Sci. Paris Série A, **271**, 949–952.

F. CHATELIN (1983), *Spectral Approximation of Linear Operators*, Academic Press, New York.

F. CHATELIN (1984), *Simultaneous Newton's iterations for the eigenproblem*, Computing, Suppl., **5**, 67–74. In Error Asymptotics and Defect Correction, Proc. Oberwolfach Conference.

F. CHATELIN (1986), *Ill-conditioned eigenproblems*, in Large Scale Eigenvalue Problems, J. Cullum and R. A. Willoughby, eds., North-Holland, Amsterdam, 267–282.

F. CHATELIN (1988a), *Etude statistique de la qualité numérique et arithmétique de la résolution approchée d'équations par calcul sur ordinateur*, Tech. Rep. F. 133, Centre Scientifique IBM–France.

F. CHATELIN (1988b), *Sur le taux de fiabilité de la méthode CESTAC*, C. R. Acad. Sci. Paris Série I, **307**, 851–854.

F. CHATELIN (1988c), *Valeurs Propres de Matrices*, Masson, Paris.

F. CHATELIN (1989a), *Comment traiter les calculs impossibles?*, La Recherche, **214**, 1268–1270.

F. CHATELIN (1989b), *Résolution approchée d'équations sur ordinateur*, Notes de DEA, Université Paris VI.

F. CHATELIN (1991), *Fiabilité arithmétique des ordinateurs*, Cours de formation permanente, Dassault- Systèmes, 20–21 Juin.

F. CHATELIN (1993a), *Eigenvalues of Matrices*, Wiley, Chichester. (Enlarged translation of Chatelin (1988c).)

F. CHATELIN (1993b), *The influence of nonnormality on matrix computations*, in Linear Algebra, Markov Chains and Queueing Models, R. J. Plemmons and C. D. Meyer, eds., Springer, New York, 13–19.

J. M. CHESNEAUX (1988), *Modélisation et conditions de validité de la méthode CESTAC*, C. R. Acad. Sci. Paris Série I, **307**, 417–422.

J. M. CHESNEAUX (1992a), *CADNA, Contrôle des Arrondis et Débogage Numérique en ADA*, Rapport MASI 92.31, Université Paris VI.

J. M. CHESNEAUX (1992b), *Descriptif d'utilisation du logiciel CADNA-F*, Rapport MASI 92.32, Université Paris VI.

B. A. CIPRA (1995), *Are eigenvalues overvalued?*, SIAM News, **28**, 8.

W. J. CODY (1973), *Static and dynamic numerical characteristics of floating point arithmetic*, IEEE Trans. Comp. C, **22**, 598–601.

J.-F. COLONNA (1992), *Erreurs d'arrondi*, Pour la science, **179**, 104–107.

G. DAHLQUIST AND A. BJÖRCK (1980), *Numerical Methods*, Prentice-Hall, Englewood Cliffs, New Jersey.

C. DE BOOR AND A. PINKUS (1977), *Backward error analysis for totally positive systems*, Numer. Math., **27**, 485–490.

A. DEIF (1990), *Realistic a priori and a posteriori error bounds for computed eigenvalues*, IMA J. Numer. Anal., **9**, 323–329.

J. W. DEMMEL (1987), *On condition numbers and the distance to the nearest ill-posed problem*, Numer. Math., **51**, 251–289.

J. W. DEMMEL (1988), *The probability that a numerical analysis problem is difficult*, Math. Comp., **50**, 449–480.

J. W. DEMMEL (1990), *Nearest defective matrices and the geometry of ill-conditioning*, in Reliable Numerical Computation, M. G. Cox and S. Hammarling, eds., Clarendon Press, Oxford, 35–55.

J. W. DEMMEL (1992), *The componentwise distance to the nearest singular matrix*, SIAM J. Matrix Anal. Appl., **13**, 10–19.

J. W. DEMMEL (1993), *Geometry and High Accuracy Algorithms*, the James H. Wilkinson Prize in Numerical Analysis and Scientific Computing award and presentation, SIAM Annual Meeting.

R. L. DEVANEY (1989), *An Introduction to Chaotic Dynamical Systems*, second ed. Addison-Wesley, Redwood City, California.

J. D. DIXON (1983), *Estimating extremal eigenvalues and condition numbers of matrices*, SIAM J. Numer. Anal., **20**, 812–814.

P. G. DRAZIN AND W. H. REID (1981), *Hydrodynamic Stability*, Cambridge University Press, Cambridge.

J. DRKOSOVA, A. GREENBAUM, M. ROZLOZNIK, AND Z. STRAKOŠ (1995), *Numerical Stability of GMRES*, BIT, **35**, 309–330.

V. DRUSKIN AND L. KNIZHNERMAN (1995), *Krylov subspace approximation of eigenpairs and matrix functions in exact arithmetic*, J. Numer. Linear Algebra Appl., **2**, 205–217.

I. DUFF, R. GRIMES, AND J. LEWIS (1992), *User's Guide for the Harwell-Boeing Sparse Matrix Collection*, Tech. Rep. TR-PA-92-86, CERFACS.

D. DUVAL (1992), *Examples of problem solving using computer algebra*, in Programming Environments for High-Level Scientific Problem Solving, P. W. Gaffney and E. N. Houstis, eds., North-Holland, Amsterdam.

A. EDELMAN (1988), *Eigenvalues and condition numbers of random matrices*, SIAM J. Matrix Anal. Appl., **9**, 543–560.

A. EDELMAN AND H. MURAKAMI (1995), *Polynomial roots for companion matrix eigenvalues*, Math. Comp., **64**, 763–776.

I. EKELAND (1984), *Le calcul, l'imprévu*, Seuil, Paris.

J. ERHEL AND B. PHILIPPE (1991a), *AQUARELS: a problem-solving environment for numerical quality*, in IMACS'91, 13th World Congress on Computation and Applied Mathematics, vol. 1, Trinity College, Dublin, Ireland, C. Brezinski and U. Kulisch, eds., North-Holland, Amsterdam.

J. ERHEL AND B. PHILIPPE (1991b), *Design of a toolbox to control arithmetic reliability*, in International Symposium on Computer Arithmetic and Scientific Computation, Oldenburg, Germany, J. Herzberger and L. Atanassova, eds., North-Holland, Amsterdam.

J. ERHEL (1991), *Statistical Estimation of Roundoff Errors and Condition Numbers*, Tech. Rep. 1490, INRIA/IRISA, Rennes, France.

K. FAN AND A. J. HOFFMAN (1955), *Some metric inequalities in the space of matrices*, Proc. Amer. Math. Soc., 6, 111–116.

A. FELDSTEIN AND R. GOODMAN (1976), *Convergence estimates for the distribution of trailing digits*, J. ACM, **23**, 287–297.

R. FLETCHER (1985), *Expected conditioning*, IMA J. Numer. Anal., **5**, 247–273.

B. FORD AND F. CHATELIN (EDS.) (1987), *Problem Solving Environments for Scientific Computing*, North-Holland, Amsterdam.

B. FORD AND J. RICE (1994), *Rationale for the IFIP Working Conference: "The Quality of Numerical Software: Assessment and Enhancement,"* to be held in Oxford, July 8–12, 1996, IFIP-WG2.5 document, Raleigh-2109.

G. E. FORSYTHE, M. A. MALCOM, AND C. B. MOLER (1977), *Computer Methods for Mathematical Computations*, Prentice-Hall, Englewood Cliffs, New Jersey.

G. E. FORSYTHE (1950), *Round-off errors in numerical integration on automatic machinery*, Bull. AMS, **56**, 61 (abstract).

P. FRANÇOIS AND J. M. MULLER (1990), *Faut-il faire confiance aux ordinateurs?*, Rapport 90-03, LIP, ENS Lyon.

P. FRANÇOIS (1989), *Contribution à l'étude de méthodes de contrôle automatique de l'erreur d'arrondi: la méthodologie SCALP*, Ph.D. dissertation, Institut National Polytechnique de Grenoble.

V. FRAYSSÉ (1992), *Reliability of computer solutions (Sur la fiabilité des calculs sur ordinateurs)*, Ph.D. dissertation, Institut National Polytechnique de Toulouse.

R. E. FUNDERLIC AND C. D. MEYER (1986), *Sensitivity of the stationary distribution for an ergodic Markov chain*, Linear Algebra Appl , **76**, 1–17.

P. W. GAFFNEY AND E. N. HOUSTIS (EDS.) (1992), *Programming Environments for High-Level Scientific Problem Solving*, North-Holland, Amsterdam.

A. J. GEURTS (1979), *On Condition and Numerical Stability*, Tech. Rep. T.H.-Report 79-WSK-04, Technological University of Eindhoven.

A. J. GEURTS (1982), *A contribution to the theory of condition*, Numer. Math., **39**, 85–96.

A. J. GEURTS (1992), Private communication.

A. R. GHAVIMI AND A. J. LAUB (1995), *Backward error, sensitivity and refinement of computed solutions of algebraic Riccati equations*, J. Numer. Linear Algebra. Appl., **2**, 29–49.

W. GIVENS (1954), *Numerical Computation of the Characteristic Values of a Real Symmetric Matrix*, Tech. Rep. ORNL-1574, Oak Ridge National Laboratory.

P. GLORIEUX (1988), *Chaos et crises dans les lasers*, Images de la physique 88, Courrier du CNRS. suppl. no 71.

S. K. GODUNOV AND V. S. RYABENKI (1964), *Theory of Difference Schemes: An Introduction*, North-Holland, Amsterdam. Translation by E. Godfredsen.

S. K. GODUNOV AND V. S. RYABENKI (1987), *Difference Schemes: An Introduction to the Underlying Theory*, North-Holland, Amsterdam. Translation by E. M. Gelbard.

S. K. GODUNOV, A. G. ANTONOV, O. P. KIRILJUK, AND V. I. KOSTIN (1993), *Guaranteed Accuracy in Numerical Linear Algebra*, Kluwer Academic Publishers, Dordrecht, the Netherlands.

S. K. GODUNOV (1992a), *Investigation into stability of almost conservative systems by means of Lyapounov functions*, Siberian Advances in Mathematics, **2**, 89–113.

S. K. GODUNOV (1992b), *Spectral portraits of matrices and criteria of spectrum dichotomy*, in Computer Arithmetic and Enclosure Methods, J. Herzberger and L. Atanassova, eds., North-Holland and IMACS, Amsterdam.

G. GOHBERG AND I. KOLTRACHT (1990), *On the inversion of Cauchy matrices*, in Signal Processing, Scattering and Operator Theory and Numerical Methods, International Symposium MNTS 89, vol. 3, M. A. Kaashock, J. H. Van Schuppen, and A. C. Ran, eds., Birkhäuser, Boston. 381–392.

G. GOHBERG AND I. KOLTRACHT (1993), *Mixed, componentwise and structured condition numbers*, SIAM J. Matrix Anal. Appl., **14**, 688–704.

D. GOLDBERG (1991), *What every scientist should know about floating-point arithmetic*, ACM Computing Surveys, **23**, 5–48.

H. H. GOLDSTINE AND J. VON NEUMANN (1951), *Numerical inverting of matrices of high order* II, Proc. Amer. Math. Soc., **2**, 188–202.

G. GOLUB AND C. MEYER (1986), *Using the QR factorisation and group inversion to compute, differentiate, and estimate the sensitivity of stationary probabilities for Markov chains*, SIAM J. Alg. Disc. Meth., **7**, 273–281.

G. GOLUB AND C. VAN LOAN (1989), *Matrix computations*, second edition, Johns Hopkins University Press, Baltimore.

G. H. GOLUB AND J. H. WILKINSON (1976), *Ill-conditioned eigensystems and the computation of the Jordan canonical form*, SIAM Rev., **18**, 578–619.

G. GOLUB (1962), *Bounds for the round-off errors in the Richardson second order method*, BIT, **2**, 212–223.

R. GOODMAN AND A. FELDSTEIN (1975), *Round-off errors in products*, Computing, **15**, 263–273.

S. GRATTON (1994), *Moindres carrés pour l'orbitographie. Etude de la stabilité*, Tech. Rep. TR/PA/94/17, CERFACS. (Rapport de fin d'études, ENSEEIHT.)

S. GRATTON (1995a), *Conditionnements hölderiens pour une racine multiple de polynôme*, Tech. Rep., CERFACS, to appear.

S. GRATTON (1995b), *Utilisation du produit de Kronecker pour le calcul de conditionnement en norme de Frobenius*, Annex of Contract Rep. FR/PA/95/28.

S. GRATTON (1995c), *On the Condition Number of Linear Least Squares Problems in Frobenius Norm*, Tech. Rep. TR/PA/95/27, CERFACS. Submitted to BIT.

A. GREENBAUM AND Z. STRAKOŠ (1994), *Matrices that generate the same Krylov residual spaces*, in Recent Advances in Iterative Methods, IMA Vol. Math. Appl., 60, G. Golub and M. Luskin, eds., Springer, New York, 95–119.

A. GREENBAUM, V. PTÁK, AND Z. STRAKOŠ (1995), *Any nonincreasing convergence curve is possible for GMRES*, to appear in SIAM J. Matrix Anal. Appl.

A. GRIEWANK (1989), *On automatic differentiation*, in Mathematical Programming, M. Iri and K. Tanabe, eds., Kluwer Academic Publishers Dordrecht, the Netherlands, 83–107.

L. H. GUSTAVSSON (1991), *Energy growth of three-dimensional disturbances in plane Poiseuille flow*, J. Fluid Mech., **224**, 241–260.

S. HAMMARLING AND J. H. WILKINSON (1976), *The practical behaviour of linear iterative methods with particular reference to SOR*, Tech. Rep. NAC 69, NPL, Teddington.

S. H. HAMMEL, J. A. YORKE, AND C. GREBOGI (1987), *Do numerical orbits of chaotic dynamical processes represent true orbits?*, J. Complexity, **3**, 136–145.

P. HENRICI (1962a), *Bounds for iterates, inverses, spectral variation and field of values of nonnormal matrices*, Numer. Math., **4**, 24–40.

P. HENRICI (1962b), *Discrete Variable Methods in Ordinary Differential Equations*, Wiley, New York.

P. HENRICI (1966), *Test of probabilistic models for propagation of roundoff errors*, Comm. ACM, **9**, 409–410.

D. J. HIGHAM AND N. J. HIGHAM (1992a), *Backward error and condition of structured linear systems*, SIAM J. Matrix Anal. Appl., **13**, 162–175.

D. J. HIGHAM AND N. J. HIGHAM (1992b), *Componentwise perturbation theory for linear systems with multiple right-hand sides*, Linear Algebra Appl., **174**, 111–129.

N. J. HIGHAM AND P. A. KNIGHT (1995), *Matrix power in finite precision arithmetic*, SIAM J. Matrix Anal. Appl., **16**, 343–358.

N. J. HIGHAM (1987a), *Error analysis of the Björck-Pereyra algorithm for solving Vandermonde systems*, Numer. Math., **50**, 613–632.

N. J. HIGHAM (1987b), *A survey of condition number estimation for triangular matrices*, SIAM Rev., **29**, 575–596.

N. J. HIGHAM (1989), *The accuracy of solutions to triangular systems*, SIAM J. Numer. Anal., **26**, 1252–1265.

N. J. HIGHAM (1990), *How accurate is Gaussian elimination?*, in Numerical Analysis 1989, Proceedings of the 13th Dundee Conference, D. Griffiths and G. Watson, eds., Longman Scientific and Technical, Harlow, 137–154.

N. J. HIGHAM (1991a), *A collection of test matrices in MATLAB*, ACM Trans. Math. Software, **17**, 289–305.

N. J. HIGHAM (1991b), *Iterative refinement enhances the stability of QR factorization methods for solving linear equations*, BIT, **31**, 447–468.

N. J. HIGHAM (1993), *Perturbation theory and backward error for $AX - XB = C$*, BIT, **33**, 124–136.

N. J. HIGHAM (1994), *The matrix sign decomposition and its relation to the polar decomposition*, Linear Algebra Appl., **212/213**, 3–20.

N. J. HIGHAM (1996), *Accuracy and Stability of Numerical Algorithms*, SIAM, Philadelphia.

D. HINRICHSEN AND B. KELB (1993), *Spectral value sets: a graphical tool for robustness analysis*, Systems Control Lett., **21**, 127–136.

H. HOTELLING (1943), *Some new methods in matrix calculation*, Ann. Math. Statist., **14**, 1–34.

T. E. HULL AND J. R. SWENSON (1966), *Tests of probabilistic models for propagation of round-off*, Comm. ACM, **9**, 108–113.

M. IRI (1991), *History of automatic differentiation and rounding error estimation.*, in Automatic Differentiation of Algorithms—Theory, Implementation, and Application, A. Griewank and G. F. Corliss, eds., SIAM, Phildelphia, 3–16.

M. JANKOWSKI AND H. WOŹNIAKOWSKI (1977), *Iterative refinement implies numerical stability*, BIT, **17**, 303–311.

B. KÅGSTRÖM AND A. RUHE (1981), *An algorithm for numerical computation of the Jordan normal form of a complex matrix*, ACM Trans Math. Software, **6**, 398–419.

W. KAHAN (1966), *Numerical linear algebra*, Canad. Math. Bull., **9**, 1983.

W. KAHAN (1972), *Conserving Confluence Curbs Ill-Condition*, Tech. Rep. 6, Department of Computer Science, University of California, Berkeley.

E. M. KASENALLY (1995), *GMBACK: A generalized minimum backward error algorithm for nonsymmetric linear systems*, SIAM J. Sci. Comput., **16**, 698–719.

T. KATO (1976), *Perturbation Theory for Linear Operators*, second edition, Springer, Berlin, New York.

C. S. KENNEY AND A. J. LAUB (1989), *Condition estimates for matrix functions*, SIAM J. Sci. Comput., **10**, 191–209.

C. S. KENNEY AND A. J. LAUB (1994), *Small sample statistical condition estimates for general matrix functions*, SIAM J. Sci. Comput., **15**, 36–61.

W. KERNER (1986), *Computing the complex eigenvalue spectrum for resistive magnetohydrodynamics*, in Large Scale Eigenvalue Problems, J. Cullum and R. A. Willoughby, eds., North-Holland, Amsterdam, 240–264.

W. KERNER (1989), *Large scale complex eigenvalues problems*, J. Comp. Phys., **85**, 1–85.

A. KIEŁBASIŃSKI (1975), *Basic Concepts in Numerical Error Analysis (Suggested by Linear Algebra Problems)*, Banach Center Publications 3, 223–232.

O. KIRILYUK AND V. I. KOSTIN (1991), *Package of routines Palina–1.30*, user's manual (in Russian).

D. E. KNUTH (1969), *The Art of Computer Programming. Vol. 2: Seminumerical Algorithms*, Addison-Wesley, Reading, Massachusetts.

U. KULISCH AND W. L. MIRANKER (1981), *Computer Arithmetic in Theory and Practice*, Academic Press, New York.

U. KULISCH AND W. L. MIRANKER (1986), *The arithmetic of the digital computer: A new approach*, SIAM Rev., **28**, 1–40.

U. KULISCH (1987), *PASCAL-SC, a Pascal Extension for Scientific Computation*, Wiley-Teubner, Stuttgart. (Information manual and floppy disks.)

M. LA PORTE AND J. VIGNES (1974), *Arithmétique des ordinateurs, Tome 1: systèmes linéaires*, Technip, Paris.

P. LANCASTER AND M. TISMENETSKY (1985), *The Theory of Matrices*, second edition with applications, Academic Press, New York.

P. S. LAPLACE (1812), *Théorie analytique des probabilités*, Paris.

A. LARGILLIER (1994), *Utilisation du théorème des fonctions implicites pour estimer les erreurs relatives dans des factorisations linéaires complexes*, Tech. Rep., Analyse Numérique, Université Jean Monnet, St-Etienne, URA CNRS 740.

J. L. LARSON AND A. H. SAMEH (1980), *Efficient calculation of the effects of roundoff errors*, Computing, **24**, 275–297.

J. L. LARSON, M. E. PASTERNAK, AND J. A. WISNIEWSKI (1983), *Algorithm 594 : Software for relative error analysis*, ACM Trans. Math. Software, **9**, 125–130.

S. L. LEE (1994), *Bounds for the departure from normality and the Frobenius norm of matrix eigenvalues*, Tech. Rep. TM-12853, ORNL, submitted to SIAM J. Matrix Anal. Appl.

S. L. LEE (1995), *A practical upper bound for departure from normality.* SIAM J. Matrix Anal. Appl., **16**, 462–468.

R. B. LEHOUCQ (1995), *Analysis and Implementation of an Implicitly Restarted Arnoldi Iteration*, Ph.D. dissertation, Rice University, Houston, Texas.

O. MARQUES AND V. TOUMAZOU (1995a), *Spectral Portraits Computation by a Lanczos Method, Normal Equation Version*, Tech. Rep. TR/PA/95/02, CERFACS.

O. MARQUES AND V. TOUMAZOU (1995b), *Spectral Portraits Computation by a Lanczos Method, Augmented Matrix Version*, Tech. Rep. TR/PA/95/05, CERFACS.

K. MEYER AND D. SCHMIDT (EDS.) (1991), *Computer Aided Proofs in Analysis*, IMA Vol. Math. Appl. 28, Springer, New York, Berlin.

W. MILLER AND D. SPOONER (1978), *Software for roundcff analysis* II, ACM Trans. Math. Software, **4**, 369–387.

W. MILLER (1976), *Graph transformations for round-off analysis*, SIAM J. Comp., **5**, 204–216.

L. MIRSKY (1960), *Symmetric gauge function and unitarily invariant norms*, Quart. J. Math. Oxford, **11**, 50–59.

R. MOORE (1966), *Interval Analysis*, Prentice-Hall, Englewood Cliffs, New Jersey.

R. E. MOORE (1991), *Interval tools for computer aided proofs in analysis*, in Computer Aided Proofs in Analysis, IMA Vol. Math. Appl. 28, K. Meyer and D. Schmidt, eds., Springer, New York, Berlin, 211–216.

R. G. MOSIER (1986), *Root neighborhoods of a polynomial*, Math. Comp., **47**, 175, 265–273.

O. NEVANLINNA (1993), *Convergence of Iterations for Linear Equations*, Birkhäuser, Basel.

S. NEWCOMB (1881), *Note on the frequency of use of different digits in natural numbers*, Amer. J. Math., **4**, 39–40.

W. OETTLI AND W. PRAGER (1964), *Compatibility of approximate solution of linear equations with given error bounds for coefficients and right-hand sides*, Numer. Math., **6**, 405–409.

M. PICHAT AND J. VIGNES (1993), *Ingénierie du contrôle de la précision des calculs sur ordinateur*, Editions Technip, Paris.

S. POLJAK AND J. ROHN (1993), *Checking robust nonsingularity is NP-hard*, Math. Control Signals Systems, **6**, 1–9.

H. A. RADEMACHER (1948), *On the accumulation of errors in processes of integration on high-speed calculating machines*, Annals Comp. Lab., Harvard U., **16**, 176–185.

L. B. RALL (1981), *Automatic Differentiation*, Lecture Notes in Comput. Sci. 120, Springer, New York.

L. B. RALL (1991), *Tools for mathematical computction*, in Computer Aided Proofs in Analysis, IMA Vcl. Math Appl., 28, K. Meyer and D. Schmidt, eds., Springer, New York, Berlin, 217–228.

S. C. REDDY AND L. N. TREFETHEN (1990), *Lax-stability of fully discrete spectral methods via stability regions and pseudo-eigenvalues*, Comp. Meth. Appl. Mech. Eng., **80**, 147–164.

S. C. REDDY AND L. N. TREFETHEN (1992), *Stability of the method of lines*, Numer. Math., **62**, 235–267.

S. C. REDDY AND L. N. TREFETHEN (1994), *Pseudospectra of the convection-diffusion operator*, SIAM J. Appl. Math, **54**, 1634–1649.

S. C. REDDY (1991), *Pseudospectra of Operators and Discretization Matrices and an Application to Stability of the Method of Lines*, Ph.D. dissertation, Department of Mathematics, Massachusetts Institute of Technology.

L. REICHEL AND L. TREFETHEN (1992), *Eigenvalues and pseudo-eigenvalues of Toeplitz matrices*, Linear Algebra Appl., **162–164**, 153–185.

J. R. RICE (1966), *A theory of condition*, SIAM J. Numer. Anal., **3**, 287–310.

J. RIGAL AND J. GACHES (1967), *On the compatibility of a given solution with the data of a linear system*, J. Assoc. Comput. Mach., **14**, 543–548.

F. ROBERT (1986), *Discrete Iterations: A Metric Study*, Springer, Berlin.

J. ROHN (1989), *New condition numbers for matrices and linear systems*, Computing, **41**, 167–169.

J. ROHN (1990), *Non singularity under data rounding*, Linear Algebra Appl., **139**, 171–174.

T. H. ROWAN (1990), *Functional Stability Analysis of Numerical Algorithms*, Ph.D. dissertation, University of Texas at Austin.

A. RUHE (1970), *An algorithm for numerical determination of the structure of a general matrix*, BIT, **10**, 196–216.

S. M. RUMP (1995), *Bounds for the Componentwise Distance to the Nearest Singular Matrix*, Research Rep., Hamburg University.

Y. SAAD (1992), *Numerical Methods for Large Eigenvalue Problems*, Algorithms and Architectures for Advanced Scientific Computing, Manchester University Press, Manchester, U.K.

J. SANCHEZ-HUBERT AND E. SANCHEZ-PALENCIA (1989), *Vibration and Coupling of Continuous Systems: Asymptotic Methods*, Springer, Berlin.

A. SARD (1942), *The measure of the critical values of differentiable maps*, Bull. AMS, **48**, 883–896.

F. SCHLESINGER (1917), *On the errors in a sum of a number of tabular quantities*, Astron. J., **30**, 183–190.

P. J. SCHMID AND D. S. HENNINGSON (1992), *A new mechanism for rapid transition involving a pair of oblique waves*, Phys. Fluids A, **4**, 1986–1989.

H. G. SCHUSTER (1989), *Deterministic Chaos: An Introduction*, VCH, Weinheim.

J. SCOTT (1993), *An Arnoldi Code for Computing Selected Eigenvalues of Sparse Large Real Unsymmetric Matrices*, Tech. Rep. RAL-93-097, RAL.

M. SHUB AND S. SMALE (1993a), *Complexity of Bézout's theorem I. Geometric aspects*, J. Amer. Math. Soc., **6**, 459–501.

M. SHUB AND S. SMALE (1993b), *Complexity of Bézout's theorem IV: Probability of Success. Extensions*, Research Rep., University of California at Berkeley.

R. D. SKEEL (1979), *Scaling for numerical stability in Gaussian elimination*, J. Assoc. Comput. Mach., **26**, 3, 494–526.

R. D. SKEEL (1980), *Iterative refinement implies numerical stability for Gaussian elimination*, Math. Comp., **35**, 817–832.

S. SMALE (1990), *Some remarks on the foundations of numerical analysis*, SIAM Rev., **32**, 211–220.

R. A. SMITH, (1967), *The condition numbers of the matrix eigenvalue problem*, Numer. Math., **10**, 232–240.

C. STEPHANOS (1900), *Sur une extension du calcul des substitutions linéaires*, J. Math. Pures Appl., **6**, 73–128.

G. W. STEWART AND J. SUN (1991), *Matrix Perturbation Theory*, Academic Press, New York.

G. W. STEWART (1971), *Error bounds for approximate invariant subspaces of closed linear operators*, SIAM J. Numer. Anal., **8**, 796–808.

G. W. STEWART (1973a), *Error and perturbation bounds for subspaces associated with certain eigenvalue problems*, SIAM Rev., **15**, 727–764.

G. W. STEWART (1973b), *Introduction to Matrix Computation*, Academic Press, New York.

G. W. STEWART (1990), *Stochastic perturbation theory*, SIAM Rev., **32**, 579–610.

G. W. STEWART (1993a), *Gauss, Statistics and Gaussian Elimination*, private communication.

G. W. STEWART (1993b), *On the perturbation of LU, Cholesky and QR factorizations*, SIAM J. Matrix Anal. Appl., **14**, 1141–1145.

I. STEWART (1993c), *1 est plus probable que 9*, Pour la science, **190**, 94–98.

J. S. STOER AND R. BULIRSCH (1980), *Introduction to Numerical Analysis*, Springer, New York, Berlin.

F. STUMMEL (1985a), *Forward error analysis of Gaussian elimination (part 1)*, Numer. Math., **46**, 365–395.

F. STUMMEL (1985b), *Forward error analysis of Gaussian elimination (part 2)*, Numer. Math., **46**, 397–415.

THE MATHWORKS (1992), *MATLAB Reference Guide*, The MathWorks Inc., Natick, MA.

A. TIKHONOV AND V. ARSÉNINE (1976), *Méthodes de résolution de problèmes bien posés*, Mir, Moscow.

K.-C. TOH AND L. N. TREFETHEN (1994), *Pseudozeros of polynomials and pseudospectra of companion matrices*, Numer. Math., **68**, 403–425.

L. N. TREFETHEN AND M. TRUMMER (1987), *An instability phenomenon in spectral methods*, SIAM J. Numer. Anal., **24**, 1008–1023.

L. N. TREFETHEN, A. E. TREFETHEN, S. C. REDDY, AND T. A. DRISCOLL (1993), *Hydrodynamics stability without eigenvalues*, Science, **261**, 578–584.

L. N. TREFETHEN (1990), *Approximation theory and numerical linear algebra*, in Algorithms for Approximation II, J. C. Mason and M. G. Cox, eds., Chapman and Hall, London, 336–359.

L. N. TREFETHEN (1992), *Pseudospectra of matrices*, in Numerical Analysis 1991, D. F. Griffiths and G. A. Watson, eds., Longman, Harlow.

L. N. TREFETHEN (book in preparation), *Spectra and Pseudospectra: The Behavior of Nonnormal Matrices and Operators*, Department of Computer Science, Cornell University.

A. M. TURING (1948), *Rounding-off errors in matrix processes*, Quart. J. Mech. Appl. Math., **1**, 287–308.

P. R. TURNER (1982), *The distribution of leading significant digits*, IMA J. Numer. Anal., **2**, 407–412.

A. VAN DER SLUIS (1970), *Domain of uncertainty for perturbed operator equations*, Comp., **5**, 312–323.

A. VAN DER SLUIS (1975), *Perturbations of eigenvalues of nonnormal matrices*, Comm. ACM, **18**, 30–36.

J. M. VARAH (1979), *On the separation of two matrices*, SIAM J. Numer. Anal., **16**, 216–222.

J. VIGNES (1986), *Zéro mathématique et zéro informatique*, C. R. Acad. Sci. Paris Série I, **303**, 1–13.

V. VOÏÉVODINE AND P. Y. YALAMOV (1990), *A new method for roundoff error estimation*, in Proc. Workshop on Parallel and Distributed Processing, K. Boyano, ed., Elsevier, Amsterdam, pp. 315–333.

V. VOÏÉVODINE (1980), *Principes numériques d'algèbre linéaire*, Editions Mir, Moscow.

J. VON NEUMANN AND H. H. GOLDSTINE (1947), *Numerical inverting of matrices of high order* I, Proc. Amer. Math. Soc., **53**, 1021–1099.

B. WALDÉN, R. KARLSON, AND J. SUN (1995), *Optimal backward perturbation bounds for the linear least squares problem*, J. Numer. Linear Algebra Appl., **2**, 271–286.

P.-Å. WEDIN (1973), *Perturbation theory for pseudoinverses*, BIT, **13**, 217–232.

N. WEISS, G. W. WASILKOWSKY, H. WOŹNIAKOWSKI, AND M. SHUB (1986), *Average condition number for solving linear equations*, Linear Algebra Appl., **83**, 79–102.

J. H. WILKINSON (1961), *Error analysis of direct methods of matrix inversion*, J. Assoc. Comput. Mach., **8**, 281–330.

J. H. WILKINSON (1963), *Rounding Errors in Algebraic Processes*, vol. 32, Her Majesty's Stationery Office, London.

J. H. WILKINSON (1965), *The Algebraic Eigenvalue Problem*, Oxford University Press, Oxford.

J. H. WILKINSON (1971), *Modern error analysis*, SIAM Rev., **13**, 548–569.

M. WRIGHT (ED.) (1989), *Aspects of Computation on Asynchronous Parallel Computers*, North-Holland, Amsterdam.

P. Y. YALAMOV (1991), *On the backward stability of Gauss-Jordan elimination*, Computing, **47**, 193–197.

P. Y. YALAMOV (1994), *Roundoff Errors and Graphs*, manuscript, Ruse Technological University, Ruse, Bulgaria.

Index